Routledge Revivals

The Middle English Harrowing of Hell and Gospel of Nicodemus

The Middle English Harrowing of Hell and Gospel of Nicodemus

William Henry Hulme

Routledge
Taylor & Francis Group

First published in 1907 for The Early English Text Society
by Kegan Paul, Trench, Trübner & Co., Ltd.

This edition first published in 2018 by Routledge
2 Park Square, Milton Park, Abingdon, Oxon, OX14 4RN
and by Routledge
711 Third Avenue, New York, NY 10017

Routledge is an imprint of the Taylor & Francis Group, an informa business

Publisher's Note
The publisher has gone to great lengths to ensure the quality of this reprint but points out that some imperfections in the original copies may be apparent.

Disclaimer
The publisher has made every effort to trace copyright holders and welcomes correspondence from those they have been unable to contact.

A Library of Congress record exists under ISBN: 8014822

For Product Safety Concerns and Information please contact our EU representative: GPSR@taylorandfrancis.com.
Taylor & Francis Verlag GmbH, Kaufingerstraße 24, 80331 München, Germany.

ISBN 13: 978-1-138-62540-2 (hbk)
ISBN 13: 978-1-138-62545-7 (pbk)
ISBN 13: 978-0-429-45992-4 (ebk)

The Middle-English

Harrowing of Hell

AND

Gospel of Nicodemus.

Early English Text Society.

Extra Series, C.

1907.

BERLIN: ASHER & CO., 13, UNTER DEN LINDEN.
NEW YORK: C. SCRIBNER & CO.; LEYPOLDT & HOLT.
PHILADELPHIA: J. B. LIPPINCOTT & CO.

The Middle-English Harrowing of Hell and Gospel of Nicodemus.

NOW FIRST EDITED FROM ALL THE KNOWN MANUSCRIPTS,
WITH INTRODUCTION AND GLOSSARY,

BY

WILLIAM HENRY HULME, Ph.D.,
Professor in Western Reserve University, U.S.A.

LONDON:
PUBLISHED FOR THE EARLY ENGLISH TEXT SOCIETY
By KEGAN PAUL, TRENCH, TRÜBNER & CO., LIMITED
DRYDEN HOUSE, 43, GERRARD STREET, SOHO, W.
1907.

Extra Series, C.

RICHARD CLAY & SONS, LIMITED, LONDON AND BUNGAY

PREFACE.

An attempt is made in the present volume (1) to make easily accessible to students of English literature all the known Middle-English versions of the *Harrowing of Hell* and the poetical *Gospel of Nicodemus;* (2) to give exact reproductions of the several manuscripts in parallel columns, so far as that is possible in print, as well as the variant readings of all previous reprints; (3) to give in the Introduction a succinct but comprehensive bibliographical account of the manuscripts in which the poems have been preserved and of all those manuscripts, so for as they are known, which contain prose versions of the Middle-English *Gospel of Nicodemus;* (4) to furnish a Glossary of obsolete and unfamiliar words.

The historical account of the rise and growth of the "Harrowing of Hell" motive and of the *Evangelium Nicodemi* in mediaeval literature and art has been made brief, and all explanatory notes have been omitted, because they are to be published in a special edition of one of the Middle-English poetical versions of the *Gospel of Nicodemus* which the present editor has about ready for the press.

I also hope to print in a future volume the most important of the ten (including the Black Letter reprint of Wynkyn de Worde) Middle-English prose versions of the Gospel, which are likewise interesting and valuable in many respects to the student of English literature and language.

The manuscript readings have been retained in the texts almost without exception, inasmuch as corrupt forms of one manuscript are generally explained by reference to the other manuscripts. If the original reading is ever changed, the manuscript form is given in the marginal notes. Few emendations have been suggested, and these are always enclosed in brackets. Resolutions of manuscript abbreviations are printed in italics. The capitals of the manuscripts have been retained, but the punctuation has been modernized. The crosses in final *ll* and the flourishes of final *m* and *n* have been ignored in the text.

The manuscripts of the *Harrowing of Hell* differ so widely and in so many respects from one another, that it would be impossible so to arrange any two of them in parallel columns as to make the lines always, or even generally, correspond without resorting to a considerable amount of jugglery in placing them. The lines of each manuscript are numbered, therefore, without reference to the numbering of the others, except that the fragment E begins with l. 29, corresponding to the line numbers of L. But E might perhaps with just as much reason be printed and numbered according to the arrangement of O, which has in fact been done by Varnhagen.

I desire in conclusion to make due acknowledgment for the assistance that I have received from many sources in the preparation of this edition. I have met with uniform kindness and consideration from the librarians (and their assistants) of the British Museum, the Cambridge University Library, the Bodleian Library, the Advocates' Library of Edinburgh, the Sion College Library, the Library of Stonyhurst College, the Worcester Cathedral Library, the Salisbury Cathedral Library, and the Library of Magdalen College, Cambridge. I am under special obligations to Mr. J. A. Herbert of the Manuscripts' Department of the British Museum, Mr. Francis Jenkinson, Librarian of the Cambridge University Library, Mr. C. W. Moule, Librarian of Corpus Christi College, Cambridge, and my friend, Dr. W. de Gray Birch, for numerous instances of help and suggestions. I am above all indebted to the enthusiastic encouragement, generously given on many occasions, by the great friend and inspirer of so much of the best English scholarship of the last fifty years, Dr. Frederick J. Furnivall.

WM. H. H.

Cleveland, Ohio (*U. S. A.*),
July 1907.

CORRIGENDA.

Sion, l. 478, *for* loured *read* louerd
,, l. 1252, *for* [leaf 32] *read* [leaf 31]
Harley, l. 632, *for* myht *read* myght
Additional, l. 819, *for* gon *read* gan
,, l. 1056, *for* sithin *read* sithen
,, l. 1104, *for* sikerly *read* sikirly
,, l. 1214, *for* now *read* nowe
,, ll. 1530, 1644, *for* paim *read* þaim
,, l. 1612, *for* mann *read* man

INTRODUCTION.

I.

THE MIDDLE-ENGLISH HARROWING OF HELL.

The earliest known attempts at reproducing the *Evangelium Nicodemi* in Middle English are in the form of poetry. And the poetical versions, as well as those in prose, are apparently independent of the Old-English translations and adaptations of the same narrative. That is to say, they are based directly upon a Latin original. If any of the Middle-English poetical or prose versions are translations from the Old French, I have not yet been able to discover the fact. There are, however, a large number of Old-French prose manuscripts of the Gospel of Nicodemus in Continental libraries which I have had no opportunity of examining. But no one of those in the British Museum[1] can, I think, be considered the original of any of the Middle-English versions.

The dramatic *Harrowing of Hell* is the earliest of the Middle-English descriptions of the *Descensus Christi ad Infernos* of which we have any knowledge. And the original manuscript of this piece (which is not in existence at the present day) could hardly have been written later than

[1] O.F. prose versions of the whole or a part of the Gospel of Nicodemus are preserved in the following manuscripts of the British Museum: (*a*) Egerton 613, ff. 13 b–21 (beginning with the account of the imprisonment and rescue of Joseph of Arimathea). The MS. is on vellum and is as early as the thirteenth century. (*b*) Egerton 2710, ff. 126–133 b, also of the thirteenth century. It contains a version of the narrative which bears considerable resemblance to that of Harl. 149. (*c*) Egerton 2781, ff. 173–189 b, of the fourteenth century, contains a free adaptation of the narrative, beginning with the story of Joseph's rescue from prison by Christ. (*d*) Harl. 2253, ff. 33 b–41 b, from about 1300, contains the same version as Eg. 2710, in different dialect. (*e*) Addit. 32,090, ff. 3–48, from the year 1445, contains an independent, complete version.

the middle of the thirteenth century.[1] The poem has been preserved in three different MSS., no one of which is later than the middle of the fourteenth century. They are: Bodl. Digby 86, ff. 119–120 b (O)[2]; Brit. Mus. Harl. 2253, ff. 55 b–56 b (L); Auchinleck, W. 4, I, in the Advocates' Library, Edinburgh (E). The oldest of the three versions seems[3] to be that which is designated by O and preserved in the Bodleian Library at Oxford, and this version is probably nearest to the original composition.[4] This MS., Digby 86, is described in detail by Dr. E. Stengel in his *Codex Manuscriptus Digby* 86, Halle, 1871, and more recently and accurately in the *Catalogi Codicum Manuscriptorum Bibliothecae Bodleianae, Pars nona*, etc., compiled by W. D. Macray, Oxford, 1883, pp. 91–97. The MS. is a vellum quarto containing 207 leaves which measure $8\frac{1}{4} \times 5\frac{1}{2}$ inches, and it was probably written during the last years of the thirteenth century. The codex is written with sometimes two columns to a page, sometimes only one column, and it contains 81 different pieces,[5] which are distributed among three different languages, English, French, and Latin. The *Harrowing of Hell* is described as No. 34 on p. 93 of the *Catalogue*.[6] The prologue to this version was printed many years ago by Wright and Halliwell,[7] and the poem has been printed recently in complete form, accompanied by a photographic facsimile of the entire MS., as well as of the other two MSS., by H. Varnhagen.[8]

[1] Dr. Eduard Mall, *The Harrowing of Hell, Das altenglische Spiel von Christi Höllenfahrt*, Berlin, 1871, p. 8; ten Brink, *History of English Literature*, II, 241 ff.; Creizenach, *Geschichte des neueren Dramas*, I, 158 f. Cf. also Wülker, *Das Evangelium Nicodemi in der abendländischen Literatur*, Paderborn, 1872, p. 76 ff.; Mall, "Zu The Harrowing of Hell," *Jahrbuch für romanische und englische Litteratur*, XIII, 217 ff.; Dr. K. Böddeker, *Altenglische Dichtungen des MS. Harl.* 2253, p. 264 ff.

[2] The designations of Mall are retained in this discussion.

[3] Cf. Wülker, *op. cit.*; Mall, *Harrowing of Hell*, p. 5 ff.; Böddeker, *op. cit.* There seems to be no good reason for placing the Auchinleck version earlier than L and O, as D. Laing would do (*Preface* to "The Harrowing of Hell" in *Owain Miles and Other Inedited Fragments of Ancient English Poetry*, Edinburgh, 1837). A careful collation of Laing's text was printed by Zupitza, Wagner's *Archiv*, I, 190 ff. Cf. Sir W. Scott, *Sir Tristrem, A Metrical Romance*, Edinburgh, 1819, Append. p. 107 ff.; especially, D. Laing, *A Penni worthe of Witte*, etc., selected from the Auchinleck manuscript. The Abbotsford Club, Edinburgh, 1857, Preface.

[4] But see Mall, pp. 1–10, Varnhagen, p. 22 ff., where the relation of the MSS. to one another and to the original is discussed at length.

[5] Stengel enumerates only 78.

[6] No. 32 according to Stengel (p. 52). From Macray's note (p. 93) one would erroneously be led to suppose that this version had been printed three times: "Impr. a J. P. Collier, anno 1836, et J. O. Halliwell, anno 1840, et, una cum *Owain Miles*," etc., whereas no one of the three editions mentioned takes any account of the Digby version.

[7] *Reliquae Antiquae*, I, 253, but the reprint contains several inaccuracies.

[8] It is difficult to understand how the editor could have imagined that any one would ever detect *The Harrowing of Hell* (or *Höllenfahrt Christi*) in the pompous

The piece, which begins on f. 119 and ends near the foot of col. 2, f. 120 b, is written in a distinct hand of the late thirteenth century, with two columns of 33 lines each to a page. The scribe made considerable effort at ornamentation, that is, by red strokes through the initial letter of each line and paragraph. This version contains 256 lines, which is 8 more than version L has and 55 more than version E. The names of the speakers or *dramatis personae* are not given in the MS.

Version L has received much more attention from modern scholars. It has been printed six times[1] (five different editions) since the year 1835, but only one of the editions, that of Varnhagen, represents an exact and careful reproduction of the MS. The Harleian MS. 2253 is a vellum folio of 140 leaves and 3 fly-leaves, one at the beginning and two at the end of the codex. The leaves measure 11½ × 7¼ inches, and the MS. contains 116 different pieces, "written by several different hands, upon several subjects, partly in Old French, partly in Latin, and partly in Old (*i. e.* Middle) English; partly in verse and partly in prose." If we omit the fly-leaves, in which two different kinds of handwriting are shown, the MS. is actually written in three different hands: (1) ff. 1–48, "written in a round text hand, perhaps by some religious person,"[2] and probably as early as the last decade of the thirteenth century; (2) ff. 49 b–140 b (*i. e.* to the end of the MS.) are, excepting one and a half columns of f. 52 b, all written in the same hand, the date of which may be placed about 1300; (3) the second half of col. 1 and all of col. 2, f. 52 b are written in a third very small hand of about the same date as the second. Then the *rectos* of the first and last fly-leaves contain extracts in Latin from an old account-book, written perhaps about 1280–1300. The *versos*

Latin of the title-page of this otherwise modest little monograph: *Regiae Friderico-Alexandrinae Litterarum Universitatis Prorector D. Carolus Ehcberg Rerum Politicarum Professor Publicus Ordinarius, etc. Cum Procancellario Reliquoque Senatu Academico Successorem Suum Civibus Academicis Commendat. Praemissa est Editionis Criticae Vetustissimi Quod Sermone Anglico Conscriptum est Dramatis Pars Prior, Curavit* Hermannus Varnhagen. Erlangen 1898.

[1] J. Payne Collier, *Five Miracle Plays, or Scriptural Dramas.* Privately printed, etc., London, 1836; J. O. Halliwell, *The Harrowing of Hell, A Miracle-Play*, etc. Now first published from the original manuscript in the British Museum. With Introduction, etc., London, 1840; and Böddeker and Mall as previously cited. A. W. Pollard reprints Mall's text in his *English Miracle Plays, Moralities, and Interludes*, etc. Fourth edition, Oxford, 1904, Appendix III, pp. 166–172. Cf. Varnhagen, *op. cit.* The editions of Collier and Halliwell both contain many inaccuracies of a minor character, while those of Mall and Böddeker are "doctored," that is to say, they are so called "critical" editions which do not follow any MS. faithfully, and which often represent merely the individual editor's peculiar conception of what the original might have been, but with whose restorations, emendations, and guesses as a whole, probably no two scholars in the world would agree.

[2] Cf. *Catalogue of the Harl. MSS. in the British Mus.*, vol. II, p. 584.

of the leaves are written in a different and somewhat later hand, and they contain passages from some Latin theological piece. None of the hands are to be placed much after the first decade of the fourteenth century.[1] The MS. is arranged in quires of 12 leaves each, the ends of the quires are indicated by catch-words and the first 48 leaves have two columns to a page; after that the number of columns to the page varies between one and two.

The *Harrowing of Hell*, which is written on ff. 55 b–56 b, is given as number 21 in the table of contents printed in the *Catalogue* and reproduced by Böddeker, and there described as "an Old English poem upon our Savior's descent into hell; and his discourses there with Sathanas, the Janitor, Adam, Eva, Habraham, David, Johan Baptist, and Moyses."[2] The compiler of the *Catalogue* adds, "I fancy this might have been made for some Interlude, to be acted by Friers or other religious persons." The piece is written in a fine large hand, with two columns of 40 to 44 lines each on a page. Böddeker printed all the English poems of this MS., with two or three noteworthy exceptions,[3] in his *Altenglische Dichtungen des MS. Harl.* 2253; but the rest of it has remained for the most part unpublished.

The most recent of the three versions seems to be E, which is preserved in the famous Auchinleck MS. (W. 4, I, ff. 35–37) of the Advocates' Library in Edinburgh. This MS. "was presented to the Faculty of Advocates by Alexander Boswell of Auchinleck,"[4] and the first writer who showed any appreciation of its value and importance was

[1] Thomas Wright (*Specimens of Lyric Poetry, composed in England in the Reign of Edward the First.* Edited from MS. Harl. 2253, etc., London, 1842. *The Percy Society*, vol. iv, Pref., p. v) thinks the date of the MS. "is fixed by the handwriting and by the contents to the beginning of the reign of Edward II. It contains political songs relating to different events in the reigns of Henry III and Edward I. The two latest are those on the Traillebastons (A.D. 1305) and the death of Edward I (A.D. 1307). It is probable that the manuscript was written in, or very soon after, the latter year." Collier (*op. cit.*) had already asserted that the MS. was "as ancient as the reign of Edward II, or Edward III," and Halliwell (*op. cit. Introd.* p. 11) says: "The play now printed occurs in a well-known manuscript on vellum, of the time of Edward II." Cf. W. W. Skeat, *The Lay of Havelok the Dane*, London, 1868, p. 88, and Mall and Böddeker, *op. cit.* Joseph Ritson (*English Metrical Romances*, London, 1802, vol. iii, p. 264) says that MS. Harl. 2253 was "written, apparently, in the time of King Edward the second, by some French or Norman scribe," etc. Varnhagen says (p. 2): Die HS. gehört der ersten Hälfte des 14. Jahrhunderts an.

[2] The names of *Dramatis Personae* are inserted in the margins of this MS.

[3] Especially *The Geste of Kyng Horn* (No. 70) and *The Prophecies of Thomas of Erceldoune* (No. 90), which have been published frequently. That is to say, Böddeker's book contains 45 out of the 116 pieces.

[4] David Laing, *A Penni worthe of Witte*, etc., Pref., p. i. This book escaped the notice of both Mall and Böddeker, otherwise the former, at least, would have been able to tell us much more than he does about the history of the MS.

Bishop Thomas Percy in his now universally known *Reliques of Ancient English Poetry.*[1] Percy gives the titles of a few of the pieces in the introductory essay[2] to vol. III. "In the Edinburgh MS. so often referred to (preserved in the Advocates' Library, W. 4. I)," he says, "might probably be found some other articles to add to this list, as well as other copies of some of the pieces mentioned in it; for the whole volume contains not fewer than xxxvii Poems or Romances, some of them very long. But as many of them have lost the beginnings, which have been cut out for the sake of the illuminations; and as I have not had an opportunity of examining the MS. myself, I shall be content to mention only the articles that follow." He then mentions four pieces, all tales or romances, to only one of which, *The King of Tars*, he gives a title; but he does give the first lines of each poem.

The Auchinleck MS. "acquired its chief notoriety in 1803, from having furnished Sir Walter Scott with the text of his elaborate edition of the metrical romance of SIR TRISTREM."[3] Laing gives us some further information as to the history of the MS. in the following words, after stating that it was presented to the Faculty of Advocates in the year 1744 by Alexander Boswell: "He was raised to the Bench, as a Lord of Session, in February 1754, and died in 1782, in the seventy-sixth year of his age. His son James Boswell was the well-known biographer of Johnson. His grandson, the late Sir Alexander Boswell of Auchinleck, was an accomplished scholar. . . . The previous history of the Manuscript is wholly unknown. It is of a square or large quarto size, of vellum, in double columns, written, as conjectured, in the North of England, not later than the middle of the fourteenth century.[4] In its original state, the volume must have been of considerable bulk, inasmuch as its folios contain 44 different articles; but, according to the numbers at the head of each leaf, there must at least have been 57 in the volume. Besides the loss therefore of 13 distinct articles, several leaves are more or less mutilated. Of the missing articles, some indeed may have been of small extent, as short legends or lays, but there remain only small portions of the two long romances of Alexander and King Richard. The mutilations are chiefly blanks occasioned by most of the small illumina-

[1] Three vols., London, 1765. I quote from the fifth edition, London, 1812.

[2] *On the Ancient Metrical Romances*, etc., pp. 25–27, 31, 34, and especially 35.

[3] Laing, p. iii.

[4] Zupitza (*Zur Literaturgeschichte des Guy von Warwick*, Wien, 1873, pp. 8–9) says that it belongs to the first half of the fourteenth century (*aus der ersten Hälfte des* 14. *Jahrhunderts*). In Herrig's *Archiv 87*, 90, Zupitza would place the MS. after 1327; while Varnhagen (p. 1) thinks it belongs to the middle of the fourteenth century. Cf. Koelbing, *Ipomedon*, Breslau, 1889, Einl. p. xl.

tions at the head of each article, carefully designed, and finished in gold and colours, having been barbarously cut out, which also entailed the loss of eight or nine lines written on the reverse of the leaves so mutilated. From a circumstance to be stated, it may be conjectured that the volume had fallen into the hands of an ignorant binder, who was in the process of cutting it up for the purposes of his trade, when so many of the illuminations were taken out, as things of no value, before the most considerable portion of the volume was fortunately rescued from complete destruction." After speaking of the circumstances[1] under which he and Turnbull printed the little "volume, entitled 'Owain Miles, and other inedited Fragments of Ancient English Poetry'" in the year 1837, Laing adds a few additional points of interest concerning the history of the Auchinleck MS.: "I was quite unaware, at that time (*i. e.* 1837), that I actually had in my own possession a fragment of two leaves of that Romance (*i. e.* 'King Richard'), which had formed part of this identical Manuscript. They were given to me several years before by a learned and reverend friend, as a specimen of old writing, but had fallen aside. At length, upon examining the leaves, to ascertain what they were, the form of writing seemed to me quite familiar, and I soon discovered that they must have originally formed part of the Manuscript in question. I lost no time therefore in making inquiry, and securing another fragment of two leaves, which I remembered having seen when the others were given me. These I found contained the first portion of 'The Life of Adam,' which is inserted in the present volume. The leaves having been employed as covers of blank paper-books, which were purchased for note-books by a Professor in the University of St. Andrews, before the middle of the last century, the writing in some parts is scarcely legible. I have not been able to ascertain whether any other volumes with similar covers may still exist; but the discovery of these few leaves is sufficient to suggest the idea that Lord Auchinleck rescued the bulk of the Manuscript from being so employed. Probably attaching much less importance to the volume than it has obtained, it was bound in the plainest manner, some of the leaves were misplaced, and, when compared with the recovered fragments, of which the parts folded over the boards are preserved, it must have suffered in the rebinding, by being rather unsparingly cut in the edges. The volume is now rebound in morocco, in a style more suitable to its worth, and the mutilated leaves have been carefully mended."

Laing then states that Bishop Percy was the first to give any account

[1] *A Penni worthe of Witte*, Pref. p. ii.

of the MS., but on information which was communicated to him by Dr. Blair. Ritson also examined the MS. very carefully, and made a list of its contents in the year 1792, at the same time transcribing select portions, "which he afterwards published in his collection of English Metrical Romances."

Sir Walter Scott's description[1] of the MS., which is reproduced[2] with a few corrections and additions by Laing, is as follows in its essential features: "This valuable record of ancient poetry forms a thick quarto volume, containing 334 leaves, and 44 different pieces of poetry; some mere fragments, and others, works of great length. The beginning of each poem has originally been adorned with an illumination; for the sake of which the first leaf has in many cases been torn out, and in others cut and mutilated. The MS. is written on parchment, in a distinct and beautiful hand, which the most able antiquaries are inclined to refer to the earlier part of the thirteenth [fourteenth] century. The pages are divided into two columns, unless where the verses, being Alexandrine, occupy the whole breadth of the quarto. In two or three instances there occurs a variation of the handwriting; but as the poems regularly follow each other, there is no reason to believe that such alterations indicate an earlier or later date than may be reasonably ascribed to the rest of the work;[3] although the satire against Simonie, No. 44, seems rather in an older hand than the others, and may be an exception to the general rule.... Many circumstances lead us to conclude that the MS. has been written in an Anglo-Norman convent.—That it has been compiled in England there can be little doubt. Every poem, which has a particular local reference, concerns South Britain alone. Such are the satirical verses, No. 21, in the following catalogue; the *Liber Regum Angliae*, No. 40; the Satire against Simonie, No. 44. On the other hand, not a word is to be found in the collection relating particularly to Scottish affairs." Then follows immediately the list of subjects in the MS. together with an extensive description of the different poems and fragments, as well as the first or last lines from each piece, keeping to Scott's notation.

The Auchinleck MS. is a medium-sized vellum quarto, the leaves of

[1] *Sir Tristrem, a Metrical Romance*, Edinburgh, 1803, Appendix, p. 107 f.

[2] *A Penni worthe of Witte*, Pref., pp. xiii–xxxi. It would require too much space to reproduce the first or last lines from the several poems, as is done in the Scott-Laing list. A more recent and trustworthy account of the entire MS. is given by Koelbing in *Engl. Studien* 7, 178–191.

[3] Turnbull says (*Legendae Catholicae, A Lytle Boke of Seyntlie Gestes*, Edinburgh, 1840, pp. v–vi): "This manuscript is supposed to have been written in some north of England Monastery about the latter end of the thirteenth or commencement of the fourteenth century, and this hypothesis appears to be warranted both by the structure of the language and the chirograph."

which measure 10 × 7½ inches. The entire volume seems to have been arranged in quires of eight leaves, since catchwords occur with considerable regularity at the end of each eighth folio. Thus there are still thirty-seven catchwords in the MS., indicating the ends of as many quires.

In its unmutilated form the *Harrowing of Hell* probably occupied ff. 35 b–37 a. But f. 35 has been torn out, probably on account of the miniature that adorned the upper margin, so that only a narrow strip, containing the beginnings of the lines of col. 1, f. 35 and the ends of the lines of col. 2, f. 35 b, now remains. Half of f. 37 has also been torn away, leaving col. 1 of the first page and col. 2 of the second almost entire. Leaf 36 remains complete and virtually uninjured, and from this leaf and the remnants of the other two leaves we see that the piece was written in two columns of 44 lines each to a page. The hand is rather small, but it is for the most part easy to read. The pages show considerable effort at ornamentation in the heavy, bright-colored flourishes of the capitals and the touches of red for the initial letters of the lines. The *Harrowing of Hell* is designated as No. XIII in the MS., and it is found as No. 8 in the descriptions of Scott-Laing and Koelbing.

A careful examination of this part of the MS. shows that at least one column (and possibly more) of the *verso* of f. 35 belonged to our poem. The concluding words of the first two lines of col. 2, f. 35 b, *mare* : *Helle fare*, might indicate that they belonged either to the *Harrowing of Hell*, or to some other poem which immediately preceded it in the MS., and of which they were the concluding lines. By comparing the first thirty lines of the London and Oxford versions with the remnants of the lines of col. 2, f. 35 b, we shall find that the similarity between this part of E and the corresponding part of L–O is closer if we take the second couplet (*helle* : *-es duelle*) of the column as the beginning of *Harrowing*. The first couplet would in that case form the conclusion of another poem. Immediately after the first couplet there is blank space on the strip for two lines, and we may very reasonably assume that this space was originally for the rubric or title of the *Harrowing of Hell*. If then the first two lines of the column with the immediately following space, as well as two other spaces of 1–2 lines each (for the speakers ?) near the centre of the column be omitted from the count, the remnants of 35–40 lines are still visible on the strip. This number (35–40) of lines, moreover, agrees quite closely with that of the corresponding lines in the other two MSS.

At the foot of the *recto* of the strip (f. 35 a) occurs the *explicit* of the poem entitled *þe deputisoun bitven þe bodi & þe soule*, and between this *explicit* and the second couplet of col. 2, f. 35 b, there would therefore be space for two columns and two lines. Supposing the columns to have had the same number (44) of lines as those of *Harrowing*, we should have 90 lines for this intervening space. And if we deduct say 5–10 lines for the space of the miniature which probably stood at the head of the second column of the *recto* (f. 35) and the same number for the beginning of col. 1 of the *verso*, which would have been torn away with the miniature, there would still be 75–80 lines in these columns in the original form of the MS. But so many lines at the beginning of E would increase the length of this version of the poem out of all proportion to that of the other two MSS. For if we assume only 75 lines for the columns in question, they would give E about 275 lines besides the 28–30 lines wanting in the conclusion, as compared with L and O. There is no good reason, however, for supposing that E contained originally 45–50 lines more than L and O. The simplest solution of the difficulty would be to assume that the two columns of f. 35 were originally occupied by a short independent poem which has entirely disappeared. Or we might accept the rather improbable supposition that col. 2, f. 35 a, was left blank, and that *Harrowing* began beneath a miniature in col. 1, f. 35 b. Varnhagen does not express himself with certainty on this point. He reckons the number of missing lines at about 76, which, he thinks, might have belonged either to an independent poem or to the *Harrowing of Hell.*[1]

II.

THE MIDDLE-ENGLISH POETICAL GOSPEL OF NICODEMUS.

THE M.E. verse translation of the *Gospel of Nicodemus* has been preserved in at least four manuscripts, all of the fifteenth century. Three of them are in the British Museum, and the fourth is in the library of Sion College. All of these MSS. must be considered copies of earlier ones, and they would all seem to go back eventually to the same original. The press marks of these MSS. are: Brit. Mus. Cotton Galba E IX (G); Brit. Mus. Harl. 4196 (H); Brit. Mus. Addit. 32,578 (A); Sion College arc. L. $40.2^{a}+^{2}$ (S). From the standpoint of kinship and similarity they fall into two, possibly three, groups: (a) G–H, (b) A–S; or (b) A, (c) S. The first group seems to be closer to the original than the other or others. It is written in the Northern dialect, as are also the other versions, but the latter group, especially A, shows a very decided Midland tendency in the

[1] Cf. *op. cit.* p. 1: Diese ungefähr 76 Verse können nun entweder ein selbständiges Gedicht gelbildet oder zu unserm Denkmale gehört haben.

word-forms. The A–S group was written between the beginning and the middle of the fifteenth century, and A is certainly the earlier of the two. The differences between A and the G–H group are so striking and so numerous, that it could not possibly have been copied from either G or H, nor could either member of this group have been copied from A. But S sometimes follows G–H exactly, sometimes it reproduces entire lines as they occur in A,—lines which have no counterpart in G–H. It is, therefore, not improbable that the scribe of S had copies of G–H and of A before him at the time of writing. It may be doubted whether the version A, in its present form, is a copy of the original of which G–H is a transcription. The discrepancies in language and style are almost too great and too numerous to justify such a conclusion. In other words, we should probably not be far from correct in assuming that A goes back through an intermediate link (y) to the common original (x).[1] Both A and S omit the sixteenth stanza (ll. 181–192)[2] of the G–H version, and both show everywhere traces of a slightly different origin. S also omits twelve lines (1747–58) near the end of the poem, as well as several other single lines or couplets, and there are numerous instances of the carelessness and ignorance of the copyist. The language and style of A are generally more modern than the same features of the G–H group.

The conclusion of the poem as represented by version A is wholly different from that of the other three MSS. That is to say, A is the only one of the MSS. which attempts to reproduce in its proper (or any) connection the letter of Pilate to the Emperor Claudius. And it omits that part of the narrative of G–H–S contained in ll. 1717–1764 (*i. e.* the concluding 45–50 lines of the poem) in which Annas and Cayphas attempt to prove to the satisfaction of Pilate that the 5500 years, mentioned by the angel to Seth at the gates of Paradise when he appeared there on his mission to get the Oil of Mercy for his father Adam, had already elapsed. But in spite of this omission and that of the stanza previously noticed, A contains thirty-six lines, or three stanzas, more than the G–H version.

There is considerable difference between the metre and rhythm of G–H on the one hand, and of A–S on the other. The latter MSS. show much greater variation in the number of syllables to the line, and A, especially, very frequently omits the alliteration altogether, which is generally

[1] This is of course only a supposition which in our present state of information about the MSS. can neither be proved nor refuted. But it is like most of the futile efforts at setting up genealogical tables where several MSS. are to be considered: its value is weakened by the personal equation, and it is subject to complete annihilation at any time by the discovery of a new MS.

[2] This stanza has nothing corresponding in the *Evangel. Nicodemi.*

present, even in the three-stress lines, of the G–H version. But the versions are all written in peculiar twelve-line stanzas, each of which is made up of two, according to Schipper, three parts, or rhythmic periods. The first two parts contain each four alternately rhyming lines, of which the odd ones have four stresses (eight syllables) and the even ones three (six syllables[1]). The third part has four alternately rhyming lines, and each line usually has three stresses (six to seven syllables). In version A there is a considerable proportion of the even lines in the first two parts of the stanza with eight syllables (four stresses), and in the last parts there are many lines that have seven syllables and a few that have eight. The rhyme scheme is, however, uniform throughout all the MSS., and is represented thus: abab,abab,cdcd. Schipper[2] gives a very clear and concise history of the development of the separate four-stress and three-stress lines, as well as of various combinations of these lines into strophes or staves. He has moreover shown that twelve-line stanzas are by no means infrequent in Middle-English literature. But he has not given any account, strange to say, of the twelve-line stanza of the Gospel of Nicodemus which was apparently developed under foreign influences and at a comparatively late date, and which is of rare occurrence. In fact, I know of no other instance in the entire range of Middle-English literature.

Schipper[3] says that eight-line stanzas with cross-rhymes and composed of four and three stresses in alternate succession are exceedingly rare in English literature. And we may suppose that our twelve-line stanza was developed from such a stanza, or by (1) doubling the first four lines, and (2) by appending a *Cauda* of four more three-stress, alternately rhyming lines to these eight. To what extent French, Provençal, and other Romanic verse forms influenced this peculiar Middle-English development, I leave for the consideration of some one better versed in the history of the metrical forms of the Middle Ages. It is worth noting that, judging from the verse form, the Middle-English poetical Gospel originated in entire independence of the Old-French versions of the same story.[4]

[1] But there are many of these lines that have seven, and a few even eight syllables. Schipper was apparently unfamiliar with this stanza when he wrote his book. See J. Schipper, *Englische Metrik*, etc., *Zwei Theile, Erster Theil: Altenglische Metrik*, Bonn, 1881, p. 421 f.; cf. Paul's *Grundriss*, II, 1072; and especially Schipper, *Grundriss der Engl. Metrik*, Wien, 1895, bk. II, p. 267 ff.

[2] Cf. *Grundriss*, 1str Theil, Cap. 4, p. 75 ff.; 2ter Theil, 2ter Abschnitt, cap. 1, p. 176 ff.; and the whole of Buch, II, p. 267 ff.

[3] *Grundriss*, p. 302; cf. ibid. p. 320; *Englische Metrik*, II, 599–600.

[4] Cf. G. Paris and Bos, *Trois versions rimées de L'Evangile de Nicodème*. Paris, 1885. (Société des Anciens Textes Français.) Moreover, the Provençal poetical *Gospel of Nicodemus* certainly exerted no influence in this direction, because it is not

The English stanzaic form which most resembles that of the *Gospel of Nicodemus* is found in several of the York Plays. There are twelve lines in this stanza which likewise consists of two (or three) parts. But the first eight lines have four stresses each—not one four-stressed followed by a three-stressed line,—while the last four lines have three stresses each, just as the Gospel stanza. The rhyme order in the two cases is precisely the same, that is, abababab, cd cd.[1] This twelve-line stanza is employed in twelve[2] different plays. There are also two plays[3] in which the rhyme order of the last four lines of the stanza is varied (abababab cb cb and abababab cd dc), and two[4] in stanzas of twelve lines in which the character of the lines as well as the rhyme order is varied. About one-third of the plays, therefore, are written in the twelve-line stanza, and in the case of the first fourteen of these twelve-line stanza plays there can be little doubt, I think, that they are imitations of the Gospel stanza.[5]

Two of the MSS. (H and S) of the M.E. poetical *Gospel of Nicodemus*, and variants from a third MS. (G), were printed several years ago by Dr. Carl Horstmann.[6] The reprints are generally reliable; but a few errors of minor importance escaped Horstmann's notice, and through a peculiar oversight he marks l. 932[7] as wanting in version S, though it is perfectly distinct in the MS. The MS. Addit. 32,578 was not acquired by the British Museum until the summer of 1885,—some three years after the date of the last of these reprints by Horstmann. It is therefore not altogether unnatural that version A was unknown to him. The MS. has in fact never been carefully and exactly described, for the description of the *Catalogue of Additions to the MSS. of the British Museum* is meagre and imperfect, and Percy Andreae[8] confines his remarks about it entirely to one article, viz.: *The Pricke of Conscience.*

It is not easy to determine which of the four MSS. has followed the common original most closely, or which is the earliest. But the age of these MSS. is in itself conclusive evidence that no one of them can be taken as

written in strophic form. Cf. H. Suchier, *Denkmäler provenzalischer Literatur und Sprache*, Halle, 1883, Bd. I, p. 1 ff.

[1] Cf. Toulmin-Smith, *The York Plays*, Introd. p. li.

[2] They are Nos. X, XI, XII, XV, XVII, XX, XXIII, XXIV, XXVII, XXXV, XXXVII, XLIV.

[3] II, XXVIII. [4] XVIII, XXXIII. Cf. Smith, *op. cit.*

[5] See below the further discussion of the relation of the *York Plays* to the M.E. poetical *Gospel of Nicodemus.*

[6] H in *Archiv für das Studium der neueren Sprachen und Literaturen, 53*, 389 ff. (1874); S in *Archiv 68*, 207 ff. (1882); the variants from G (as compared with H) in *Archiv 57*, 73 ff. (1877). [7] See *Archiv 68*, 217.

[8] *Die Handschriften des Pricke of Conscience von Richard Rolle de Hampole im Britischen Museum.* Berlin, 1888.

the original version. For, while no one of them probably originated earlier than about 1400, there are good reasons for believing that the poetical *Gospel of Nicodemus* was in existence as early as the first quarter of the fourteenth century. Craigie[1] has proved it to be more than probable that certain parts of the York Plays follow the M.E. poetical Gospel rather than the Latin *Evangelium Nicodemi.* He has indeed produced such an array of parallelisms between the poetical version H and those plays of the York cycle which represent Christ's passion and descent into Hades, that there cannot be any doubt about the intimate connection between the two productions. The resemblances are of such a nature as to make it almost certain that the author of the plays borrowed extensively from the poetical Gospel, and not *vice versa.* Craigie's theory as to the relationship may be gathered from the following passage:[2] "The above parallels are quite sufficient to prove that the author of the plays cited was familiar with the northern version of the *Gospel of Nicodemus.* From the general character of his borrowings it seems most probable that he had parts of it by heart, and utilized these when opportunity or memory served. Had he been working directly from a written copy, his borrowings would probably have been more numerous and closer to his original. That the translator and the dramatist were one and the same person is less likely; style and vocabulary are distinctly against such a supposition. It may be noted too that while many of the plays are written in a stanza resembling that of the Gospel, the precise metre of the latter is not adopted in a single case. The difference is that in the latter the even lines have only three stresses (six syllables) while in the Plays they have four." A few of the most striking parallelisms from Craigie's long list must suffice here. In the second stanza of the Gospel we have a register of the names of the accusers of Christ:

Simon, Zayrus and Caiphas,
  Datan and Gamaliell,
Neptalim, Leui and Iudas,
  With þaire accusinges fals and fell,
Alexander and als Annas,
  Ogaines Ihesu þai speke and spell;
Bifore Sir Pilate gan þai pas,
  þaire tales vntill him gan þai tell.[3]

[1] *The Gospel of Nicodemus and the York Mystery Plays*, in *An English Miscellany.* Presented to Dr. F. J. Furnivall, Oxford, 1901, p. 52 ff.

[2] Pp. 60–61.

[3] I have followed G instead of H, and have introduced capitals where they are required, and omitted italicised resolutions of MS. abbreviations.

The order of names here given does not follow that of the Latin original.[1] A similar list of witnesses appears in Play xxxiii, 113, in the following order:

> Simon, Zarus, and Judas
> Datan and Gamaliell,
> Neptalim, Leui, and Lucas
> And Amys þis maters can mell
> to-githere
> þer tales for trewe can þey telle
> Of this faytour þat false is and felle.[2]

"Cayphas" was necessarily omitted from the first line, since he is speaking; "Annas also disappears, being a leading person in the play itself"; while Lucas and Amys are probably inventions of the dramatist.

The sixteenth stanza of the Gospel, beginning with the third line,

> "þe fende þan thoght if he war slayn
> He suld saue men of sin," etc.,

contains certain ideas which have nothing corresponding in the Latin. "The same explanation of the intercession made by Pilate's wife on behalf of Jesus is adopted in Play xxx, 159, but the wording of the scene is original."[3]

Take again the following passage (ll. 1189–96):

> I prechid and said: "All Neptalym land
> And Zabulon land withall, . . .
> Men in mirknes of ded walkand
> Light vnto þam schine sall."
> þus I said whils I was lifand,
> I see it now bifall.

These lines are a part of the exulting prophecy of Isaiah at the approach of Christ in Hades, with which compare the following from the speech of Isaac (*i. e.* Isaiah), Play xxxvii, 51–56:

> I prechid in Neptalym, þat lande,
> And Zabulon even vntill ende.
> I spake of folke in mirke walkand,
> And saide a light shuld on þam lende,
> This lered I whils I was leuand,
> Nowe se I God þis same hath sende.[4]

[1] As printed by Tischendorf, *Evangelia Apocrypha*, second edition, Leipzig, 1876. The Latin was also printed by Horstmann along with his edition of version H, together with notes on the differences between the English and the Latin.

[2] See Toulmin-Smith, *The York Plays*, pp. 323–4.

[3] Craigie, p. 57. It is worthy of remark that it is this same stanza which is omitted from A–S.

[4] Craigie, p. 59; Smith, p. 375.

One more example from the list furnished by Craigie's study will be sufficient to show the validity of the contention. The prophecy of John the Baptist, which follows soon after that of Isaiah in the Gospel (1237 ff.), runs thus :

I baptist him right with my hend
In þe water of flom Iordan ;
þe haly gaste on him gan lende
In a dowue liknes þan ;
þe voice of þe fader doun was send
And thus to speke bigan.

Very similar lines are spoken by Johan Baptist in Play xxxvii, 75–80 :

I baptiste hym with bothe my hande
Euen in þe floode of flume Jordanne ;
þe holy goste fro heuene discende
Als a white dowue doune on hym þanne ;
þe Fadir voice, my mirthe to mende,
Was made to me euen als manne.[1]

Returning to the question of the probable date of the original version of the *Gospel of Nicodemus*, we may now assume that it is earlier than the York Plays. Miss Toulmin-Smith thinks[2] the date of composition of these plays may "safely be set as far back as 1340 or 1350, not long after the appearance of the *Cursor*," and Hupe believes that the *Cursor* was written between 1255 and 1280. If, therefore, Miss Toulmin-Smith and Hupe[3] are approximately correct in their proposed dates for the composition of the York Plays and of *Cursor Mundi*, then the poetical version of the *Gospel of Nicodemus* was probably first translated not far from the beginning of the fourteenth century. Craigie thinks[4] "there can be little doubt . . . that the translation is much earlier than [the beginning of the fifteenth century]; in all probability it belongs to the first half of the fourteenth century."

Besides these four manuscript versions of the Middle-English *Gospel of Nicodemus*, another version was for a long time supposed to be preserved in the Pepysian collection of Magdalen College Library, Cambridge. Wülker,[5] Hortsmann[6] and Brandl[7] have all treated the subject upon the supposition

[1] Cf. Craigie, p. 60 ; Smith, p. 376. Special consideration of the general influence of the *Gospel of Nicodemus* upon the mediaeval drama will be found in the editor's study of the *Harrowing of Hell* as an inspiring force in mediaeval life, art and literature, which is shortly to be published.

[2] *Op. cit.* Introd. p. xlv. Craigie says (*op. cit.* p. 61): "In any case, it is scarcely possible to fix its date (*i. e.* of Gospel) so precisely as to exclude the supposition that the *York Plays* are, as a whole, to be dated *c.* 1350."

[3] Cf. *Cursor Mundi*, E. E. T. S. 99–101, p. 186 f.

[4] *Op. cit.* p. 61. [5] *Op. cit.* p. 18–19. [6] *Archiv 53*, 389.

[7] Paul's *Grundriss der germanischen Philologie*, II, 630.

that this was the oldest and perhaps best (as far as the poetry is concerned) of all the known versions. But no one of these scholars apparently made any attempt to examine the MS. for himself. And Bernard[1] was perhaps responsible for the wide circulation given to this one of several current errors[2] about the *Gospel of Nicodemus.* For he records No. 37 among the manuscripts of Samuel Pepys as "Nicodemus's Gospel in English Verse, of about the year 1300. Pergam. fol."[3] Bernard had no doubt seen the first page of the MS. upon which the words "Nycodemus his gospel" actually appear. A cursory examination of the piece so entitled shows at once that it really (in the form as preserved in MS. Pepys 2014) has nothing to do with the *Evangelium Nicodemi*,[4] but is a fragmentary version of the well-known poem of *Titus and Vespasian, or The Destruction of Jerusalem.*

The Cotton MS. Galba E IX is a large vellum folio of 114 leaves which measure 13 × 8½ inches. It is arranged in quires of twelve leaves each, the ends of the quires being indicated in every case by catch-words. The first quire wants one leaf, and the last contains only four leaves (counting two fly-leaves). The MS. is written in a fine large hand (or hands) of the first half of the fifteenth century, and it has two columns of 47–48 lines each to a page. Capitals, especially those at the beginning of the first line of each column and paragraph initials, are often profusely ornamented with large flourishes of black and yellow, which are in many cases so constructed as to represent the faces of angels, men, demons, leaves of trees, flowers, etc. A careful examination of the chirography of the MS. shows that six different scribes (at least, hands) were concerned in its composition, but all of the handwritings except two present a general appearance of uniformity at first sight. The first of the hands extends to f. 48 b, the second to within a few

[1] Edward Bernard, *Catalogi Librorum Manuscriptorum Angliae et Hiberniae,* Oxford, 1697, vol. II, p. 208, No. 6756.

[2] These will be noticed and corrected in another connection.

[3] Wülker does not give Bernard as his authority, though he quotes the exact words of the catalogue, cf. p. 19.

[4] In its complete form this poem does contain (ll. 395–666) the principal features of the Gospel, but these lines are wanting in the Pepysian MS. The fragment has 3114 lines out of more than 5000, and it was recently printed by R. Fischer (*Archiv 111*, 285–298, and *112*, 25–45) under the misleading title *Vindicta Salvatoris. Mittelenglisches Gedicht des 13. Jahrhunderts.* Cf. J. A. Herbert, *Titus and Vespasian, or The Destruction of Jerusalem*, London, 1905. The Roxburghe Club, *Introduct.* p. xxiii–xxiv; also, Fritz Bergau, *Untersuchungen über Quelle und Verfasser des mittel-englischen Reimgedichts. The Vengaunce of Goddes Deth* (*The Bataile of Jerusalem*), Diss. Königsberg, 1901, and the review of the same by W. Suchier, *Archiv 108*, 199–206; W. Suchier, *Ueber das afrz. Gedicht von der Zerstörung Jerusalems*, Diss. Halle, 1899, and *Zeitschr für roman. Philologie*, Bd. xxiv–xxv; F. Kopka, *The Destruction of Jerusalem*, etc., Diss. Breslau, 1887.

lines of the head of col. 1, f. 50,[1] the third through f. 51 b, the fourth to f. 76, the fifth hand extends through the *Pricke of Conscience* (ff. 76–113), and the last three pages (fly-leaves) of the MS. (ff. 113 b–114 b) are written in a sixth hand which differs altogether from any of the preceding.[2]

Excepting Horstmann[3] and those students who have followed him, the consensus of the best recent scholarly opinion would place the date of Galba E IX in the early years of the fifteenth century. T. Wright said[4] half a century ago, "The manuscript (*i. e.* Galba E IX) which has preserved them (*i.e.* the Songs of Minot) belongs to the earlier part of the fifteenth century, probably to the reign of Henry V;" while Ritson[5] was of the opinion that it was "written in the time of Richard II or towards the close of the fourteenth century, and not, as appeared to Warton, who knew nothing of the age of MSS. and probably never saw this, 'in the reign of King Henry the Sixth.'" Morris[6] says: "The handwriting of the Cottonian (Galba E IX) manuscript is generally assigned to the reign of Henry V, but there are good reasons for placing it not later than the commencement of the fifteenth century." W. Scholle[7] probably did not see the MS. and therefore rests content with the citation of the opinions of other well-known scholars. Prof. Herford[8] assigns it to the early years of the fifteenth century, and Hall,[9] who discusses the question at considerable length, says: "The handwriting of this MS. is of the first twenty years of the fifteenth century. The evidence offered by the poem printed at p. 101 would be in favour of a date immediately before the Battle of Shrewsbury in 1403. For the enthusiastic partisan of the conspirators against Henry the Fourth would hardly have written in such a strain after the battle which shattered the hopes of his party. At the utmost we cannot carry the *composition* of the concluding portion of this piece down later than 1407, and it is difficult to conceive of its being copied as it stands later than the date which marks the definite triumph of Henry the Fourth." Craigie[10] is of the opinion that "both manuscripts (*i.e.* Galba E IX and Harl. 4196) of the Gospel belong to

[1] F. 49 is in fact about one half-inch broader than the other leaves of the MS.

[2] It is therefore incorrect to say that the entire MS. is written in one and the same hand; cf. J. Hall, *The Poems of Lawrence Minot*, second ed., Oxford, 1897, Introd. p. ix.

[3] See under the description of Harl. 4196.

[4] *Political Poems and Songs*, London, 1859, I, 58, footnote.

[5] *Metrical Romances*, III, 229.

[6] *The Pricke of Conscience*, p. iv. Campbell (*The Seven Sages of Rome*, Boston, 1907, Introd. p. lxvii, footnote) is in error when he reckons Morris with those scholars who "date the MS. in the second half of the fourteenth century."

[7] *Laurence Minot's Lieder*, *Quellen u. Forschungen*, Heft 62, Strassburg, 1884, Einleit. p. viii.

[8] *Dict. Nat. Biogr.*, art. "Lawrence Minot."

[9] *Op. cit.*; cf. pp. 101–109.

[10] Cf. *op. cit.* p. 61.

the early part of the fifteenth century, and are thus not much (if at all) older than the manuscript of the *York Plays.*" Campbell says (*op. cit.*): "The date of the manuscript is early in the fifteenth century."

A complete list of the poems contained in this valuable MS. is given by Hall,[1] but a brief description of the contents may be added here for the sake of convenience to students of Middle-English literature.

The *recto* of the first leaf is blank except for the words "Chaucer[2] *exemplar emendate scriptum.*" The second leaf is from an entirely different MS., it is in Latin and apparently belonged to a book of hours. On f. 3 a there are a few faded lines which seem to indicate that the scribe of the sixth hand probably began there to copy the short pieces which he afterwards entered on ff. 113 b–114. There are also a few recipes or inventions on the same page in a different hand which have been crossed out. The *verso* of f. 3 is blank. The actual contents of the MS. begin therefore with f. 4.[3] The most important poems of the list are, besides *The Gospel of Nicodemus: The Romance of Ywaine and Gawayne* (ff. 4–25), *The Proces of the Seuyn Sages* (ff. 25 b–48 b), *The Poems of Lawrence Minot* (ff. 52–57 b), and *The Pricke of Conscience* (ff. 76–113).

The Gospel begins on 57 b and extends to within a few lines of the head of col. 2, f. 66 b. The rubric is, "Hic incipit euangelium nichodemi." There are a few stanzas in a much later hand just after the end of the Gospel and on the same page:

> "What shal happen alse weene
> After MCCCCC lx. yerne:
>
> When mametri is beate downe
> An þe godspel trwe Ifownde
> Then shall begin holly wrte to be senne.
>
> In eache mans breste
> There dooth it rest,
> What shall betide
> Of þe wordle wide
> They haþe all byt (?) ȝeste.

[1] *Op. cit.* pp. vii–viii.

[2] The name "Richard Chawfer" occurs on the *verso* of the last leaf in the volume. It seems to have been these words which attracted the attention of Tyrwhitt to the MS. and brought about the discovery of Minot's poems. See Ritson, *Poems written on Interesting Events in the Reign of King Edward III, Anno MCCCLII, by Lawrence Minot*, 1795, pp. vii, viii; cf. Hall, *op. cit.*, Scholle, *op. cit.*

[3] Throughout this discussion all references to MSS. will be according to the present pagination. But in the case of Galba E IX the older pagination may be obtained by deducting three from the present numbers.

He that casteth of the olde
  Before he know the newe,
Maye weepe in the winter
  When frostes dooth inswe.

All olde things ar not ill
  Where wise men doo weue;
Som newe thinges ar scharce good
  And that is trwe."

There is a peculiar piece at the end of the MS. (f. 113 b) which has, I think, never been printed in full and which runs as follows:

"The horss hath xxv propertes, þat ys to say: He hath iiii off a lyon, iiii of an ox, iiii off an asse, iiii off an hare *and* iiii of a fox, and v of a woman.

Aft*er* a lyon, prowd-herted, brod-brestid, iiii good leg*is*, *and* a stowte stern. After the ox, out(?)-ribbed, low-brawned, schort-pasterd *and* well Ifed. Aft*er* the asse, well-mouthid, well-wyndyd, streght-bakked (?) *and* rownd-foted. Aft*er* the hare, steep yen, wyght off fote, tornyng on litell grownde, ii god filetts. Aft*er* the fox, prik-eryd, fayr-sided, schorte trottyng, and a litell hed. Aft*er* a woman mery of chere, brod-buttokyd, and esy to lep on, good at long-rynnyng, *and* steryng vnder a man.[1]

Heded as an ox;
Tayled as fox;
Comly as a kyng;
Nekkyd as a dukyng;
Mowythyd as a kliket;
Witted [as] a wodkok;
Wylled as a wedercoke."

The Harleian MS. 4196 is also a folio on vellum and very large, like Galba E IX. It contains 258 leaves measuring $15 \times 9\frac{1}{2}$ inches and having two columns of 47–49 (usually 48) lines each a page. The MS. is bound in quires of eight leaves each, the ends of the quires being indicated by catch-words. There are two leaves (one probably a fly-leaf) missing from the first quire, two from the fourth, and one from the thirteenth (ending with f. 99). One entire quire has been lost after f. 107, and

[1] A similar scrap is preserved in Brit. Mus. MS. Lansdowne 762, f. 16 (printed by Wright and Halliwell in *Reliquiae Antiquae*, I, 232–233): "A good horsse must have xv. propertyes and condicions, that is to witte, iij. of a man, iij. of a woman, iij. of a ffox, iij. of an hare, and iij. of an asse. Of a man, bolde, prowde, *and* hardy; of a woman, fayre-brested, fayre of here, and esy to lepe vpon; of a fox, a faire tayle, short eres, with a good trotte; of an hare, a grete eye, a drye heed, *and* wele rennyng; of an asse, a bigge chynne, a flat leg, *and* a good hone. Wele traveled wymen or wele traveled horsses were neuer good."

there are nine leaves in the twenty-ninth quire (ending with f. 230). The MS. belonged to the noted antiquarian and scholar Wanley in the early part of the eighteenth century, and the following words in his hand are written at the top of the first page: "19 die mensis Novembris A. D. 1725." This was probably the date when Wanley acquired the MS., since it was his custom to enter the dates on which he purchased MSS. and books in his diary. Early in the seventeenth century the MS. was probably the property of William Browne, the well-known poet and author of *Britannia's Pastorals*, since the name "Wm Browne 1622" occurs on the upper margin of f. 1.

There are three handwritings of the same general character and of about the same age in this MS., all of them being large, bold, and very distinct and belonging to the early years of the fifteenth century. The first of these hands extends from the beginning to f. 165, the second from f. 165 to the beginning of the *Gospel of Nicodemus*, from which point to the end of the MS. we have a third handwriting quite different from the preceding one. That is to say, it is much blacker and bolder and the ornamentation is of a different character. Most of the ornamentation is the result of making the capitals and initials of columns and paragraphs unusually large (so as to extend over three or more lines), and of colouring them with gold, blue, and red. But the third scribe employs gold and blue very sparingly, and confines his ornamentation mainly to large flourishes in black and red for the initial letters of columns and paragraphs.

Horstmann[1] and Wülker[2] place this MS., as well as Galba E IX, in the fourteenth century, without, however, offering any proof whatever.[3] The two MSS. are undoubtedly of about the same age, though Dr. G. F. Warner of the British Museum thinks that Galba E IX is perhaps a little earlier. The same palaeographist and other experts of the MSS. department of the Museum whom I have consulted, as well as all modern English scholars of note, place both MSS. in the first half of the fifteenth century. The hands are decidedly later than any of the well-known fourteenth century specimens, such as we find in MS. Harl. 2253 and Egerton 613, for example. The language is, indeed, somewhat archaic for the fifteenth century, but this may be accounted for in two ways. In the first place, the transcribers of the two MSS., as an examination of the versions of the *Gospel of Nicodemus* shows, were undoubtedly very careful

[1] *Archiv 53*, 389. [2] *Op. cit.* p. 19.

[3] Hortsmann in fact (*Altenglische Legenden*, Neue Folge, Einleitung, p. 78) confidently asserts that the MS. originated about the middle of the fourteenth century. Other German scholars have generally followed Horstmann and Wülker.

in trying to reproduce the peculiarities of their original. Secondly, the MSS. are written in the Northern dialect, which withstood the influences of modernisation much longer than Southern and Midland English. Horstmann holds[1] (against Wülker) that version H is better, more original, than version G. Here again Horstmann's judgment is not to be trusted. For a careful comparison of the two versions, together with the opinion of Dr. Warner, proves clearly that version G is a better, a more exact reproduction of the original than H. In the former there are not nearly so many serious omissions as in the latter, and the scribe of Galba E IX manifested on more than one occasion an appreciation of rhythm and metre which was evidently wanting in the copyist of Harl. 4196. If we tabulate the evidence then in favour of version G, we may arrange it under three different heads: (1) the opinion of one of the best-known specialists in palaeography, (2) the rhymes of G are more exact than those of H, (3) G does not contain nearly so many serious omissions as H. Moreover, since the omissions (generally of a single word) in the two versions almost never correspond, we may definitely and emphatically assert that neither of the two is a copy of the other. And as neither of them can possibly represent the original MS., we are safe in saying that they could not have been by the same author.[2] Again, the same scribe could not have transcribed the two versions, for the handwriting of the one is quite different from that of the other.[3]

Horstmann has given a careful description of the contents of about half of Harl. 4196 (*i. e.* as far as the *Gospel of Nicodemus*), but for some reason he failed to say that the same MS. contains a version of Hampole's

[1] Cf. *Archiv 57*, 73. [2] Cf. Hortsmann, *Archiv 57*, 73.

[3] The following instances will sufficiently illustrate the differences above referred to: G has only three or four omissions of single, short words (*day* l. 38, *ay* l. 536, and *ane* l. 855). It also has the following apparently incorrect forms, as against the correct ones of H: *in what* for *I ne wate*, l. 459; it is not easy to say which MS. is correct in l. 603, where G has simply, *His clathes of him þai don*, and H, *His clothes þai dof, on him þai don*, they may represent different renderings; A–S omit this thought; G *Iestas* for *Iesmas*, (H) l. 637; G *quit* for *tyte*, (H) l. 1016. H omits: *Ihesus* l. 209, *goddes* l. 390, *many* l. 522, *þan* l. 649, *done to* l. 1085. Both G and H omit *dred(e)* l. 909, A–S have the word. H shows the following incorrect forms: *sene* for *schene* l. 125; *schape* (allit. with *skathe*) for *skape* l. 380; *als yhe can* for *als he can*, l. 437; *þis* for *his*, l. 587; *And answer* for *ane answer*, l. 654; *sir clerkes* for *þir clerkes* (A þes, S *þire*), l. 689; *uoys* (so Horst.) for *noys* (S *noys*), l. 707; the MS. reading might be either *uoys* or *noys*; rhymes *sethen—hethen—feyne—þethen*, l. 1069 ff. (G. *seine—hein—fein—þeine*); *þis* for *þi*, l. 1164; *coniornd* for *coniord*, l. 1165; *myknes* for *mirknes*, l. 1193; *symon* for *simion*, l. 1093 and 1203; rhymes *toke—luke* for (G) *toke—loke*, l. 1209; *forthermer* for *foreriner* (forerunner), l. 1246; *dwell* for *well*, l. 1292; *bandell* for *bandes*, l. 1417; *þat* for *þou*, l. 1497; *will* for *sall* (rhyme *all*), 1506; *destroit* for *destroid* (rhyme *noyed*), l. 1509; rhymes *toke—boke—luke—note* for *toke—boke—luke—noke*, l. 1639 ff.; *þare þai* for *þan þai*, l. 1653.

Pricke of Conscience.[1] The first 205 leaves contain a series of North English poems in the form of "Homilies on the Gospel lessons for Sundays and Festivals, and on the Legends of the Saints."[2] The *Gospel of Nicodemus* begins (f. 206) with the same rubric as in Galba E IX: "Hic incipit Eua*n*geliu*m* Nichodemi," and it extends to the foot of col. 1, f. 215. The *Pricke of Conscience* then follows (f. 215 b) with the words (in a different hand), "This Booke here following is callyd the pryck of Conscience," and extends to the end of the MS.[3]

The MS. Additional 32,578 was purchased by the British Museum "at Sotheby's (Fuller Russell sale) 30 June 1885." It apparently belonged to several different people between the seventeenth and the nineteenth centuries. This fact is to be gathered from several different names that are written at various places in the margins of the MS. There are, for example: "Thos. Eyr's Booke" in a late hand (f. 2), "Francis Britland"[4] (f. 17), "William Richardson" (f. 33 b), and "Thomas Stead" (ff. 64 b, 76 b, 103, 109 b), which are all probably the names of seventeenth century owners of the MS. The name "John Pride" also occurs on f. 103 b, and "Thomas Steade," "Nicholas Steade" are scribbled several times on the same page. At the top of the page the word "Banker" is written unusually large, and just beneath it are the following lines in a late sixteenth or an early seventeenth century hand:

"O lord, I am not poffte in mind,
I have noo scornfull eye,
I do not exercise myselfe
In thinges that be to hye."

But the most important name that is found in this MS. is undoubtedly that of "Robert Farnelay" in the colophon to the *Pricke of Conscience*, because there is no reason to doubt that it has some connection with the origin

[1] *Altenglische Legenden*, Neue Folge, Einl. p. 78. It has of course long been a well-known fact, but it is certainly very desirable that the first editors of parts of valuable MSS. give some account of the contents of the entire MS. in question. It might inspire others to enter the work of editing inaccessible texts, and would certainly save them much time and labour.

[2] From Mr. J. A. Herbert's manuscript notes of a new and revised edition of Ward's *Catalogue of Romances in the Department of Manuscripts in the British Museum*, which the author kindly placed at my disposal. Two of these legends are about the Holy Rood, (1) *The Story of the Holy Rood* (ff. 76 b–80 b); (2) *Finding of the Cross* (ff. 149–151). Cf. Morris, *Legends of the Holy Rood*, London, 1871.

[3] For a description of this version of the *Pricke of Conscience* and an extensive comparison with those of other MSS. in the British Museum, see Andreae, *op. cit.*; Bülbring, *Transactions of the Philological Society* for 1889–90, p. 261 ff.

[4] On f. 17 a the words "Fran. Britland his Book Anno Dom*i*ni 1695, Anno Dom*i*ni 1696," are written in a large distinct hand.

of a portion at least of the MS. The *Dictionary of National Biography* contains two of the names, Thomas Eyre and William Richardson, and the accounts of their lives and the time in which they lived agree very well with what we should expect in the possessors of the MS. in question.

The MS. is a paper quarto containing 140 leaves which measure $8\frac{1}{4} \times 5\frac{1}{8}$ inches, and it is bound in quires of sixteen leaves each. But according to the present arrangement of the quires, the sixth has twelve leaves, the seventh eleven, and the last[1] only one leaf; the ends of the quires are always indicated by catch-words. The volume is written in two different hands, the first and (somewhat) earlier one extending through the *Pricke of Conscience* (f. 103 b), and the second from that point to the end of the MS. They are both clearly fifteenth century hands, and they are small and distinct, but not elegant. The volume contains only English poetry, which is written in one column of thirty-six to forty-four lines to a page. The initial letter of each line and capitals generally are ornamented with a simple stroke of red, while the first letter of each paragraph is unusually large and it is written in red ink with many flourishes.

The contents of the MS. are: (1) *The Pricke of Conscience* (ff. 1–103 b), the first lines of which are so badly faded that it is almost impossible to make them out. The poem has the following conclusion:

"To þe whilke place he vs alle brynge
þat for oure hele on rode gan hynge. Amen!"

After this we have the important colophon which has already been mentioned: "Explicit tractatus qui dicit*ur* stim*ulus* Consciencie, Anno D*omi*ni mill*esi*mo CCCC^{mo} quinto, sec*und*um manu*m* Roberti ffarnelay Capell*ani*."[2] The name "Roberti" has been altered by a later hand to "Johannes," and the words "manent*is* in Bolton" have been added. The name Farnelay is also introduced into the last line of the second piece (A poem on the Creed, ff. 104–105):

"W*it*houtyn any mysse, Mary, þou pray
þat we may come to blisse.—Ame*n*! q*uo*d ffarnelay."[3]

[1] According to Andreae (*op. cit.*) four leaves are wanting in the *Pricke of Conscience* somewhere between ff. 80 and 93, and the first 182 lines of the poem are also wanting. The margins of all the pages from f. 17 b to 27 b are covered with a prose religious piece in a different hand, and the confession to God of some pious priest. A similar piece in the same hand occurs on the margins of ff. 47 b–50 a.

[2] The following Latin sentences also occur at the end of the *Pricke of Conscience*: "Laus tibi rex Ch*r*iste, quem librum explicit iste"; and near the bottom of the page (f. 103 b) in red: "ffini! ffinito libro sit laus et gl*or*ia Ch*r*isto.—Amen!"

[3] The following invocation in red is written at the top of the page (f. 104): "Assit principio S͞ca Maria mea!"

Now, there is no valid reason why we should not accept 1405[1] as the date of the *Pricke of Conscience* part of the MS., and the other portion cannot be much later. This date would probably make version A a little older than G–H, but it is of course next to impossible to determine with anything like exactness the chronology of several different MSS. which were written in the same century and in different parts of England.

The Creed poem has the colophon, "Explicit Credo in Anglicis." The third piece (ff. 105 b–116), which is an English poem in 784 lines, begins with the rubric, "Incipit templu*m* Do*m*i*n*i," and the first two lines run:

"Gode þat alle thynge first began
Has giffen his g*ra*ce in diuerse gyse."

It ends:

"Als he of noȝt all*e* thynge began
Gif vs þe blisse þat lastes ay.—Amen!
Explicit templu*m* Do*m*i*n*i."

The *Gospel of Nicodemus* (ff. 116 b–140 b) is the fourth poem of this MS., and it begins without any rubric or heading at the top of the page.

The volume ends with a short moral-religious poem (f. 140 b) in three eight-line stanzas with a common refrain and a *moral* or *l'envoi* in four lines, which has never been printed, so far as I have been able to discover. It may, therefore, be given in full here:

"In a semely someres tyde,
  Als I gan walke in a wilde woude,
Vndr*e* a bowe I sawe abyde
  A Company of clerkes gude;
In a stody als þai stode
  þus þai gan mene in þair*e* spekynge:
'In ilke man*er*e of ma*n*s mode
  Mesure is best of all*e* thynge;

Crist þat all*e* thynge has vndr*e* cure—
  Heuene & erthe and also helle—
All*e* he made vndr*e* mesure,
  As holy writte wytnes welle.
þou spare no pont (?) of þair*e* spelle,
  Bot leue wele in þis lernynge;
And take þis tale as I þe telle,
  þat mesure is best of all*e* thynge.

[1] Dr. G. F. Warner and Mr. J. A. Herbert both think that "1405" is intended to represent the date of the *Pricke of Conscience*, and both agree in placing G–H in the first half of the fifteenth century.

To litill*e* or to gret excesse,
  Bothe arne wike and vicyous
And greue god bothe, as I gesse,
  ffor bothe þe p*ar*tise arne p*er*illouse.
þen were a mene full*e* v*er*tuouse
  And p*ro*ued prisse in p*re*chynge;
And þ*er*efore bothe in hille and house
  Mesure is best of all*e* thynge.'

God g*ra*unt þat his g*ra*ce so grete
  Be wele mesured till*e* ilka man,
And to his g*ra*ce he take hym mote
  W*ith* crafte to kepe hym as he kan!"

The version S is preserved in a MS. of Sion College Library which has the press-mark arc. L. 40. $2^{a}+{}^{2}$ (*olim* "17," "18.6" and "arc. 2.19."). On the cover the contents of the volume are designated as, "Of Auricular Confessions, Passion of Xt, Legend of the Virgin Mary, Of know Man's self." The MS. is paper and at one time contained 133 leaves, but one of these (f. 31) has been torn away so as to leave only a narrow strip with a few words from the beginning of several of the lines on the *verso* still legible.[1] The leaves measure $8\frac{1}{2} \times 5\frac{1}{2}$ inches, and the MS. is therefore about the size of Brit. Mus. 32,578. Likewise the handwriting, quality of the paper, and general appearance resemble the British Museum MS. It is in English poetry throughout, and has only one column of from twenty-eight to forty-five lines to a page. As there are very few catchwords, it is rather difficult to determine anything about the arrangement of the leaves into quires. The MS. is described by Bernard[2] under the colophon *Librorum Manuscriptorum Bibliothecae Sionensis, ab incendio Londiniensi* A.D. 1666 *vix ereptae*,—it being one of sixty-eight MSS. which were by some good fortune preserved from the destructive Great Fire of London.[3] Bernard then gives the contents, which have been copied on a fly-leaf of the MS. in a modern hand: "A Discourse touching Auricular Confession, in the Northern Dialect.

"The Passion of our Saviour, out of Nicodemus's Pseudo-Gospel.

"A Legend of the Virgin Mary's sorrows, as supposed to be revealed by her to St. Bernard in a Dialogue with him.

[1] The missing leaf contained sixty-nine lines.

[2] Cf. *op. cit.*, II, 106, No. 4081.

[3] Horstmann (*Archiv 68*, 207) gives no information of any consequence about this MS.; nor does Wülker (*op. cit.*, p. 19), except to say incorrectly that there is a prose translation of our piece in Sion College, Cod. 17 (*Und im collegio Sionensi cod.* 17 *ist eine prosaübertragung unsrer Schrift*): "The passion of our Saviour, out of Nicodemus's gospel," the title being an inexact copy from Bernard, who has "Pseudo-Gospel." E. Gibsion's ed. of Bernard adds: "Accuranto S. wadhamensi," as to history of these MSS.

"A Treatise of Knowing a man's self, all written about Edw. III.'s time, 4to."

So far as it goes this description is very good, but Bernard did not recognize in the last piece a version of Hampole's extremely popular poem, *The Pricke of Conscience.* The MS. is in a fifteenth century hand, which bears a later character than those of Harl. 4196 and Galba E IX.

The first piece begins:

"Not yheme of þam of with þam to mete,
for all geme þai bittir, þai ar swete,"

and ends:

"bot þe loue of god þat es clene,
Of werldly luf þat here es sene."

At the top of the next page (f. 13) the following heading appears on a red-framed scroll:

"Of þe passioun of crist als wittenes Nichodeme."

The Gospel continues to the bottom of f. 38 b, one leaf (as already stated) having been lost.

The third piece, which Bernard calls "The Legend of the Virgin Mary's Sorrows, etc.," begins at the top of f. 39:

"Why forsakes þou me, whye?
Hider I come with þe rede of þe."

The poem is written in stanzaic form.

The *Pricke of Conscience,* which begins at the top of f. 48 and extends to the end of the MS., has no title or heading, except that copied in pencil on the upper right-hand margin of the page from the table of contents, "A Treatise of Knowing a Man's self." The poem begins with the usual prologue, "þe myght of þe Fader almyghty," etc., and ends abruptly (f. 133 b) with line 9220 (according to Morris's edition), "Als wele þai þat sal be farre."[1]

III.

PROSE VERSIONS OF THE GOSPEL OF NICODEMUS IN MIDDLE-ENGLISH LITERATURE.

Nine different MSS. of the whole or a part of the Gospel in Middle-English prose are at present known.[2] They are (in chronological order,

[1] This version of the *Pricke of Conscience* is described and classified by K. D. Bülbring, *Englische Studien,* xxxiii, 2 ff., but no attempt is made to give any further description of the MS. As compared with the Morris edition 404 lines are wanting at the end of the Sion MS.

[2] New MSS. are likely to be discovered at any time, since there are so many cathedral and other libraries in England of which there is no complete catalogue.

as near as can be determined): (1) Magdalen College, Cambridge, Pepys 2498 (pp. 459–463); (2) British Museum, Egerton 2658 (ff. 15 b–18); (3) Stonyhurst College, B. XLIII (ff. 83–96); (4) Salisbury Cathedral Library, 39 (ff. 129 b–147); (5) British Museum, Additional 16,165 (ff. 94 b–114 b); (6) Oxford, Bodleian 207 (ff. 120 b–124); (7) British Museum, Harley 149 (ff. 255–276); (8) Worcester Cathedral Library, No. 172 (ff. 4–16); (9) Cambr. Univ. Libr. Mm., 1. 29 (ff. 8–16).[1] Three of the MSS. (4, 5, 7) contain each a translation of the entire *Gospel of Nicodemus*, and the same was apparently once true of a fourth (No. 8), that is, before it had lost several of its leaves. The other five have a tolerably literal version of that part of the Gospel which is especially concerned about the life experiences of Joseph of Arimathea (*i.e.* they all begin with chap. xii. of the Latin *Evangelium Nicodemi* as printed by Tischendorf, p. 365). It seems indeed plausible that these translations were made because of special interest in the legend of Joseph of Arimathea, rather than in the story of Christ's descent into Hades. There is also an Old-English version of the same portion of the *Evangelium Nicodemi*, the MS.[2] of which belongs to the early twelfth century. And a careful examination[3] of the numerous MSS. of Latin versions of the apocryphal Gospel that are preserved in many libraries of England would no doubt result in the discovery of the Latin original of these Old- and Middle-English versions. The Egerton and Stonyhurst MSS. also contain a free translation of portions of the first chapters of the Gospel, but the work is of a character to suggest that the author was not especially interested in closely following or reproducing his original. It should be noted that the Stonyhurst, Egerton, and Bodley versions all go back to a common original, but they are each written in a different dialect. The Salisbury and Additional recensions also had a common origin. From the standpoint of relationship among the several versions the MSS. may be divided into the following groups: (*a*) Egerton, Stonyhurst, Bodley; (*b*) Salisbury, Additional; (*c*) Pepys 2498; (*d*) Harley 149; (*e*) Worcester Cathedral; (*f*) Cambridge Univ. Libr.

The version contained in MSS. Salisb. and Addit. was made by the well-known fourteenth century writer, John Trevisa, but neither of the MSS. can be considered the original. In fact, we know that the Addit.

[1] The present pagination is given in every case.

[2] Vespasian D xiv; see *The Old English Gospel of Nicodemus*, Mod. Philol. I, 79 ff.

[3] It is to be expected that the new edition of the Latin *Evangelium Nicodemi* promised by that excellent scholar, E. von Dobschütz, will contain a thorough study of all these MSS., and that much light will thus be thrown upon the question of relationship between the English and Latin versions.

version, as we now have it, is a copy in John Shirley's handwriting, and that of the Salsb. MS. has too many omissions and other mistakes of carelessness or ignorance to be even considered in the light of an original Trevisa. Moreover, the handwriting cannot be earlier than about the middle of the fifteenth century—that is to say, too late for Trevisa.[1] But at least two points of an external character speak in favour of Trevisa's authorship of the translation: (1) Shirley ascribes it to Trevisa: "Maistre[2] Johan Trevysa haþe here in mynde þat some tyme þe Greekes maden Ioustes and tournamentes and oþer pleyes of maystryes and of strenkeþe oones in fyve yere vnder þe hille called Olympias and cleped þe playes Olympias."

(2) Trevisa's name is inserted in his characteristic manner at the same place in both MSS.: "Alleluya, Trevysa, alleluya is to meene," etc. In the Salisb. MS. "Alleluia, Teruisa, Ame*n*, ys to mene," etc.[3]

And (3) The style bears, in spite of the distortions of the copyists, much similarity to that of Trevisa's universally recognized works. The relationship which exists among Egerton, Stonyhurst and Bodley has already been noticed. Each of them is the work of a different scribe, and there is no possible means of determining which is nearest the original. The other three MSS. represent versions which seem to have been made in entire independence of one another, as well as of the versions already considered. Harley 149 is the latest of the complete versions, and it is the most modern in arrangement and style, as well as the most interesting in the way it reproduces the narrative. The handwriting of the Cambridge Univ. Libr. MS. proves it to be perhaps the most recent of all the MSS. with which we are acquainted.

IV.

DESCRIPTION OF THE PROSE MANUSCRIPTS.

A. As they at present exist the translation in the Pepys MS. represents the earliest M.E. prose version that is known. It was probably written about the beginning of the fifteenth century, as we learn from an entry on p. 370 of the volume: "The age of this book by conferring with another copy was wreten when K. Henry the .4. had business agaynst the Welshman an° 1401." According to Miss Paues, who consulted Dr. Montague James on the subject, "The MS. belongs to about the year 1400," and the note just quoted is "apparently in the hand of the well-

[1] John Trevisa (1326–1412).
[2] MS. 16,165, f. 94 b. This sentence does not occur in the Salisbury version.
[3] Fol. 144 b.

known collector of the Parker MSS., Stephen Batman († 1584), D.D., domestic Chaplain to Archbishop Parker."[1]

The title on the cover of the large codex ("Wickleefs Sermons MS.") is altogether misleading, because the homilies are not the work of Wyclif at all, as we are in fact told by a note written in a modern hand on the page preceding that which contains the table of contents: "These sermons are not Wickliff's, neither matter, nor style, nor manner are at all like his; neither was the author any Wicklivite. Indeed, the Language seems to be older than Wickliff."[2] The "Table of Contents" is written in the same hand as the note, and it is described with much attention to details so far as it goes, but it is not complete. As Miss Paues does not give the MS. table of contents in her description, it will be worth while to reproduce it here:

"1.	The History of the Life of Christ, with a comment there upon	page 1
2.	The Mirrour,[3] being a comment or Sermons upon the Gospels, throughout the year	p. 45
3.	Sayings of wise men	p. 212
4.	The ten commandments	p. 217
5.	A comment upon the Apocalypse	p. 227
6.	The Psalter in English with Gregory's comment	p. 263
7.	The canticle, confitebor tibi, etc.	p. 361
8.	The Song Moses	p. 362
9.	The Canticle of Isaiah	p. 364
10.	The song of Zachary	p. 368
11.	The Magnificat	p. 368
12.	The nunc dimittis	p. 368
13.	The Athanasian Creed	p. 369
14.	The Canticle upon the Mass	pp. 371, 373
[15.]	Several old Rules[4]	p. 371, etc."

[1] Cf. A. C. Paues, *A Fourteenth Century English Biblical Version*, Cambridge, 1902, Introd. p. 57; cf. pp. 65–69. It was through the kindness of Miss Paues that I learned about the Pepys MS. and was enabled to transcribe it. She printed a brief account of the volume in *Englische Studien*, xxx, 344–346, under the title "A XIVth century Version of the 'Ancren Riwle.'"

[2] The label on this MS. may have led W. Cave or his authority, Seller (*Scriptorum Ecclesiasticorum*, etc., Oxford, 1740–43, vol. II, p. 18, col. 2), erroneously to attribute a translation of *Ev. Nicod* to Wyclif. Cf. Wülker, p. 20 f., Forshall and Madden (*Wycliffite Vers. of the Holy Bible*, Preface), Arnold (*Select English Works of John Wyclif*, 3 vols. Oxford, 1869–72), F. D. Matthew (*The English Works of Wyclif, hitherto unpublished*, London, E. E. T. S., 1880), know nothing of such a translation, nor is it mentioned by Wharton, the reviser of Cave, in his list of Wyclif's works. Cf. Cave, *op. cit.* II, Append., pp. 63–65; J. Loserth, *Iohannis Wyclif Sermones.* Now first edited from the MSS. with critical and historical notes, etc. London. The Wyclif Soc., 4 vols. 1886.

[3] Cf. MS. Harl. 5085.

[4] According to Forshall and Madden (Pref. p. iv) MS. Pepys 2498 contains an English translation of the Psalms (cf. Paues, *op. cit.* p. lvii).

The MS. is a large folio on vellum measuring 13½ × 9½ inches, and it is written in a late fourteenth or early fifteenth century hand without any attempt at ornamentation. It contains 464 pages (*i. e.* 232 leaves, but the MS. is numbered by pages) with two columns to a page, besides two paper fly-leaves at the beginning and two at the end. The volume is in quires of eight leaves each, as indicated by catch-words, and it was apparently written by one scribe.

The Gospel of Nicodemus begins near the top of col. 2, p. 459, with the heading "Nicodemus Gospell" in a late hand, and it extends to p. 463. The beginning of the piece is as follows:

"þE gode man & the noble Prince Nichodemus, þat priuelich was Ihe*s*us deciple for drede of þe wicked Iewes, I schal telle ȝou a litel book þ*at* he made of þe passiou*n* and of his vparisyng þat fel. On þat ilche day þat he aros, þe bisschopes & þe princes & þe p*re*stes & þe maisters of þe lawȝe come*n* into her Synagoge, and bispeken þe deþ hard of Ioseph of Aramathie þat hij duden in prisou*n* opon þe day biforé, & hadden enseled þe dore & þe keyes vnder her seales, þat were ȝouen to Cayphas & to Annas, Bisschopes of þe lawe, and seiden, etc."

At the end of the Gospel (p. 463) there is a colophon which runs: "Of þe vprist of Crist, as Nichodem*us* ga*n* telle, here now make ich ende. God schilde vs all fro*m* helle!"[1]

B. The Egerton MS. 2658 is a large, thin vellum folio of eighteen leaves which measure 13 × 9 inches, the first of which has been considerably injured by fire or water, so that it is difficult to make out the words. It is written in a fine large hand with two columns of 50–54 lines each to a page, and it must once have been a beautiful piece of chirographical work. The initial letters of sentences and paragraphs are often very large, and they are profusely ornamented in gold and purple, blue and red, or blue, gold and red, but always so as to produce a pleasing effect to the eye. The MS. was purchased by the British Museum from a Mrs. J. Boyd on April 21, 1887. According to the *Catalogue of Additional and Egerton Manuscripts* (for the years 1882–1887, p. 378) the contents of the MS. are, (1) "The History of the Passion and Resurrection and ascension of our Lord, professing to be a translation from St. Bonaventura as appears from the colophon (f. 15 b): Explicit liber Aureus de passione et resurrecione *domi*ni *per* dominum Bonaventuram Cardinalem cuius anime propicietur deus." This is "followed by (2) a version of the Gospel of Nicodemus, or the Harrowing of Hell."

[1] A note on p. 189 suggests that the translation of the Gospel of John in this MS. may be the work of John Trevisa.

But according to the Stonyhurst MS. (which contains the same pieces, or piece), the "History of the Passion" is not separated from the "Gospel of Nicodemus." In fact the colophon about St. Bonaventura does not occur in the Stonyhurst MS. The Bodley version omits the "History of the Passion," etc., altogether and begins with the story of Joseph of Arimathea's deliverance from prison, as it is narrated in the *Evangelium Nicodemi*, chap. xii ff. This account begins in Egerton 2658 immediately after the colophon without any heading or rubric: "Now turne we aȝen to þe p*ro*ces aforhonde, how it bifell of Ioseph of-Aramathye which þe Iewes hadde enp*ri*soned þe Sat*er*day. Þe morwe vpon here Sabot day þei forȝat not Ioseph of Aramathie, whiche þei hadde yputte ynto þe stronge stonen house."

The Stonyhurst MS. has the same beginning, while the Bodl. MS. omits the first sentence and begins: "The Iewes the morowe vpon her Sabot Day," etc. Pilate's letter to the emperor Tiberius does not appear in this translation, but it is mentioned near the conclusion of the story: "And all*e* Pilate lete write a*n* epistle to the Citee of Rome, and to Tyberius Cesar of all*e* Cristes passiou*n*." The last words in the Egerton MS. are: "Now Ihe*s*u for his muche myȝt ȝeue vs grace such*e* beleue to haue, wher þurȝ we mowe come to endelees blysse! Amen." After this a later hand has added: "And brynge vs all*e* blys." Beneath these last words (f. 18) there is appended in a sixteenth century hand, "The history of the blessed Scriptures, George Theaker." Theaker is no doubt the name of a sixteenth century owner of the MS.

C. The Stonyhurst MS. is perhaps a little older than Bodl. 207.[1] The volume is a small vellum quarto containing 122 leaves (one fly-leaf at the end) which measure $6\frac{1}{2} \times 4\frac{1}{2}$ inches. The MS. is bound in quires of ten leaves each as far as p. 90; the remainder is in quires of eight leaves, excepting the last leaf. The ends of the quires are indicated throughout by catch-words.

The contents as indicated by rubrics or otherwise are: (1) "The Life of St. Catherine in English prose" (f. 1). Rubric: "Here begynnyth the right excelent and most glor*i*ous lyf and passyon of þe ryȝt blyssed virgyn Seynt Kateryne." The first page has been so blackened by fire or water that it is almost impossible to determine the reading. But the first three pages apparently constitute the prologue, for there is another heading near the bottom of f. 2: "Now folwyth the begynnyg of Seynt

[1] Mr. J. A. Herbert of the MSS. Department of the British Museum has kindly examined both the Egerton and the Stonyhurst MSS., and he thinks the former might be placed about 1450, and the latter some ten years later.

Katyrine, the ȝere fro þe incarnacyon of Cryst Ihesu ij C," etc. The piece ends (f. 19 b) with the colophon: "Here endyth the lyf of the glorious virgyn and martyr Seynt Kateryne."

The next leaf (f. 20) was left blank, and (2) "Passio domini nostri Ihesu Christi, sit Nostra salus et proteccio" follows on f. 21. This collection of episodes from the lives of Christ and the Virgin extends to f. 96 and embraces (ff. 83–96) a portion of the *Gospel of Nicodemus.* The third piece is a religious poem (ff. 96 b–97 b) written in praise of Christ, in eight four-line stanzas:

(1)

"Ihesu for þi wurthy wounde
That went to þin hert-rote,
For synne þat hath my soule bounde,
Lete þi blyssyd blod be my bote.

(2)

Ihesu for þi wundys smerte
Of þe feet & of þe handyn twoo,
Make me meke & lawe of hert
& þe to loue as I schuld doo.

(3)

Ihesu for þoo doolful teerys
That þou weptyst for my gylt,
Here and spede my preyeȝerys
And spare me þat I be not spylt.

(4)

Ihesu þat art heuene Kyng,
Sothfast god & man also,
Ȝeue me grace of good endyng,
And hem alle þat I am holdyn to.

(5)

Ihesu, lord, þat madyst me
& wyth þi blyssed blod me bouȝt,
Forȝeue me þat I haf greuyd þe
Wyth wurd, worke, wyl and thouȝt.

(6)

Ihesu in qwam is alle my trost,
þat deyst upon þe rode-tre,
Wythdrawe my hert fro fleschly lust,—
From couertyse & from vanyte.

(7)

Ihe*su* Cryst, to þe I calle
þat art fad*yr* ful of myȝth;
Kope me þ*at* I ne falle
I*n* fleschly synne as I haue tyȝt.

(8)

Ihe*su*, for þi blyssed blode,
Bryng þe sowlys into blysse
Of qwom þ*at* I haue ony goode,
& spar*e* he*m* þ*at* haue doo amysse."

The fourth piece has the rubric, "Etas beate Marie Virginis" (f. 97 b), and ends with the colophon (f. 98), "Qui sc*ri*psit carmen / sit benedictus. Amen." The fifth and last piece is called, "The Charter of the Abbey of the Holy Ghost," and has the rubric, "Here begynnyth þe charter*e* of þe abbey of þe holy gost." And then the description begins: "Here is a book þat spekyth of a place þat is clepyd þe abbey of þe holy gost, þe qwiche schulde be fownded in clene co*n*science. In qwiche abbey, as þe book tellyth, schulde dwellyn xxix gostely ladyes, amonges qwom Charite is abbesse, Wysdam p*ri*oresse, and Mekenesse supprioresse. þer is also pou*er*te, Clennesse, Tempe*ra*u*n*ce, Sobyrnesse, Penaunce, Buxu*m*nesse, Simplesse, Misericord, Largesse, Resoun, Re*u*fulnesse, Meditacion, Orison, Deuocion, Contemplacion, Drede, and Gelusye."

This piece must not be confused with another that has a very similar title, "The Abbey of the Holy Ghost," and which was printed by Perry[1] many years ago from the Thornton MS. of Lincoln Cathedral library. Horstmann[2] has also printed the account from the same MS., and immediately following, "þe Chartre of þe Abbeye of þe Holy gost,"[3] from MS. Laud 210 (f. 136 ff.), supplemented by the version of the Vernon MS.[4] Excepting the last three or four lines the Stonyhurst MS. contains the entire piece.[5]

[1] *Religious Pieces in Prose and Verse*, London, E. E. T. S., 1867, pp. 48–58. Revised Edition, 1889, pp. 49–59.

[2] *Yorkshire Writers*, vol. I, pp. 321–337. Horstmann does not call attention to Perry's editions.

[3] Ibid., pp. 337–362. Horstmann thinks *The Abbey of the Holy Ghost* is probably a work of Richard Rolle, but *The Charter*, etc., is, he says, "the work of another author, not a Northerner; its plan is similar to that of *The Castle of Love.*" This treatise is found in Laud. MS. 210, f. 136 ff. (fragmentary), and in the Vernon MS. "joined to the original treatise, so that the two have coalesced into one. The same combination is followed by the later MSS., which are mostly derived from Laud-Vernon."

[4] Beginning with f. 360. Cf. Horstmann, *op. cit.* p. 356 ff.

[5] The MS. breaks off thus: "And almithy god for his m*er*cy ȝeve vs grace for to kepe fayre and clene þe abbeye of . . ." Cf. Horstmann, p. 362. Horstmann knew

D. Manuscript No. 39 of Salisbury Cathedral library is described by Sir E. Maunde Thompson[1] as follows:

"No. 39. Vellum; $10\frac{1}{8} \times 7$ inches, 149 ff. XV. cent.

1. Imperfect tract, containing meditations of S. Bernard (?). f. 1.
2. Speculum Sacerdotum. f. 11.
3. Treatise on the Lord's Prayer, Ave Maria, and Apostles' Creed, by John de Waldeby [*flor. circ.* 1392]. f. 20.

The part relating to the Creed is addressed to Thomas [De la Mare] Abbat of St. Albans.

4. The Gospel of Nicodemus in English [Prose]. f. 129 f.

The volume seems to have lost a large portion at the beginning; the original foliation commencing with 179. On f. 149, 'Liber [Thome] Crycetur precii xxvj s. viij d.' At the end is written Cyrcetur's form of bequeathing the book. On f. 342 is a half-erased note, which is also to be found in other volumes owned by Cyrcetur: 'Liber Thomae Cyrcetr, post cujus decessum liberetur alicui seculari clerico, sacerdoti, et predicatori, ut celebret et oret pro anima ejus et pro precedentibus possessoribus, ac pro quibus tenentur, et omnibus fidelibus, etc., continue dum liber duraverit, semper disponatur post obitum occupantis, ut occupans oret pro ultimo possessore et possessoribus ac omnibus fidelibus vivis et defunctis.'

The form of bequest[2] is in the same hand as (or one very similar to it) that of the immediately preceding Gospel of Nicodemus, which is the only English piece in the MS., the others being in Latin. Fol. 147 b and f. 148 were left blank, while there are four lines in Latin and in a different hand from the preceding form of bequest near the top of f. 148 b: 'Melius *est* ante tempus prouidere quam post causam remedium petere, Tum dormis vigilia studias operare vel orassat sic ut nulla fine transithora.'"

The *Gospel of Nicodemus* begins without any heading or rubric near the top of the page (f. 129 b). It was evidently transcribed by a care-

nothing about this MS., and he fails to mention three British Museum MSS. in the list (p. 321): Harl. 5272, Addit. 22,283, Stowe 39,—the additional MS. having the date "circ. 1390."

[1] *A Catalogue of the Cathedral Library of Salisbury*, London, 1880, pp. 9–10. The contents of this excellent Catalogue are reproduced by H. Schenkl (*Bibliotheca patrum latinorum Britannica*, VI, 1–45; cf. pp. 12–13 for this MS. Printed as No. X. in Wiener, *Sitzungsberichte der Philosophisch-historischen Classe*, Bd. 131, Wien, 1894).

[2] Fol. 147 contains the form of bequest also, but it differs somewhat from the above: Liber Thome Cyrcetr, post cuius decessum liberetur alicui deuoto sacerdoti qui vtitur predicatori die verbum ut celebret et oret pro anima eius et pro quibus tenentur et omnibus fidelibus, *etc.* Continue dum liber duraverit semper disponatur post obitum ocupantis ut ocupans oret pro ultimo possessore ac possessoribus precedentibus nec non et fidelibus viuis defunctis.

less and probably ignorant scribe, since there are several important omissions, as well as not a few instances of corrupt word-forms in the MS. The scribe frequently struck out and inserted words to suit his fancy. The Addit. 16,165 version is written with much care and neatness as compared with the Salisbury version, and it may be a better reproduction of the original (in spite of its Shirleyan peculiarities). But now and then the Salisbury version seems to be the more exact, and it is certainly to be placed earlier. The Salisbury MS. shows few traces of any attempt at ornamentation, the scribe being apparently devoid of much artistic feeling.

E. The Additional MS. 16,165 is a quarto containing 258 leaves,[1] all of which, excepting the first three and the last one, are paper. The vellum leaves are a little smaller than the others, measuring 11 × 8 inches; the paper ones measure $11\frac{1}{2} \times 8\frac{1}{2}$ inches. The entire volume is put together in quires of twelve leaves each, the end of each quire being indicated both by catch-words and by Roman numerals. The first quire however ends with f. 17, showing that five leaves including perhaps the three vellum ones have been inserted. An insertion of one leaf has also been made at the beginning of the ninth quire (f. 102), and another of two leaves occurs in the twelfth quire, but it is not easy to say where. Two leaves are missing from the eighteenth quire, that is to say, it contains only ten leaves.

The MS. was the property of the noted collector John Shirley in the fifteenth century, the entire volume being in fact in Shirley's own hand. The name "Shirley," written very large and with many ornamental flourishes in black and red, occurs near the top of the first fly-leaf, and just beneath it are the French words *ma ioye.* On the same page there are also some household recipes, a couple of lines in Latin badly faded, and some proverbial verses which run:

"Man, if þow wys arte,
Of þy gode take þy parte
Or þow hens weende.;
ffor if þowe leue þy part
In þe sekutours warde,
þy parte [shal be] no parte
At þe latter ende."

Fol. 1 b was left blank. The MS. is partly in prose, partly in verse;

[1] Not pages as Miss Hammond says; cf. *The Departing of Chaucer*, Mod. Philol. I, 331–336. The leaves of the MS. are interesting on account of their watermarks, according to which the volume is made up from at least seven different brands of paper.

but it is all English, excepting a few short Latin pieces here and there. According to the British Museum *Catalogue of Additional Manuscripts* the MS. was written about the middle of the fifteenth century. We may be sure that it could not have originated much later than this, for Shirley died in the year 1456.[1]

The contents of the volume are: (1) A poem by Shirley, called "þe prologe of þe kalundare of þis litell booke" (ff. 2–3), and beginning:

> "If þat þou list for to entende
> Of þis booke to here legende."

It ends (f. 3 b):

> "And euery womman of hir loue
> Prey I to god þat sitteþe aboue. Explicit."

Following this there is a Latin stanza of four lines, beginning, "Non homo letens tibi copia si fluateris," to the right of which the name "Shirley" appears on the margin.

(2) The second piece (*i.e.* the first one of the MS. proper, for the first three leaves are really fly-leaves) which begins at the top of f. 4 is Chaucer's translation of Boethius's *De consolatione philosophiae.* The heading is "Boicius de consolaci*one* prosed in Englisshe by Chaucier," while at the top of the double pages almost throughout the MS. are written the words, "Boycius in prosa translated by Geffrey Chaucier." For the first thirty-three leaves the pages are ornamented with large red, or black and red, capitals at the beginning of pages and paragraphs, with a few random strokes of red here and there. The "Boicius" translation extends to near the bottom of f. 94, and (3) *The Gospel of Nicodemus* begins at the top of the following page. This piece is introduced at the conclusion of the Boethius as follows: "And þus endeþe þe translacou*n* of Boece, sometyme oon of the chief Senatours of the senate of Rome, translated by þe moral and famous Chaucyer, which first enlumyned þis lande with and eloquent langage of oure rude englisshe meders tonge. And filowyng begynneþe þe translacou*n* of Nichodeme out of latyn into englisshe, laborred by maystre Iohan Trevysa, Doctour in Theologye, at þe instance of Thomas, some tyme lord of Berkley."

[1] Grohman (*The Master of the Game, by Edward, Second Duke of York.* The Oldest English Book on Hunting. Edited by Wm. A. and K. Baillie-Grohman. London, 1904) prints a letter from the late Sir Henry Ellis in which he says (cf. Introd., p. xxvii): "The MS. (*i.e.* 16165) is indisputably of the middle of the fifteenth century, completely corroborated by the title of a ballad written by Shirley contained in one of Thoresby's MSS., described in his *Ducatus Leodiensis,* dated in 1440." And the author says in his Appendix ("Bibliography"), p. 239, that the MS. "was probably copied about the year 1450."

Two points of interest are contained in this heading: (*a*) Shirley's testimony as to Trevisa's authorship of the translation, (*b*) the work of translation was undertaken at the instance of Thomas Lord Berkeley.

(4) The fourth piece begins at the top of f. 115, and is entitled, "Of þe boke of huntyng made by Edward duc of Yorke."[1] The first leaf (f. 115) is taken up with an extended Table of Contents: "Here beginneþe þe table of þe Chapitres þ*a*t beþe contened in þe Booke of huntyng, þe whiche is cleped þe Maystre of þe game, contreued and made by my lord of York þat dyed at Achincourt þe day of þe batayle in his souerain lordes p*ro*uince." At the beginning of the history, near the top of f. 116, there is a kind of dedication to King Henry IV (?): "Into þonour and reuerence of yowe, my right worshipful and drede lorde, Henry by þe grace of god."

This interesting book on hunting in the Middle Ages ends on f. 190 as follows: "and many dyuers gentil hunters did my bysynesse in þis rude maner to put þe Crafft, þe termes and þexercyse of þis sayde game more in remembraunce openly to þe knowlegge of alle lordes, ladyes, gentylmen, and wymmen,[2] affter þe custumes and maners vsed in þe hyenable court of þe Realme of Engeland."

(5) "And here filowyng begynneþe a Right lusty amerous balade, made in wyse of complaynt of a Right worshipfull Knyght þat truly euer serued his lady, enduryng grete disese by fals envye and malebouche, made by Lydegate" (ff. 190 b–200 b). Begins:

"IN MAY whanne *flourra* þe freshe lusty qwene."

Ends (f. 200 b):

"Exyles beon þat I may not atteyne
Rekouer to fynde of myn aduersite. Explicit."

(6) A Latin "tract on the duties and obligations of priests" (ff. 201–206).

(7) "The dreme of a Trewe lover, made by daun Iohn [Lydgate] of þe tempull of glasse, þat shall next folowe þe house of fame" (ff. 206 b–241 b).[3] The poem is in two parts and the heading in French runs:

[1] Another and different version of this unique treatise was recently published in a magnificent edition by Grohman (cf. *op. cit.*), with an exhaustive bibliography of mediaeval books on hunting, and with numerous illustrations reproduced from manuscript miniatures. [2] *and wymmen* repeated in the MS.

[3] The full title does not occur at the beginning of the poem, but it is written at the top of f. 207. This poem has been erroneously attributed by some to Stephen Hawes, and it was printed by W. de Worde under the title of *The Temple of Glas.* Cf. *Catal. of Additions to the Department of MSS. in the British Museum*, 1846–1847, pp. 155–6. "The Compleynt" begins on f. 231: "Ellas for thought and Inwarde peyne."

"Et en sy finé vn petit abstracte appellez regula sacerdotalis et comence vne soynge moult plesaunt, fait à la request dun amoreux *par* Lidegate, Le Moygne de Bury." Begins:

> "For thought compleynt and generous hevynesse."

Ends: "þis is al and some my lady dere
And I youre man frome yere to yere.

Here endeþe þe Dreme and þe compleynt of þe desyrous seruant in loue; and filowyng (8) begynneþe þe compleint of Anelyda, þe feyre Qweene of Cartage. Vpou*n* þe Chiualrous Arcyte of þe royal blode of Thebes descend" (ff. 241 b–243 b). Begins:

> "SO thirlleþe with the poynt of Remembraunce."[1]

Ends (f. 243 b):

> "And þus endeþe here, þe compleynt of *Anelyda*."

(9) "And filowyng begynnen two verses made in wyse of balade by Halsham Esquyer" (f. 244): Begins:

> "þe worlde so wyde, þeyre so remuable."

This poem is followed (10) on the same page by a "Balade by Chaucer" (?), which begins:

> "Hit is no right alle oþer lustes to leese."

(11) Another "Balade by Chaucer" begins about the middle of f. 244 b:

> "Of alle þe craftes oute, blessed be þe ploughe."

(12) Some Latin verses begin near the middle of f. 245: "Deuotissima suffragia p*ro* mulierib*us* inpregnand*is*."

(13) A "Balade made of Isabelle Countesse of Warr[wyk] and lady de Spenser by Richerd Beuchamp Eorlle of Warrewyk." The poem begins (f. 245 b):

> "I can not half þe woo compleyne
> þat doþe my woful herte streyne."

(14) "Prouerbe usually attributed to Chaucer" (ff. 245 b–246 b).

(15) "Invocacou*n* by Lydegate to Saynte Anne" (ff. 247–248). Begins: "þou first moeuer þat causest euery thing."

(16) "Balade made by Lydegate at þe Departyng of Thomas Chaucyer on Ambassaade into ffrance" (ff. 248–249 b).[2]

(17) Near the middle of f. 249 b there is another ballad dedicated to

[1] This is the second part of the well-known poem of Chaucer, the first part following at the end of the MS. (ff. 256 b–258 b).

[2] This poem was printed with a considerable introduction by Miss E. P. Hammond, *Mod. Philol.*, I, 331 ff.

Thomas Chaucer: "Amerous balade by Lydegate on þe kynges ambassade into ffraunce."

(18) The "Devynale p*er* Pycard" (f. 251 b). Begins:

"Take þe seventeþ in ordre sette."

(19) "Balade of wymens constance; Balade made by Lydegate" (ff. 252–253 b). Begins:

"þis world is ful of Varyaunce."

(20) "Amerous balade by Lydegate þ*a*t haþe loste his thanke of wymmen" (ff. 253 b—254 b), beginning:

"In honnour of þis heghe fest of custums yere by yere."

(21) "Complaynte Lydegate," or "þe comendacou*n* of wymmen" (ff. 255–256). Begins:

"FFul longe I haue a seruant be."

(22) Four Latin lines on the "Doctrina Sacerdotis" (f. 256).

(23) A "Balade of Compleynte" (f. 256 b). Begins:

"Compleyne ne koude, ne might myn he*r*t neuer."

(24) "Balade of Anelyda Qwene of Cartage, made by Geffrey Chaucyer" (ff. 256 b–258 b).

The *Gospel of Nicodemus* has the following beginning (f. 94 b): "Whanne Pilatus was ruler and Iuge of þe Iuwery, and Rufus and Leo weren consuls, and Annas and Cayphas p*r*inces of preostes of þe Iewes, þe eghtyenþe Kalendes of Aueryll, þat is þe fyve and twentyeþe day of þe moneþe of Marche, þe yeer of þe Empe*r*our Tyberius Cesar eghtyenþe, þe veorþe yeer of þe Olympias two hundreþe and tweyne, hit was edoon indeed, as þe story telleþe, of þe passyoun of þe Croys and of þe resurreccou*n* of oure lord Ihe*su*. Maistre Iohan Trevysa haþe here in mynde þat some tyme þe Greekes maden Ioustes and tournamentes and oþer playes of maystryes and of strenkeþe, oones in fyve yere vnder þe hille called Olympias, and cleped þe playes Olympias. And for þey had suche playes but oones in fyve yere vnder þe mountaigne Olympias, þe first fyve yeere in which þey hade suche pleyes, þey cleped þe first Olympyas, and so forthe, so þat and as cryst dyed in þe ferthe yere of þe Olympias, two hundred and tweyne, þanne hit foloweþe in þe book þat Nichodemus wrought þis story and wrot it, þe which begynneþ in þis maner in l*ett*res of hebrewe."

The Salisbury version follows the introduction as given in Addit.

16,165 to the words, "Maistre Iohan Treuysa[1] haþe," which it omits. But it employs the following words instead: "Here haue mynde *þat* sumtyme," etc.

F. The Bodleian MS. 207 contains a late fifteenth century[2] version of the same portion of the *Gospel of Nicodemus* as that which is found in the MSS. Eg. 2658 and Stonyhurst XL B. The volume consists of 128 vellum leaves which measure 13 × 9½ inches. It shows the writing of three different but contemporary hands and contains no other ornamentation than rubrics and red initials. Inside the bottom cover the name "Thomas Wetherston" is twice written, but nothing further appears to be known about the history of the MS.

The *Gospel of Nicodemus* (ff. 120 b–124) is preceded by a piece entitled, "The Mirror of the blessed life of our Lord Jesus Christ," and it is followed by a Middle-English version of the *Cura Sanitatis*[3] account of Velosian's embassy to Jerusalem in behalf of his master, the Emperor Tiberius Cesar. The Bodley version has a different conclusion from that of the Egerton and Stonyhurst MSS. That is to say, it gives an English version of Pilate's letter to the emperor "Claudius Cesar," which the other versions merely mention.[4] There are numerous other differences in the use and arrangement of the words, which seem to prove conclusively that the Bodley version, though the latest of the three, was not copied from either of the others. They all seem to go back to a common original which has probably been lost.

G. The most complete and readable one of the Middle-English prose versions of the Gospel is perhaps that of the Harleian MS. 149 (ff. 255–276). It is also comparatively late and shows more traces of modernization than any of the versions which we have as yet described.

The volume is a thick paper folio containing 281 leaves and three vellum fly-leaves (one near the middle and two at the end of the MS.). The leaves measure 11 × 8½ inches and they are without ornamentation. The MS. is really divided into two distinct parts, the first part extending through fol. 182, after which the first vellum fly-leaf is found. The handwriting in the two parts is different, as is also the quire arrangement. The first part was apparently originally bound in quires of sixteen leaves,

[1] There is no foundation whatever for the supposition that Trevisa's translation was reprinted by W. de Worde (1509, and after) and later by Cousturier (cf. Max Förster, *Archiv 107*, 321). The versions are entirely different productions. Cf. p. lvii ff. for a full description of De Worde's reprint.

[2] The handwriting would place the MS. about the year 1470.

[3] Cf. Brit Mus. MS. Harl. 149 (ff. 276–279 b).

[4] In Egerton and Stonyhurst the letter is referred to as having been written to "Tyberius Cesar."

while the quires of the second part have twelve leaves each. Several of the quires in Part I are imperfect, that is, they contain either fewer or more than sixteen leaves. The first quire, for example, has only eight leaves, the third eighteen, and the last quire of the first part has fifteen leaves. In the last part all the quires have twelve leaves each, except the concluding one which has six, inclusive of the two vellum fly-leaves. The first part of the MS. shows three different but contemporaneous hands, the first extending to the bottom of f. 22 b, the second from f. 23 to the head of f. 60, the third extends only through f. 60 a, after which the second hand continues to the end of the first part. The whole of the second part is written in one and the same hand, which belongs distinctively to the second half of the fifteenth century.

The *Catalogue of Harleian MSS. in the British Museum* gives quite an accurate description of the contents of Harl. 149, which are:[1] 1. "A Dialogue between Dives and Pauper, wherein the X Commandments are explained. Perhaps this Treatise was composed by Henry Parker" (ff. 7–182 b). The first six and a half leaves contain an extensive analysis of the contents of the piece. 2. "Medicamenta nonnulla contra Sciaticam et Hydropem" (f. 6 b). 3. "The Booke of Goode Maners, or of Goode Condityons, composed (in Latin?) by Frere Jacques the Grete (per Jacobum Magni) of the Relygeon of St. Augustyn" (ff. 183–252). 4. "Hereaftyr followeth the Cene that oure Lorde made with hys Dyssyplys" (ff. 252–254). 5. "The Story of the Passyoun whych Nychodemus wrote in Ebrew, and yn Latyn, fyve year aftyr the Passyoun of Ihesu Cryst" (ff. 254–263). 6. "Serteyn Storyes of thynges done aftyr hys Passyioun" (ff. 263–276). This is not a separate piece, but a continuation of the *Gospel of Nicodemus*, in which Carinus and Leucius tell about Christ's harrowing of hell. But the scribe seems to have considered it an independent production, since he wrote (near the top of f. 263): "Here endyth the Passyou*n* of Ih*esu* Cryst and Folowyth Serteyn storyes of thynges Done aftyr hys Passyou*n*," as did also the compiler of the *Catalogue*. 7. "A Story of the Veronycle" (ff. 276–279). 8. "A Tretys betwene Saynt Petre and Symon Magus" (ff. 279–280). 9. The Obyte of Pylat (f. 280 b). 10. The Decollacyoun of S. Petre and S. Paule (f. 280 b). 11. The Worthy Tokene goyng before the general Doom (in Latin f. 281).

The first part of the *Gospel of Nicodemus*, which bears the title "Nichodemus his gospell" (f. 255, at head of page) and which is divided

[1] The order and wording of the *Catalogue* are followed for the most part; only occasionally I have added a few supplementary words.

into twenty chapters, corresponds in general to the *Acta Pilati* I[1] as printed by Tischendorf. The "Serteyn Storyes," or the second part, which is not divided into chapters, is a translation of the *Descensus Christi ad Inferos.* The translator however refers to several other sources, especially the canonical scriptures, the legends of St. Andrew, St. James "the More" and "the Lasse," St. Thomas (cf. f. 267), and St. Bartholomew. In the first part the scribe always indicates the beginning of a chapter by the proper numerals and by paragraphing, that is, by setting in the first line of the new chapter. This part actually ends (f. 262 b) with the story of the blind Longinus who pierced the side of the dead Christ with a spear that was placed in his hands by the Jews. And the "Serteyn Storyes" begin (f. 263) with the report of the Centurion to Pilate about the "merveyles þ*a*t wer schewed at þat tyme," while the narrative of "Caryus and Lucyus" does not begin till f. 269.

This version begins (f. 255) as follows: "Cap^{m} i. It felle yn the xvth yere that Thybery Cesar had be*n* Emp*er*oure of Roome, And yn þe xixth yere of Herode, sone to Herode whych was kynge of Galylee, and yn þe viiith kalendes of Apryle, whych ys the xxviiith day of Marche, And yn þe iiiith yere o þe Erle of Ruffyn and Lyou*n*, and yn þe same yere also that Anna and Cayphas wer bysschoppes, and yn þe vth yere aftyr þe passyou*n* of Ihesu Cryst, that Nychodem*us* wrote thys story bothe yn Ebrew and yn Latyn . . . . Cap^{m} ii. Anna and Cayphas, Sobna, Dathan, Gamalyel, Syr, Leuy, and Alexandre, Iewes fulle of trecherye, and wyth hem Iudas Skaryothe, the falce awmonere of Ih*e*su Cryst, came to Pylate ayenst Ih*e*su and Accused hym seyenge thys wyse."

The translation ends (f. 276) with the proof offered to Pilate by "Anna and Cayphas" that the 5500 years which the angel Michael mentioned to Seth on the latter's visit to Paradise had already elapsed, and that the Messiah should therefore appear.[2] The colophon runs, "Et sic est finis Deo gracias."

H. The eighth of the known MSS. of the Middle-English prose *Gospel of Nicodemus* is preserved in the library of the Dean and Chapter of Worcester Cathedral and has the press-mark Fol. 172. The volume is a paper folio containing 216 leaves, six of which (three at the beginning and three at the end) are fly-leaves. Sixteen leaves have been lost from the beginning of the MS., as is indicated by the early foliation, the old number on the first leaf being "xvii." In the upper left-hand margin of the first page the words, "There wantith sixteen leaves," are written in a late hand.

[1] Tischendorf's divisions are however different.
[2] Cf. the conclusion of the poetical versions G–H.

The leaves of the MS. measure 11 × 8 inches, and the volume is bound in quires of twelve leaves each, the ends of quires always being indicated by catch-words. But the first quire has only six leaves besides the three fly-leaves. The paper of the MS. is all (excepting the fly-leaves) of the same quality and brand, the water-mark being a large Gothic P surmounted by a cross or trifolium. At the beginning the upper parts of several leaves have been severely injured—blackened, or rather browned —so that it is sometimes almost impossible to get the correct reading. The brown diagonal, defacing bar extends with steadily decreasing intensity through a large portion of the MS. All the pieces of the MS. are in English prose,—the last piece, which is an imperfect version of the Psalter, having the verses alternately in Latin and in English. It was all written by the same scribe, and, indeed, so far as the pieces are translations from Latin originals, the translation seems to have been done by the same person. The handwriting is, to be sure, late—not much earlier than 1485,— but several of the pieces bear fourteenth century dates. However, the dates may very easily have been attached to the Latin originals. The copy of the *Gospel of Nicodemus*, which I transcribed and examined with considerable care, bears the marks of an original translation and not of a copy of an earlier version.

So far as I have been able to discover no complete catalogue of the MSS. in the Worcester Cathedral Library has ever been published, and the several partial, imperfect descriptions all omit any mention of the MS. Fol. 172.[1] The contents are of a miscellaneous character, and many of the pieces are of great historical value; some of which, like the version of Peter Alfunsi's *Disciplina Clericalis* and "The Statutes of the Blissed Lord and Bisshop, Blac Rogier," are otherwise unknown in Middle-English versions.[2]

The table of contents on the *recto* of the first fly-leaf does not record half the pieces of the MS., it omits in fact the two most valuable works

[1] T. R. Nash (*Collections for the History of Worcestershire*, II, App., p. 94 f., 1782) says nothing about it; nor does J. Noake in his chapter on the history of the Worcester Cathedr. Library (*The Monastery and Cathedral of Worcester*, London, 1866, pp. 406–467). H. Schenkl does not appear to have described the Worcester Cathedral Library in the various reports of the MSS. of early religious literature that he has been publishing for about fifteen years in the *Sitzungsberichte der philosophisch-historischen klasse der Kaiserl. Akademie der Wissenschaften* of Vienna.

[2] Through the kindness of Mr. W. H. Stevenson, of St. John's College, Oxford, I learned (but too late for reference) that a *Catalogue of the Manuscripts preserved in the Chapter Library of Worcester Cathedral*, compiled by the Rev. John Kestell Floyer, M.A., F.S.A., and edited and revised by Sidney Graves Hamilton, M.A., Fellow and Librarian of Hertford College, Oxford, was published in the year 1906 by the Worcestershire Historical Society.

in the volume. It is therefore especially important that a complete list of the contents be given. The inside of the first cover and the lower part of both pages of the first leaf contain some account of the life of Richard Rolle of Hampole, and a list of the MSS. which contain his works, evidently copied from the catalogues of Bale, Bernard and Leland, in a modern hand. The table of contents, in the same hand, is as follows:

"p. 29. explicit Passio Nichodemi.

p. 30. The libel of Richard Hermit of Hampol, of the rule of good living in 12 chapters.

p. 46. A treatise against ghostly temptations, the twelve degrees of humility.

p. 61. The deeds or Acts of the Apostles.

p. 85 b. Of Life contemplative and of the words therof, it endeth p. 129.

p. 181 b. Part of the Psalter Latin and English."

1. The first piece in the MS. is a fragmentary prose version of the *Gospel of Nicodemus*, the first lines of which are almost illegible (ff. 4–12, *olim* xvii–xxv). The *Explicit Passio Nichodemi* on f. 16 (*olim* xxix) should have been written near the top of f. 12. 2. A short account of the discovery of Joseph of Arimathea by Titus in a prison at Jerusalem and of the death of Pilate (a kind of *Paradosis Pilati*, f. 121–2 b). 3. The story of the origin of the cross, in which an account is given of Seth's mission to Paradise for the Oil of Mercy and of his receiving three apple-seeds from the Angel Michael, etc. (ff. 13–16). 4. A short homiletic or ecclesiastical piece follows (p. 16), which begins: "It was wont to be doubted of sum whi Tithes bien yevon to holichirche. It is in Reproef of al wikked and cursed spirites; of al the feithful men, of trew cristen people tithes bien yoven into holi chirche," etc. 5. "This is the libel of Richard hermyte of hampol of the Amendement of mannes lif, other ellis of the Rule of goode livyng and it is departed in .XII. chaptres" (ff. 17–32 b). The description of the contents of the piece then follows, and the first chapter begins: "Tarie the noght, man, to be conue*r*ted vnto the lord god, nother delay the noght from day to day," etc. The twelfth chapter ends (f. 32 b) with the colophon, "Explicit Ricardus de Ampull."[1] 6. A short description of the "office of a Bisshop" (f. 33). 7. "A treati

[1] Horstmann does not record any such "libel" in his list of the works bearing Hampole's name (cf. *Yorkshire Writers*, II, Introd., p. xl f.).

agenst gostly temptaciouns"[1] (ff. 33 b–44). Begins: "Ure merciful lord god Ihesu chasticith his chieldren and suffrith hem to be tempted for many profitable skillis and to their profite." 8. Hic incipiunt duodecim gradus humilitatis (ff. 44–46 b). Begins: "Seynt Gregory tho doctour saith, that without mekenes it is vnlieful to truste of foryevenes of thi synne." Colophon: "Expliciunt .XII. gradus humilitatis." 9. A series of four short narratives which are in part adaptations from certain of the *Dialogues* of Caesarius of Heisterbach[2] (ff. 46 b–48). The rubrics of these "narratives" are: (a) Narracio de periculo differendi penitenciam, (b) Alia narracio, (c) Narracio *contra* confessos de peccatis *sed* non contritos, (d) Narracio de peccatore penitente *et* Saluate. Tho fables begin respectively: "Ther was a worthi man and a Riche whos name was Crisaurius, and as plentivous as he was of worldly goodis, also ful he was of synne and vice, in pride, in lechery, in covetise," etc.

"Ther was.ij.scoole felawes of the whiche oon entred into Religioun," etc.

"Cesarius the grete clerk telleth that ther was a man in Parice, a young man that yaf al to lechery," etc.

"Ther was a thief in a grete desert, leader and maister of many," etc.

10. "The dedis of Apostels" (ff. 48–72), a version of the Acts of the Apostles which was unknown to the editors of the "Wycliffite Bible." But it is undoubtedly a late version of the Purvey translation of the Acts as the following parallels will show:

Purvey's Dedis of Apostlis.	*Worcest. MS., fol.* 172, *Dedis.*
Here begynneth prolog on the Dedis of Apostlis.[3]	The prolog on the dedis of Apostels.[4]
Luk of Antiochie of the nacioun of Sirie, whos preisyng is teld in the gospel, at Antioche he was a worthi man of leche craft, and afterward a disciple of Cristis apostlis, and suwede Poul, the apostle.	Luke of Antioche of the nacioun Sirie, whos praiseng is told in the gospel, at Antioche he was a worthy man of lechecraft and afterward a disciple of Cristes apostels and sued Poul thapostel.

[1] Cf. "A tretyse of gostly batayle," Horstmann, *op. cit.*, p. 420 ff., which is however not the same production.

[2] Cf. Mrs. Mary M. Banks, *An Alphabet of Tales*, E. E. T. S., 126–127, where Middle-English versions of numerous Tales from Caesarius of Heisterbach appear; also A. Kaufmann, *Caesarius von Heisterbach, Ein Beitrag*, etc. Cöln, 1862; the same author, *Wunderbare und denkwürdige Geschichten aus den Werken des Cäsarius von Heisterbach, Ausgewählt, übersetzt, usw. Vierter Theil, Annalen des historischen Vereins für den Niederrhein.* Heft. 47, Köln, 1888; Anton E. Schönbach, *Studien zur Erzählungsliteratur des Mittelalters. Vierter Theil: Ueber Caesarius von Heisterbach*, I. *Sitzungsberichte der philosophisch-historischen Classe der kaiserlichen Akademie der Wissenschaften*, Bd. 144, Abh. IX. Wien, 1902.

[3] Cf. Forshall and Madden, *The Wycliffite Versions of the Holy Bible*, IV, 507, 508, and 593.

[4] Fol. 48, and f. 72.

Purvey's Dedis of Apostlis. Cap. I.	*Worcest. MS., fol.* 172, *Dedis.* C^{m} P^{m}.
Theofle, first Y made a sermoun of alle thingis, that Ihesu bigan to do, etc.	Theofile, first [I] made a sermon of al thynges that Ihesu bigan to do, etc.
Colophon: *Here endith the Deedis of Apostlis.*	Here enden the deedis of apostlis.

11. "The Book of Contemplacioun, or The Divine Cloud of Vnknowing" (ff. 72 b–116). The heading at the beginning of this piece runs: "That the inner havyng of a man shuld be like to the vtter." Then in a different hand, "Venite exultemus domino." Begins: "Gostly brother in Ihesu Crist, I praie the that in þe callyng whiche our lord hath callid the to," etc. The treatise is divided into ninety-three chapters.[1] 12. At the top of the next page (f. 116 b) stands the following invocation (red): "Ihesus be oure spede, Amen." This page and the following have been crossed through with heavy strokes, but the piece seems to be a series of invocations to God accentuated by Pater Nosters. 13. Another religious piece begins on f. 117 with the heading, "UI vertuous questiouns and answers of vj holy doctours of tribulacioun paciently taken in this world." 14. On f. 117 b there are a few prayers and "Masses" of the Popes Gregory and Innocent which have been partially crossed out. 15. What is perhaps the most important piece in this MS. begins without rubric or heading at the top of f. 118 b. But the first words of the piece reveal the fact that it is a fifteenth century English version of Peter Alfunsi's *Disciplina Clericalis*, a noted and interesting collection of mediaeval tales or fables, supposed to have been told by an Arab father on his deathbed to his son, for the latter's instruction and guidance. This is, I think, the only Middle-English version so far known of anything approaching the complete *Disciplina Clericalis*, although several of the tales are incorporated in the fifteenth century English translation of the *Alphabetum Narrationum*,[2] which was until recently[3] thought to be the work of Etienne de Besançon. The Latin version exists in a large number[4] of MSS., and the Old-French[4] poetical version appears to

[1] The *Book of Contemplacion* is preserved in the following MSS. of the British Museum: Reg. 17, G. xxvi (fifteenth cent.), Reg. 17 D V (fifteenth cent.), Reg. 17 G. xxvii (seventeenth cent.), Harl. 674, 954 and 2373. It has been ascribed to William Exmeuse, Maurice Chawney, and to Walter Fitz-Herbert.

[2] Recently edited by Mrs. Mary M. Banks from the Brit. Mus. MS. Addit. 25,719 for the E. E. T. S., under the title, *An Alphabet of Tales*, etc. Two Parts. Part I, London, 1904; Part II, London, 1905.

[3] Cf. Mr. J. A. Herbert's article in the *Library*, Jan. 1905.

[4] Cf. Ward, *Catalogue of Romances*, II, p. 235 ff.; M. Roesle, *Le Castoiement d'un Père a son Fils*, etc., Munich, 1899; G. Paris, *Romania*, I, 106.

have been extremely popular.[1] The Middle-English version of the *Disciplina* contains 24–25 tales, which do not however follow the order of any of the Latin and French MS. versions described by Ward. The piece begins: "Petir Alfons seruaunt of Ihesu Crist, maker of this booke, with thankynges I do to god, the whiche is first and without bigynnyng. To whom is the bigynnyng and the end of al goodenes, the fulfillyng," etc. After a short prologue, the stories are introduced: "Therfor Enoch the philosophre, whiche in Arabik tung is named Edriche, saide to his sone: 'The dreede of god be thy busynes, and lucre and wynnyng shal come to the without any labour.'" The *Disciplina* extends to about the middle of f. 138 a. 16. The next piece is an English version of the well-known "Epistle of Alexander the Great to Aristotle," and it is introduced by the rubric, *Incipit epistola Alexandri Magni Regis Macedonum ad Magistrum Suum Aristotilem* (ff. 138–148). Begins: "Alwey I am myndeful of the also among the preeks and doubtes of our batels, most diere comandour, and after my Moder and Susters most acceptable," etc. Ends with an "Epitaphum" in twenty-two Latin verses:

> "Primus Alexander, pillea natus in vrbe
> Quem comes Antipater, confecto melle veneno," etc.

17. At the top of f. 148 b an ecclesiastical piece begins, which contains certain regulations for the government of the dominions of the Church of Rome: "That the Pope with other prelatis of holichirche hath power to make divers lawes to edificacioun of holichirche, and to accuse theym that brekith hem, may be proeved both bi thold lawe and bi the newe." After a brief introduction, a series of thirty-nine ecclesiastical laws are given (ff. 148 b–154 b). 18. This piece is followed by another ecclesiastical work of great importance to the history of the Church and of the life of London in the thirteenth and fourteenth centuries. The heading of the piece is as follows: "The statutes of the blissed Lord and Bisshop, blac Rogier"[2] (ff. 155–163). The prologue to the list of "statutes" begins: "To the Bisshop of London of the comfort of the

[1] An Icelandic version of twenty-seven stories from the *Disciplina Clericalis* was published by H. Gering, *Islendzk Æven tyri, Isländische Legenden, Novellen und Märchen*, 2 Bände, Halle, 1882–3, Bd. I, pp. 163–198. The best edition of the Latin *Disciplina* is by W. V. Schmidt, Berlin, 1827, and this edition is reproduced by Migne, *Patrol. Lat.*, vol. *157*, col. 671–706.

[2] According to Ric. Newcourt (*Repertorium Ecclesiasticum Parochiale Londonense: An Ecclesiastical Parochial History of the Diocese of London*. London, 1708, I, 13) Roger, surnamed Niger, was probably consecrated a bishop in June 1229, and died in September 1241. On p. 58, Newcourt says: "Roger Niger, Bishop of London, in the time of King Henry III, made certain Statutes, and prescrib'd them to the Rectors and Priests of the Archdeaconry of London; which are in a certain old Manuscript-Book of Statutes in the publick Library of the University of Cambridge."

lord Petir, Archedeken of London, made and direct to al the Persons, vicars, and parasch priestes in the Citee of London constitute." There are in all thirty-three different articles of the statutes, which deal with about all the phases of English (*i. e.* London) religious life in the latter years of the Middle Ages. 19. What appears to be a charter of an Archbishop of Canterbury begins on f. 163 b: "Will*iam*,[1] bi divyne suffraunce Archebisshop of Caunterbury, of al Inglond Prymat, and of the Apostels seete legate, to our welle beloved sone, Thomas Bekaton,[2] Doctour of Lawe, Archedeken of London, and Deane in the chirche of our lady at the Bowe of London," etc. This document ends near the top of f. 165 a with the exact date of its origin: "Yeven in our Manor at Lamblith, the .xi. kalendis of Decemb*er*, the yeere of our lord MCCC-LXXXVII, and of our translacioun the vii." 20. On ff. 165–5 b there is another ecclesiastical document of some historical consequence, of which the rubric runs: "The tenour folowith of Constitucionns memoratief." 21. "Thiese bien the constitucionns provincial of the Archebisshop of Caunterbury, Robert of Wynchelsey"[3] (ff. 165 b–166). This document concludes with the date of its execution: "writen Anno do*mi*ni Milesimo CCCCXLVII." 22. The last piece of the Worcester MS., fol. 172, is a late Middle-English interlinear (Latin-English) version of the Psalms, of which only the first seventy-one chapters and nineteen verses of the seventy-second chapter have been preserved (ff. 166–313 b). At first there is a prologue: "Here bigynnyth a prolog vpon the psautier," which extends to the bottom of f. 168. Then at the top of the following page there is a long rubric: "Here bigynneth the psautier the whiche is comunely vsed to be rad [in] holichirche service, for it is a booke of grete deuocioun and of high gostly conceivyng; in whiche booke men fynden ful moche wetnesse and parfite vndirstondyng of gostly Comfort. Also þis booke shewith the meedis of iust men and the meedis of uniust men, the Reward of everyman after his travaile." The MS. ends after cap. LXXII, 19, the last verse being: "How bien thei made into desolacioun, the faileden sodainly, thei perissheden for their wickidness." A comparison of this verse with the same one in the Purveyite[4] translation

[1] This is apparently the "Willielmus de Courtney" described by Newcourt (*op. cit.* p. 19). He was "Bishop of Hereford," whence he "was translated to London, 1375, Sept. 12." . . . "In 1381, August 10, this our Bishop was made Lord-Chancellor, and in January following, translated to the See of Canterbury."

[2] "Thomas Baketon occurs Arch-Deacon of London in 1382 and 1335."—Newcourt, I, 61, Note C.

[3] This is probably the Robert Gilbert described by Newcourt (*op. cit.* pp. 22–23). He became Bishop of London in May 1436, and in October of the same year Archbishop of Canterbury. He died July 27, 1448.

[4] Cf. Forshall and Madden, II, 811.

shows that the Worcest. MS. 172 version is probably a later form of the same translation, with the addition of the Latin text.

As has already been intimated, the translation of the *Gospel of Nicodemus* in the Worcester MS. was undoubtedly made in complete independence of all the other English prose versions that we have described. The margins of each page in the MS. contain from two to four Latin sentences or clauses, corresponding to particular passages in the text. The translator probably had a Latin original before him, and a comparison of the marginal passages with Tischendorf's edition of the *Evangelium Nicodemi*[1] shows clearly that it was the D^b text. The translator was not very familiar with this kind of work, and he frequently shows that either the meaning of the Latin word, or of the English, or of both, was quite unfamiliar to him.[2] This fact accounts for the comparatively large number of strange, un-English words that occur in the translation. At times however the translation is in good, vigorous, original English.

I. Another late fifteenth (possibly early sixteenth) century English version of the *Gospel of Nicodemus* has been preserved in the Cambridge University Libr. MS. Mm. 1. 29 (ff. 8–16). The volume is a paper quarto of fifty-nine leaves, besides three fly-leaves at the beginning and eleven at the end, which measure 8 × 5¾ inches. It belonged apparently to one "Thomas Earl, Minister of S. Mildred's, Bredstreet," in the latter half of the sixteenth century, since it is called "his Note Book wherin are set down the Episcopal & Archidiaconal Visitations in London, together with the Courses taken with the Puritans & Papists, during the said Writers Incumbency, that is from the year 1564 to 1600. And many other cursory Notes of Church Matters under the Reignes of K. Henry VIII & K. Edward VI." The other pieces according to the memorandum (on the *recto* of the third fly-leaf) are: "The Gospel of Nicodemus." "Notes concerning Puritan Controversies, with collections out of Tindal, Barnes, Calvin, Joh. Fox, etc. concerning Ceremonies"; "Notes concerning Papists and Jesuits."

At the end of the volume there are a few pages of promiscuous notes, a part of which consists of a list of words apparently copied from glosses of older MSS. As the above note and the table of contents are in the

[1] Second edition, Leipzig, 1876, p. 333 ff.

[2] Cf. "Lo, I have wrapped hym in cleene sendal and put hym [in] my monument and set the stone to the Doore of the spelunc, Denne, or Grave or Sepulcre" (f. 5 b) with the (D^b) Latin: Ecce in monumento meo posui et involvi eum in sindone munda et apposui lapidem magnum ad ostium speluncae (Tischendorf, *op. cit.* p. 366).

well-known hand of Humphrey Wanley, the MS. was no doubt at one time the property of that famous antiquarian.[1]

The version of the *Gospel of Nicodemus* (ff. 8–16) begins with the story of Joseph's begging the body of Christ and wrapping it "in a shining Syndonia," and laying it "in the new grave or stoun sepulture where neaver man was layed."

The piece begins on f. 8 of the MS. with a rubric or rather heading at the top of the page in the centre: "*De* Resurrectione domini." To the left of this are the words: "Sermones dormij secure, S*ermo* parati de tempore . . . 105." On the left margin of the same page we read: "Nichodem*us* Ghospel . . . Expl-translatid." Below the heading and in the centre of the page there is the following dedication: "To the Christian Reader grace, mercy and peace in god, By Jesus Christ our Savyour in the Holye Spyrite of god,—iij parsons, one onelye God—Amen." The dedication is in the same hand as the text, while the heading and the following words to the right of the dedication are later: "James Pynner, Taylour"; on the left margin beneath the title (*i. e.* Nichodem*us* Ghospel), "1590"; and further below in red ink, "1509."

The author (or scribe) of the translation then tells us something about the origin of the piece: "Because the fables of that Romain papall sinagogue ys not now exstant, thought somtym Impryntid in the Inglishe tounge vnder the Tytle of Nychodem*us* Ghospell, I have Agayn written thee same ovt of their oude postill*es*, As John Herolt,[2] Sermones discipulij (*sic*), Sermo 146, 1 F. Sermones Dormi, Sermo 30^{iii}, . . De Resurrectione Do*mi*ni." Then under this in the later hand: "Jacobus de voragine, whose wordes follow thus." After this the translation begins: "It is Read in the ghospell of nychodemus, That After that the Iwees and Romaines had crucified our Lord Iesus chryst, That there was A good and Iust man By name Iosephe of Arathemathia, A cytti of Iwrj, w*hiche* loked for the kyngdome of god and [was] not consenting nor willinge to accord vnto the accusations of the Iwes Agaynst christ. This man Requyred pylat and Requestyd of him the Bodye of christ Iesus," etc.

At the end of the piece (f. 16) the following words occur in red: "Vide Liber Beliall," and to the right of this, the name "Jacob de Theranie" (*sic*). On the following page the colophon has been crossed out, but "sic est" remains and the other words have been traced over in

[1] *The Gospel of Nicodemus* as preserved in this MS. may have been copied from some early print (cf. Förster, *op. cit.*), but there is no such volume known.

[2] The *Sermones discipuli de tempore et de sanctis* of the German Dominican friar, John Herold (or Herolt, *flor.* 15th cent.) were published at Nuremberg in 1480 and 1492, and at Mayence in 1612.

a later hand. Afterwards the scribe appended a curious note by way of comment and admonition: "Behold goodlij christian Reader this nychodemus, no nychodemus; this ghospell, no ghospell; this vnwritten verytij, no verytij / But a verytable lye, a lucyflerian fable, old wyves tale and detestable lye, vnsavery salt for the downg hill, and to be tred on vnder fotte of men. This aucthor whosoever of sermondes dormi secwre preache thus and sleap saffely. A mynister of Antychrist wrote this in latin and Imprinted thee sam after in anno 1517 at lyons, 16 of November. Whether it was peter Vigeneye, Herolt, Barland I know not. But this you can surely wytnesse *with* me: No lyttell leven of popische doctrynes are Bwylded as fyrst the avthoritij of sacred scriptures countyd vnperfecte, *with*out this nychodemus, Blasphemouse spyrit of lyinge, Be an eptyd also coequall *with* them, O Sathanas, whiche pluckyng vs from the scriptures wold aprove the Resurectyon of christ By this devyses, etc."

J. In conclusion I must call attention briefly to the early Black Letter editions of the English *Gospel of Nicodemus.* The popularity of the apocryphal account of Christ's passion and descent into Hades among Englishmen of the early sixteenth century is clearly shown by the considerable number of editions of the Gospel that was published. It was printed by Julyan Notary, London, 1507,[1] Wynkyn de Worde, 1509,[2] John Skot, London, 1529, and so on. The De Worde version was apparently the standard edition throughout the next two centuries,[3] and no one has as yet discovered an original for it. It follows none of the known Latin manuscripts and editions, and it differs in many essential features from any of the M.E. versions with which we are at present acquainted. One peculiarity of this text appears in the prologue, where the printer asserts that his original is a French version made by Bishop Turpin: "It befell in the .XIX. yere of the seygnorye of Tybarye cesarye Emperour of Rome, And in the Seygnorye of Herode that was the sone of Herode, whiche Was kynge of Galyce, the .viii. kalendes of Apryll, the whiche is the .xxv. daye of Marche, the iiij yere of the

[1] A copy of this rare book is in the library of Archb. Marsh, Dublin.

[2] Reissued in the years 1511, 1512, 1518, 1532. A copy of the first edition is preserved in the Cambridge University Library and in the Bodleian. Cf. Lowndes, *Bibliographical Manual.* London, 1864, vol. III, pp. 1688–89.

[3] Editions appeared 1620 (?) at Rouen by Coustourier-Warrin; 1767 at London by John Wilson; 1775 (?) at New Castle as one of William Garrett's collection of Chap-Books. Judging from the prologue of Wilson's edition as reproduced by Thilo (*Proleg.* p. cxlv f.; it is not in the British Museum) this text is also a reprint of the De Worde edition; or it is at any rate based upon the same original. That part of the Gospel which refers especially to Joseph of Arimathea was printed also in Black Letter by De Worde (date not given), and in abbreviated form from "The Kalendre of the New Legende of Englande" by Richard Pynson (1516). Cf. Skeat's *Joseph of Arimathie*, E. E. T. S. No. 44, p. 25 ff., London, 1871.

sone of Uelom whiche was counseyller of Rome. And Olympius had ben afore two hondred yere and two. This tyme Ioseph and Annas were lordes aboue all Iustyces mayres and Iewes. Nychodemus whiche was a worthy prynce dyde wryte this blessyd storye in hebrewe. And Theodosius the Emperour dyde it translate out of hebrewe into latyn. And bysshop Turpyn dyde translate it out of latyn into Frensshe. And here after ensueeth this blessyd storye."

The text has the following beginning (p. 2): "ANas and Cayphas. Symeon. Datan. Gamaliel. Iudas. Leuy. Neptalim. Alysaunder. Zarius. And many other Iewes came to Pylate and accused our lorde Ihesu cryste in many thynges / and thus they sayd / we knowe hym well that he is the sone of Ioseph the carpenter / and was borne of Marye," etc. The conclusion of De Worde's print runs: "Thus our scrypture bereth wytnes of hym that shall be the sone of god / & a kynge of the people of Israhell / but after the passyon of Ihesu we & our prynces meruaylled of the tokens & wordes that were done by hym / & so we loked our storyes & counted all the lygnage downe to Iosephs lygnage / & the lygnage of Marye that was moder of Ihesu / & so we haue accounted that fro that tyme that god made þe worlde & Adam the fyrst man vnto Noes flode is two M. & V. C. yere And fro the flode to Abraham is thre M. and V. C. yere / and fro Moyses to Dauyd is V. C. yere / and fro the transmygracyon of Babylone to the incarnacion of Ihesu cryste is foure .C. yere / and thus is the accounte in all V. M. yere. All these thynges and meruaylles dyde Pylate wryte for to be redde of all them that sholde come after. And than Pylate wrote a lettre to the cyte of Rome / and to Claudio the Emperour, etc. Thus endeth Nychodemus gospelle. Enprynted at London in Fletestrete at the sygne of the sonne by Wynkyn de Worde / prynter vnto the moost excellent pryncesse my lady the kynges moder In the yere of our lorde god .M. CCCCC. ix. the .xxiij. daye of Marche."

Now, a casual comparison of the prologue, and the beginning and conclusion of the text with those of the Trevisa version (MS. Addit. 16,165) shows that no other connection can possibly exist between the two versions than that of being different translations of one and the same story.[1] The Latin MSS. on which the two versions were based may indeed belong to the same group, just as do the D^{abc} and *ed. pr.* of Tischendorf. But the Latin MSS. themselves are unknown,[2] unless

[1] Cf. Förster's statement: "Es scheint das (*i. e.* the Trevisa version) dieselbe zu sein, welche 1509 (und öfter) von W. de Worde . . . gedruckt ist" (*Archiv* *107*, 321).

[2] This version baffled so brilliant a scholar as Thilo, who says of it (*Codex Apocryphus*, Proleg. p. cxlvi): "Quot-quot ego codd. Latinos evolvi, eorum nullus

perchance von Dobschütz has discovered them.[1] A more important point of difference between the De Worde translation and all other known versions of the *Gospel of Nicodemus* is to be found in a unique and very interesting story that is introduced in connection with the entombment.

Joseph of Arimathea, it is related, went to the market-place of Capernaum on the day of the crucifixion in search of a shroud for the body of Christ. There he met by chance Syndonia, the daughter of Levy (or Livy) and his wife, humble citizens of Capernaum. This maiden had been forced by the death of her father to learn some trade by which she could support herself and her invalid mother. She therefore began early to learn the art of weaving in silk, and one day about the time of the death of Christ she made by some miraculous means which she could not explain a wonderful piece of silk. When she showed this scarf to her mother the latter was also amazed, and after questioning the daughter as to how she made it, the mother bad her wash herself and go with the cloth into the market-place and sell it, in order that she might buy provisions and other articles for the following feast-day. At the same time the mother commanded that she sell the cloth to no man before she learned his name and for what purpose he wished to use it.

So Joseph in looking over the market discovered Syndonia and her wonderful fabric. He asked, and willingly paid, the price; but before closing the bargain the girl fell upon her knees before Joseph and besought him to tell her his name and the purpose for which he intended to use the cloth. Joseph readily complied, telling her that a great prophet had just died in the country and that he wished to wrap his body in the cloth before he deposited it in the tomb. Then he in turn inquired after her name and that of the weaver of the cloth, and upon receiving the answer that it was Syndonia, he said to the girl: "Now after you I shall name this cloth, for this cloth shall be named Syndonia."[2]

The story concludes with an account of how the mother was restored to health and strength as a result of the use to which the marvellous

similem huic obtulit prologum, in quo mentio fieret Turpini illius archiepiscopi Rhemensis Caroli magni aetate, cujus nomini famosam historiam de gestis Caroli initio sec. xii, suppositam esse constat. Conjicias inde, quod continuo aliis documentis confirmabimus, evangelium Nicodemi aliquo modo cum fabulis mediae aetatis Romanensibus quas dicunt conjunctum esse." Gaston Paris gives no information about such a work from the pen of Bishop Turpin in his monograph, *De Pseudo-Turpino* (Paris, 1865).

[1] My own belief is that the original of De Worde's text is to be found among the numerous Latin MSS. of the *Evang. Nicod.*, which are preserved in English libraries and which have not been carefully examined.

[2] This word is evidently from the Latin (Greek) *sindon* ("in sindone munda." *Ev. Nic.* Tischendorf, p. 366), which means a kind of linen cloth.

piece of cloth was put, and how she married a "worthy duke" and her daughter became "Empresse of Rome."

I have been able to find only a few traces of this story in mediaeval Christian literature, but it must have been a well-known legend;[1] at any rate, it does not occur in any other version of the Gospel that I have examined.

The text as printed by De Worde does not have the pages or the divisions (chapters) numbered; nor does the Warrin-Cousturier edition. But De Worde's little book contains fifty-two pages, and there are thirteen divisions of the text; there is the same number in Warrin-Cousturier and in the eighteenth century chap-book of William Garret. It is in the seventh division or chapter that the Syndonia story occurs. This chapter has the heading: "How Centurio tolde Pylate of ye wonders that was at Crystes passyon & the same Pylate tolde the Jewes therof, and of the precyous cloth that our lorde was buryed in."[2]

V.

BRIEF ACCOUNT OF THE ORIGIN AND GROWTH OF THE DESCENT LEGEND.

THE Gospel of Nicodemus is in its complete form composed of two parts which are known as (1) the *Acta Pilati* and (2) The *Descensus*

[1] Godefroy (*Dictionnaire de l'ancienne langue Française*, vol. vii [Paris, 1892], p. 417) describes the word "Sidoine" as "= suaire," and gives the following quotation: "Icele glorieuse pucele qui fila la sindoine dont la chars Dé fut envolopee (Maurice, Serm., MS. Poitiers 124, 1d 207o)." C. U. Chevalier reproduces (*Étude critique sur l'origine du St. Suaire de Lirey-Chambéry-Turin*, Paris, 1900, Append. p. 46 ff.) a *Tenor Officii Sanctae Sindonis Jesu Christi* in which the following sentence occurs (p. 56): "Mulier sapiens Sindonem fecit et vendidit, quam Joseph ab Arimathia mercatus est." There is also a reference to the Syndonia legend in the poem entitled, *The lyfe of Joseph of Armathia*, printed by Richard Pynson in the year 1520, and reprinted by Prof. Skeat in his *Joseph of Arimathie.* The last three lines of the third stanza (Skeat, p. 37) are:

> "And wrapped his body / in a clothe called sendony;
> Ryche was it wrought, with golde & sylke full pure,
> Joseph of a mayd it bought / in Aromathy cyte."

[2] The story is told on p. 22 ff. of the 1509 edition. John Ashton is in error when he says (*Chap-Books of the Eighteenth Century*, London, 1882, pp. 30-31, where he merely reproduces the title and Table of Contents from the Chap-book), "This is a translation by John Warren, priest, of this apocryphal Gospel." The Warren edition is nothing more than a slightly modernized reprint of the De Worde text. Ashton is also entirely wrong in asserting that the Chap-book text "varies very little from that given by Hone." As a matter of fact Wm. Hone simply reprinted (*Apocryphal New Testament*, London, 1820) a translation of the *Evang. Nicodemi* which was made by the Rev. Jeremiah Jones near the end of the seventeenth century from Grynaeus's edition (*Orthodoxographa*, vol. I, p. 643 ff.), and published

Christi ad Inferos.[1] According to the best authorities[2] these two parts originated at different times and in entire independence of each other. The *Descensus* is the older of the two, and it probably received its literary form as early as the second or third century, while the *Acta* did not exist in anything like its present form before the latter half of the fourth century, or even the early fifth century.[3] The earlier is also the more important of the two parts, so far as their influence upon mediaeval literature and art is concerned. It contains a vivid, dramatic description of Christ's descent into Hades in the time between his crucifixion and resurrection, of his breaking down the gates of hell, of his binding of Satan and of his deliverance of the patriarchs and prophets from their long imprisonment there. The story of Christ's underworld mission is related by two men who are purported to have risen from the dead, and who were in the realm of Hades when Christ entered its gates as conqueror and deliverer. These two men, who are usually[4] called Lucius and Carinus, are represented as being the sons of a prominent Hebrew named Simeon. From their names it has been surmised[5] with considerable ground for justification that the author of the *Descensus* was a certain Lucius Charinus who flourished in the second century and who seems to have written several other apocryphal treatises.[6]

The *Acta Pilati* gives an account of the trial of Christ before Pilate, of the crucifixion, of the entombment by Joseph and Nicodemus and of the miraculous escape of Joseph from the prison where he had been confined by the Jews because he buried the body of Christ. The story

---

in numerous editions along with an extensive and valuable criticism of the apocryphal books of the New Testament, having the title, *A New and Full Method of Settling the Canonical Authority of the New Testament*, etc., 3 vols., Oxford, 1727; cf. vol. II, pp. 223–299. Hone divides the text into chapters and verses. He also states in his "Preface" to the *Gospel of Nicodemus* (p. 44 f.), that his text is a translation from the *Orthodoxographa*. Thilo is wholly wrong, as well as unjust to the admirable critical work of Jones, in suggesting (*Prolegom.* p. ix.) that his book is little more than a rehash of Fabricius.

[1] This sketch can only give a bare outline of the development of the story and its importance. No attempt is made to give an exhaustive list of the literature on the subject in the footnotes.

[2] M. Nicolas, *Études sur les Évangiles Apocryphes*, Paris, 1866, p. 254, 361 ff.; Lipsius, *Die Pilatus-Akten*, p. 1 ff.; J. Monnier, *La Descente aux Enfers, Étude de pensée religieuse d'art et de littérature*, Paris, 1905, p. 91 ff.

[3] Lipsius, *op. cit.*; von Dobschütz, Hastings's *Dictionary of the Bible*, III, 544 ff.

[4] The names are omitted from the Greek version printed by Tischendorf, *op. cit.*, pp. 323–332. Cf. Lipsius, *Die apokryphen Apostelgeschichten und Apostellegenden*, Braunschweig, 1883–1890, vol. I, p. 112 ff.

[5] Jeremiah Jones, *op. cit.*, vol. I, p. 210 f.; Lipsius, *op. cit.*, p. 117; Beausobre, *Histoire du Manichéisme*, tom. I, p. 374; Maury, *Croyances et Légendes*, p. 297; Harnack, *Geschichte der altchrist. Lit.*, I, 116–123.

[6] Lipsius, *op. cit.*; Harnack, *op. cit.*

told in the *Acta* is based mainly upon the description of the passion in the canonical Gospels, with several apocryphal additions.

The literary account of Christ's descent into Hades was developed from a belief which doubtless prevailed in apostolical times that he descended into the underworld to preach, or to bring salvation, to the dead, just as he had brought salvation to the living by his mission on earth. But the conception of God appearing as a conqueror in the lower regions of the world antedates the Christian era. It was familiar to the psalmist,[1] as well as to the authors of Isaiah[2] and Hosea.[3] It is, in fact, not improbable that the Hebrew and Christian conceptions of Jahve and Christ visiting the kingdom of the dead and overcoming Satan and his hosts are merely later developments from the Babylonian, Persian, Egyptian and Grecian belief in the descent of the spirits of the dead into a region of darkness and gloom.[4] In other words, the notion is intimately bound up with the oriental belief in the immortality of the soul, which appears to have become a definite feature of the Jewish religion for the first time after the Babylonian captivity.[5] But the mediaeval legend about Christ's descent was no doubt immediately inspired by certain passages of the New Testament, the most important of which are found in the First Epistle of Peter: "Being put to death in the flesh, but quickened in the spirit; in which also he went and preached unto the spirits in prison, which aforetime were disobedient, when the longsuffering of God waited in the days

[1] *Ps. 24.* The verses beginning: "Lift up your heads, O ye gates; and be ye lift up, ye everlasting doors; and the King of Glory shall come in."

[2] Cf. chap. *42*, 7; *45*, 2; *53*, 8–9. [3] Chap. *6*, 2; *13*, 14.

[4] Some of the most important works on the subject are: G. Maspero, *The Dawn of Civilization: Egypt and Chaldea.* Translated by M. L. McClure. Ed. by A. H. Sayce. Fourth edition, London, 1901 (cf. p. 83 ff.); E. A. W. Budge, *Egyptian Ideas of the Future Life*, London, 1899 (p. 111); Georg Beer, *Der biblische Hades*, Berlin, 1902; R. H. Charles, *A Critical History of the Doctrine of a Future Life*, London, 1899 (p. 33, 36, etc.); D. W. Bousset, *Die Religion des Judentums im neutestamentlichen Zeitalter*, Berlin, 1903 (p. 272); L. W. King, *Babylonian Religion and Mythology*, London, 1899, (p. 38, 179 ff.); J. Darmsteter, *Sacred Books of the East*, vol. 23, Oxford, 1883 (p. 320); E. Stave, *Ueber den Einfluss des Parsismus auf das Judentum*, Haarlem, 1898; E. A. W. Budge, *The Book of Paradise*, etc., vol. I, London, 1904 (Introd., p. 44 f.); M. Jastrow, *The Religion of Babylonia and Assyria*, Boston, 1898 (p. 563 ff.); E. Schrader, *Die Keilinschriften und das alte Testament*, 3rd ed., Berlin, 1903 (p. 561 ff.); E. A. W. Budge, *Babylonian Life and History*, London, 1884 (p. 139 ff.); Paul Carus, *The History of the Devil and the Idea of Evil*, London, 1900 (p. 42 f.); A. J. W. Brandt, *Die mandäische Religion, ihre Entwickelung und geschichtliche Bedeutung erforscht*, etc. Leipzig, 1899 (pp. 34, 72 ff., 168 f., 182 f., 213 f., etc.); J. G. Frazer, *The Golden Bough*, 2nd ed., London, 1900 (vol. III, p. 151 ff., etc.); J. Darmsteter, *Ormazd et Ahriman, leurs origines et leur histoire*, Paris, 1877 (p. 123 ff.); E. Rohde, *Psyche*, 3rd ed., Leipzig, 1903 (I, 45 ff.); Monnier, *op cit.* (p. 5 ff.).

[5] Stave, *op. cit.*, p. 145 ff.

of Noah" (iii. 19). "For unto this end was the gospel preached even to the dead that they might be judged according to God in the spirit" (iv, 6).[1] These verses and others from the New Testament of similar import[2] became the "texts" for numerous sermons or homilies by the early Church fathers, and they were thus developed and enlarged upon, until we have the *Descensus* in outline in sermons of Clement of Alexandria and others.[3]

The fact of Christ's descent was almost universally accepted by the early orthodox Christians, but there was much controversy among them as to the purpose of his mission to the dead and its general significance. On this point, as well as on other points, the theologians of the Greek or oriental Church differed from those of the Church of Rome.[4] But through the discussions of the theologians the belief in the descent was strengthened and popularized, and it thus gradually became a doctrine and dogma of the Church. It was, moreover, at the time[5] when these controversies were most ardent that the *Descensus* was probably written. Though apocryphal in character, this document undoubtedly aided materially in spreading the descent story throughout the Christian world. The formal recognition of the conception as a part of the Christian faith occurred about the middle of the fourth century, when the Fourth Synod of Sirmium[6] introduced the clause "He descended into Hades" into the Symbol or Apostles' Creed.[7] It was probably not far from that time that the *Acta Pilati* was composed and combined with the *Descensus*, thus constituting the complete *Evangelium Nicodemi*. But it has not yet been discovered who the author of the important treatise was, nor are any of the circumstances of its composition certainly known.

There is no known manuscript of any version of the whole or any part of the *Evangelium Nicodemi* which can be placed earlier than the fifth century. The oldest manuscripts of the story that have been preserved are in Latin and Coptic, and these manuscripts are possibly as

1 Revised Version.

2 Cf. *Acts 2*, 24, 31; *Rom. 10*, 7; *Ephes. 4*, 9; *Matth. 27*, 52–53.

3 Cf. Alfred Maury, *op. cit.*, p. 320 ff.; Nicolas, p. 303 f.

4 Tertullian, Irenaeus, and Hippolytus were the leaders of one party; Clement of Alexandria and Origen of the other.

5 Cf. Monnier, *op. cit.*, p. 91 f. See J. Turmel, *La Descente du Christ aux Enfers*, Paris, 1905, for a careful and succinct account of the descent motive in patristic literature.

6 A.D. 359.

7 See Schaff, *The Creeds of Christendom*, II, 46; Zahn, *Das Apostolische Symbol*, Berlin, 1893; A. Hahn, *Bibliothek der Symbolen*, 3rd ed., Breslau, 1897; Harnack, *Das Apostolische Glaubensbekenntniss*, Berlin, 1896; McGiffert, *The Apostles' Creed*, New York, 1902; Monnier, *op. cit.*, p. 147 ff.

early as the fifth century.[1] But the story was probably first written in the Greek language, although the Greek versions of it that are now known are considerably later than the Latin and Coptic.[2] From the fifth century on the story must have rapidly become very popular, if the numerous Latin manuscripts[3] now in existence and the many references to it in mediaeval art and literature signify anything in respect to popularity. After that time all the prominent theologians and historians of mediaeval Christianity show an intimate knowledge of the *Evangelium Nicodemi* in their writings. Moreover, the descent motive and other episodes of the Gospel were employed in a familiar way by most of the important religious poets.[4]

By the tenth century the story of Christ's descent into Hades had permeated all Christian literature and art.[5] Very soon after Byzantine reforms had softened the asceticism of the Church authorities so far as to allow the person of Christ to be treated as a legitimate[6] subject in art, artists began to chisel scenes of the passion and resurrection on marble and stone columns. And the Harrowing of Hell usually, and Longinus piercing the side of the dead Christ with a spear often, had prominent places among these portrayals. Painters in miniature and workers in mosaics[7] and the plastic arts found much inspiration in the same subjects. The scenes occur with special frequency in the illuminated manuscripts[8] and all kinds of ornamental ivory work devoted to

[1] See on this point von Dobschütz, *op. cit.*; Lipsius, *op. cit.*; G. Paris and A. Bos, *op. cit.*, *Introd.*, II–IV; Tischendorf, *op. cit.*, *Prolegom.* L, iv ff.

[2] Von Dobschütz, *op. cit.*; Tischendorf, *op. cit.*

[3] There are about twenty MSS. in the Brit. Mus. alone.

[4] References are given by Monnier, *op. cit.*, pp. 141–2.

[5] The present writer is collecting materials for a monograph on *The Harrowing of Hell in Mediaeval Art*, which he hopes to publish at an early date.

[6] The development and influence of Byzantine art has been admirably treated by Dr. Carl Schnaase in his *Geschichte der bildenden Künste im Mittelalter.* 8 bde, 2te Auflage, Düsseldorf, 1869–1879 (cf. vol. III, pp. 212–213, 193 ff., 256, etc.).

[7] The earliest known attempt to reproduce the Harrowing of Hell in mosaics dates from the beginning of the eighth century, and was formerly preserved (now lost) in the Oratory of Pope John VII at Rome (Eugene Müntz, *l'Oratoire du pape Jean VII*, *Revue archéologique*, Sept. 1877, cited by Monnier, p. 197). Other mosaics of Harrowing are in the Cathedral of Torcello, near Venice (early twelfth century), and a fine one on the central dome of St. Mark's, Venice, which in its original form also belongs to the early twelfth century. There is also a mosaic in St. Praxeds, Rome (ninth century), which represents Christ delivering Adam and Eve into the hands of the archangel Michael, according to the specifications of the *Evang. Nicod.* 25. (Cf. F. Kraus, *Christliche Archaeologie*, vol. II, p. 349.)

[8] Manuscript miniatures of Harrowing as early as the eleventh century are known to be in existence, and the scene has been preserved in scores of MSS. dating from the eleventh to the sixteenth centuries. There are about forty such MSS. in the British Museum (cf. Birch and Jenner, *Early Drawings and Illuminations . . . in the British Museum*, p. 178). According to De Waal (*Die Apokryphen in der*

Christian subjects, that were produced between the twelfth and sixteenth centuries.[1] Artists in enamel[2] and stained glass,[3] and painters in oil were at a very early date caught by the magnetism of the scene which represents the victorious Christ with the banner of the cross in one hand treading the shattered gates of hell and Satan under foot, while he mercifully extends the other hand to Adam, Eve, and the patriarchs and prophets and bids them come forth from their infernal dungeon. The legend inspired some of the most beautiful work of Fra Angelico,[4] Taddeo Gaddi,[5] Memmi, Albrecht Dürer,[6] and many other artists of the late Middle Age and the Renaissance. Indeed, there is no branch of mediaeval and renaissance art[7] which does not give evidence of the strong hold the story had acquired on the minds and hearts of men throughout Christendom.

---

altschristlichen Kunst, *Römische Quartalschrift*, 1891, p. 194 ff.) a painting of Harrowing preserved in St. Clement's, Rome, belongs to the ninth century. And P. Germano (*Röm. Quartalschrift*, 1891, p. 290 f.) describes another painting similar to that of St. Clement's and places it before the year 1000 (cited by Monnier, p. 198, footnote).

1 A Byzantine ivory representing the scene and belonging to the twelfth century is preserved in the Museum of Antiquities (*Grünes Gewölbe*) at Dresden. The Musée de Cluny in Paris possesses several ivory diptyches, triptyches, and shrines of the fourteenth-fifteenth centuries, on the sides of which Harrowing is carved.

2 The best known and most beautiful piece of enamel work in which Harrowing is represented is on the *Pala d'Oro* of St. Mark's, Venice, belonging to the last quarter of the tenth century (cf. Schnaase, III, 256).

3 The Harrowing of Hell is one of several scenes describing the passion on one of the stained windows (fifteenth or sixteenth century) in the rear end of the church of St. Germain l'Auxerrois, Paris.

4 One on the walls of one of the cloister cells of the old St. Mark's monastery, Florence.

5 A magnificent painting on the north walls of the beautiful Spanish chapel of Santa Maria Novella, Florence.

6 It is included in each of Dürer's two notable series of wood-cuts, known as the "Little Passion" and the "Greater Passion," and also in a series of copper engravings from the year 1512.

7 The Harrowing scene is found as a miniature illumination on a Vatican Evangeliarium of the year 1128, which formerly belonged to the Emperor John (Schnaase, III, 274). It was formerly on the bronze or brazen doors of the churches St. Benevento, St. Paolo-Fuori in Rome, and of the cathedral of Pisa (Jameson-Eastlake, *The History of Our Lord as Exemplified in Works of Art*. Fourth ed., London, 1881, vol. II, p. 257). It was a favourite decoration on "Exultet Rolls," one of which in the library of the monastery of S. Maria Sopra Minerva at Rome dates from the eleventh century; another fine one in the Barberini Library, Rome, belongs to the twelfth century (Schnaase, IV, 695 ff.). It occurs in bas-reliefs on columns, pulpit-supports, etc., one such having been preserved on the pulpit-support of the church of St. Bartholomew at Pistoia, and another splendid one from the early thirteenth century on a column in the east portal of the Baptistery at Pisa (Schnaase, VII, 268, footnote 3, 269). It forms one of the bas-reliefs on a marble column twenty feet high which stands in front of the cathedral at Gaeta (Estelle M. Hurll, *The Life of Our Lord in Art*, Boston, 1898, p. 5). It appears in a thirteenth century fresco on the lunette at the eastern end of the transept of the cathedral at Braunschweig (Woltmann and Woermann, *History of Painting*, edited by Sidney Colvin, vol. I, p. 309).

Nowhere was the influence of the Harrowing of Hell felt more powerfully than in the mediaeval drama.[1] Inasmuch as the early religious plays were largely inspired by a desire to reproduce in an impressive and concrete form all the phases of Christ's passion and resurrection, it is natural that the vivid description of the conquering Christ storming hell, binding Satan and rescuing the patriarchs, which is found in the *Gospel of Nicodemus*, should have appealed strongly to the imagination of the primitive play-wrights of the Middle Ages. Thus the plays which were concerned with the Easter-tide, especially the so-called cyclical mysteries, usually included the Harrowing of Hell among those scenes devoted to the representation of the passion and resurrection. The dragon mouth and other symbolical representations of the entrance to hell became in the course of time impressive parts of mediaeval stage furniture. And the antics of Satan and his minions on the stage formed no doubt one of the most attractive features of the plays.

Specimens of Harrowing plays have been preserved in all those European literatures in which any serious effort was made to develop a religious drama in the Middle Ages. One of the earliest attempts to dramatize the scene is found in the Norman-French play of *Adam*.[2] It also became one of the most popular scenes of the German Easter plays.[3]

[1] The best book on the subject of the mediaeval drama is by W. Creizenach, *Geschichte des neueren Dramas*, vols. I–III, Halle, 1893–1903; cf. also A. W. Ward, *A History of English Dramatic Literature*, 2nd ed., 3 vols., London, 1899; Petit de Julleville, *Les mystères*, 2 vols., Paris, 1880.

[2] Cf. Creizenach, I, 130; Monnier, p. 215–216. On the Harrowing of Hell in the mediaeval German drama, see Creizenach I, 112 ff., where numerous other references are given.

[3] The *Evangelium Nicodemi* was very popular in other kinds of early French and German literature besides the drama. Three poetical versions in French and one in German have been published in recent years. One of the French recensions (ed. Paris and Bos, *op. cit.*) is the work of Chrétien (not de Troies, Paris and Bos, *Introd.* p. xiii), another of André de Coutances (cf. Paris and Bos, *Introd.* p. xvi ff.), while the third (*ibid.* p. xlvi ff.) is by an anonymous poet. All three translations belong to the thirteenth century. The German rhymed version, the work of Heinrich von Hesler (ed. Karl Helm, Tübingen, 1902), is much longer (5400 lines) than any other known poetical (the longest French version, that of Chrétien, contains 2190 lines) translation of the *Evang. Nicod.* Hesler's work probably belongs to about the end of the thirteenth century (cf. K. Helm, *Untersuchungen über Heinrich Hesler's Evangelium Nicodemi*, Beitr. xxiv, 85–185). Several prose versions of the Gospel are known to exist in unpublished form in both early French and German MSS. in the Bibliothèque Nationale, Paris, British Museum, and Royal Library, Berlin (cf. Wülker, *op. cit.*), and the story of Christ's descent was extensively employed by early German and French poets and writers of sermons.

Translations of the *Evang. Nicod.* in both verse and prose have been preserved in Provençal (H. Suchier, *op. cit.*), and at least two prose versions are recorded in early Italian (Wülker, *op. cit.*, p. 33).

The story was translated into various Slavic literatures at an early date, and some

But in no other literature do we find the dramatic Harrowing of Hell so extensively and artistically developed as in Middle-English. It is in fact the subject of the earliest specimen[1] of the English religious drama which is thus far known, and which is printed in this volume. It is also described by one of the plays or scenes in each of the four great cycles[2] of English mysteries, as well as by the "Ancient Cornish Drama."[3] Moreover, the influence of the *Gospel of Nicodemus* is seen in many other scenes[4] of the cyclical mysteries besides those especially devoted to the presentation of the Harrowing of Hell. And so long as these mystery plays held the English stage, that is, until about the end of the sixteenth century, the Harrowing scenes probably retained their popularity.

The influence of the *Evangelium Nicodemi* was felt in English literature long before the period of the religious drama. The Gospel was doubtless introduced into England in the Latin version not very long after Christianity began to flourish there. For early English writers like Bede[5] show perfect familiarity with its contents. And the early Christian poets utilize the story and paraphrase it in a number of their productions. An extensive account of the descent of Christ is contained in the so-called Cadmonian poems, while the greatest of all Old-English religious poets, Cynewulf, refers to the Harrowing of Hell in several[6]

---

of these versions have been made accessible to a limited number of students during the last few years. Cf. M. Soperanskij, *The Slavic Apocryphal Gospels* (Proceedings of the Eighth Archaeological Congress at Moscow, 1890), vol. II, 1895; *The South Slavic Evang. Nicod.*, edited by Daničić from a Servian MS. (*Starine*, iv, 131–149). An early Bulgarian version was edited a few years ago by G. Polivka in *Starine*, xxiv, 112 ff. Other references are given by Harnack, *Altchristliche Lit.* I, 907–908.

[1] I cannot here give an account of the discussion that has been conducted by scholars for many years as to whether the *Harrowing of Hell* is a drama or not. Cf. on the subject Collier, *Annals of the Stage*, II, 213; Wright, *The Chester Plays*, *Transact. Shakes. Soc.* for 1843, Introd. p. 14; also *Transact.* for 1847, p. 211; Mall, *The Harrowing of Hell*, p. 47 ff.; Böddeker, *op. cit.*, pp. 264–5; Wülker, *op. cit.*, p. 79; Klein, *Geschichte des Dramas*, XII, 350; ten Brink, *op. cit.*, II, 241 ff.; Pollard, *The Towneley Plays*, Introd. p. 25; Ward, *op. cit.*, I, 89–90, 25, footnote; Jusserand, *A Literary History of the English People*, I, 443, 460; Creizenach, I, 158 f.; Chambers, *The Mediaeval Stage*, I, 83; II, 74.

[2] It is No. 37 of *The York Mystery Plays* (ed. Toulmin-Smith, pp. 372–395), No. 25 of *The Towneley Plays* (ed. England and Pollard, pp. 293–305), No. 33 of *The Coventry Mysteries* (ed. Halliwell, pp. 329–330), and No. 18 of *The Chester Plays* (ed. Wright, vol. II, pp. 71–83).

[3] Ed. Norris, vol. II, p. 11 ff.

[4] Cf. Nos. 29–30, 32–33, 36 of *The York Plays*; Nos. 23–24, 26 of *The Towneley Plays*, etc.; the influence is especially noticeable in the Cornish drama.

[5] *Hist. Eccl.* V, 12; *Comm. on Ep. 1 Pet. 3*, 19.

[6] In addition to *Christ and Satan*, ll. 366–664, cf. *Elene*, ll. 179–182; 293–297; 905–913; *Phoenix*, ll. 417–423; *Guthlac*, ll. 1074–1077; *Panther*, ll. 55–64; *Credo*, ll. 25–32.

different connections, and he reproduces much of the description in his poem on *Christ.*[1] Cynewulf, in fact, or one of his school of poets, devoted an entire poem to the subject, though only a fragment of it has been preserved.[2]

In the later centuries of Old-English literature the *Evangelium Nicodemi* was turned into the Old-English prose, which is preserved in at least three[3] different manuscripts. Besides this the story of the descent was frequently employed by writers of Old-English homilies[4] and lives of saints. The Gospel probably reached the climax of its popularity in England during the thirteenth and fourteenth centuries. In these centuries we find a great many poems that refer to or reproduce episodes from the *Evangelium.* And one of the longest, most important Middle-English poetical productions[5] paraphrases at great length the entire story. Besides this there are several translations in both poetry and prose known to be in existence. These translations kept a strong hold upon Christian sentiment in England until about the middle of the sixteenth century, if we are justified in drawing a conclusion from the large number of Black Letter editions of one of the translations that appeared during the first half of the century.[6]

While the Harrowing of Hell is in its literary and artistic significance the most important episode of the *Gospel of Nicodemus,* there are several other legends which became the inspiration of much that is good in mediaeval literature and art, and which seem to trace their origin, or, at any rate, their popularity back to this apocryphal gospel. Some of the most interesting of them are the stories of the blind Longinus piercing the side of the crucified Christ with a spear and recovering his sight through the blood that fell on his eyes; of St. Veronica and the miraculous handkerchief; of Seth's mission to Paradise for the Oil of

[1] Ll. 558–585 are especially important; cf. also ll. 140 f., 730 f., 1159 f., and Cook, *The Christ of Cynewulf*, Boston, 1900, pp. 143–144, etc.

[2] On the authorship of this poem see Cook, *op. cit.*, Introd. p. 129; also ten Brink, *op. cit.*, I, 56; Wülker, *Grundriss*, p. 187; Stopford Brooke, *History of Early English Literature*, pp. 425–6; J. Cramer, *Quelle, Verfasser und Text des altenglischen Gedichtes Christi Höllenfahrt*, *Anglia*, XIX, 137–174; J. H. Kirkland, *A Study of the Anglo-Saxon Poem, The Harrowing of Hell*, Halle, 1885.

[3] Cf. W. H. Hulme, *The Old English Gospel of Nicodemus.* Edited with Introduction and Notes. *Publications of the Mod. Lang. Assoc. of America*, XIII, 457 ff.; see also *Modern Philology*, I, 579 ff.

[4] See *The Blickling Homilies*, ed. Morris, p. 85 ff.; and *The Homilies of the Anglo-Saxon Church*, ed. Thorpe, I, 26–28, 94, 108, 216, 218, 228, 248, 460; II, 80, 606–608. See above, pp. xv ff., xxxii ff.

[5] *Cursor Mundi* (ed. Morris, E.E.T.S. No. 62), ll 17,259–18,628.

[6] See above, p. lvii f.

Mercy[1] and the apple-seeds whence the Holy Rood was believed to have sprung; of the pardoned thief in Paradise; of Antichrist.[2]

The Longinus legend exerted a strong influence on both literature and art in the Middle Ages. It seems especially to have permeated the early literature of Scandinavia, furnishing the model and inspiration for the Balder myth in Old Norse poetry.[3] Longinus and the Bleeding Lance were also one of the mainsprings in developing that part of the Arthurian legends which is especially concerned with the search for the Holy Grail.[4] The Vernicle was, moreover, frequently described and painted by mediaeval poets and artists,[5] while the Antichrist legend vied with the Harrowing of Hell in the influence it exerted upon the religious drama of the Middle Ages and the early renaissance.[6]

There can be little doubt, I think, that the conception and description of the underworld which we find in the *Evangelium Nicodemi* appealed very strongly to the Celts at an early period in their history and gave colour and tone to their mystical religious beliefs.[7] While it is

[1] See on this subject *The Tree of Life* (*from the German of Dr. Piper*), *Journal of Sacred Literature*, IV, 376 ff.; VI, 27 ff.; Morris, *Legends of the Holy Rood*, London, 1871; C. M. Gayley, *Plays of Our Forefathers*, New York, 1907, p. 246 ff.

[2] See especially *The Antichrist Legend, A Chapter in Christian and Jewish Folk-lore*, englished from the German of W. Bousset . . . by A. H. Keane, London, 1896.

[3] Cf. Bugge, *Studien über die Entstehung der nordischen Götter und Heldensagen.* German, translation by O. Brenner, Munich, 1889, pp. 32–38; Bugge-Schofield, *The Home of the Eddic Poems* . . . London, 1899, Introd. p. 43 ff. There is also an Old-Norse translation of the *Evangelium Nicodemi* (cf. C. R. Unger, *Heilagra Manna Sogur*, etc., 2 vols., Christiania, 1877, vol. II, pp. 1–20).

[4] Cf. Richard Heinzel, *Ueber die französischen Gralromane* (*Denkschriften der Kaiserlichen Akadamie der wissenschaften, Philosophische-historische Classe*, Bd. 40, Wien, 1892, p. 6, 9–11, 105, etc.); Birch-Hirschfeld, *Die Sage vom Graal*, pp. 13, 15 ff.; A. Nutt, *Studies on the Legend of the Holy Grail*, London, 1888, pp. 8–9, 11–12, 15, 19–20, 22, 24, 102–104, 115, 218, 220–221.

[5] See especially Karl Pearson, *Die Fronica*, Strassburg, 1887, where a large number of Veronica pictures of Christ are reproduced from the MSS. as an appendix; Von Dobschütz, *Christusbilder, Untersuchungen zur Christlichen Legende*, etc., Leipzig, 1899; C. W. Chevalier, *op. cit.*

[6] Cf. Creiznach, I, 78 ff. No. 24 of *The Chester Plays* (ed. Wright, pp. 150–177) is entitled *Antichrist.*

[7] See Alfred Nutt, *The Happy Other-world in the Mythico-Romantic Literature of the Irish* (in *The Voyage of Bran*, etc., 2 vols., the Grimm Library, London, 1895 and 1897, vol. I, p. 115 ff.). The influence of the *Evangelium Nicodemi* on early Irish literature is shown by the fact that it exists in an Old-Irish translation preserved in the well-known *Yellow Book of Lecan* (ed. Atkinson for the Royal Irish Academy, p. 141). It is also found in the form of passions or homilies which are preserved in the *Lebar Brecc, or Speckled Book*, a vellum manuscript of the fourteenth century. They have been translated into English and edited by Robert Atkinson, M.A., LL.D., under the title, *The Passions and the Homilies from Leabhar Breac*, etc. Todd Lectures, 2 vols., Dublin, 1887, "Passions," 19–20. See also a Middle-Cornish poem on *The Passion of Our Lord*, published together with an English translation by Whitley Stokes, *Transactions of the Philological Society* for 1860–61, Appendix, pp. 1–79.

not easy to point out specific instances of the indebtedness of St. Patrick's *Purgatory*, *Tundale's Voyage* and the *Voyage of Bran* to the apocryphal story, there is nevertheless such a similarity of conception and sentiment between the Celtic and Latin-Oriental productions that we are almost forced to believe in some connection between them. Dante certainly owed much of his wonderful conception of Purgatory to the descriptions of the *Evangelium*,[1] and it is probable that Milton studied the same legend and drew considerable inspiration from it for his portrayal of the character of Satan in *Paradise Lost*.[2]

[1] Cf. *Inferno*, IV, 37, 38; XII, 33 f.; IX, 122 f.; XXI, 106 f.; Monnier, 175 f.
[2] See Walter Raleigh, *John Milton*, London, 1900, p. 168 ff.

The Harrowing of Hell.

The Harrowing of Hell.

Digby MS. TEXT O.

Hou ih*es*u c*ri*st herowede helle [leaf 119]
Of harde gates ich wille telle.
Leue frend, nou beþ stille,
Lesteþ þat ich tellen wille
Ou ih*es*u fader him biþoute
And adam hout of helle broute.

In helle was adam and eve
þat veren ih*es*u crist wel leve,
And seint iohan þe baptist
þat was neweu ih*es*u crist,
Dauit þe p*ro*phete and abraham,
For þe sunnes of adam;
And moni oþer holi mon
Mo þen ich ou tellen con;

Abbreviations.—B = Boeddeker; C = Collier; H = Halliwell; M = Mall; L = Laing; Varn = Varnhagen.

1. Lines 1–2 in red ink; *de* in *herowede* above line; Varn. *herewede.*

8. (Hal. = Wright-Halliwell, *Reliq. Antiq.* i, 253.) Hal. M. Varn. *weren.*

10. Hal. *newen.* 12. Hal. *Adem.*

The Harrowing of Hell.

Harley MS. Text L. | *Auchinleck MS.* Text E.

Alle herkneþ to me nou ! [leaf 55, bk.]
a st*ri*f wolle y tellen ou
of ih*esu* ant of Sathan,
þo ih*esu* wes to helle ygan
fforte vacche þenne hys,
ant bringen hem to parays.
þe deuel heuede so muche pouste
þat alle mosten to helle te ;
nas non so holy p*ro*phete
seþþe Adam & eue þen appel ete,
ant he were at þis worldes fyne,
þat he ne moste to helle pyne ;
ne shulde he neuer þenne come
nere ih*esu* c*ri*st godes sone.
vor þat wes seid to Adam a*n*t eue,
þ*at* were ih*esu* c*ri*st so leeue ;
ant so wes seyd to habraham,
þat wes sothfast holy man ;
an[t] so wes seid to dauyd þe kyng,
þ*at* wes of cr*is*tes oune ofspryng ;
ant to Iohan þ[e] baptist,
þ*at* folewede ih*esu* c*ri*st ;
ant to Moyses þe holy whyt,
þe heuede þe lawe to ȝeme ryht ;

2. M. *wille I.* Mall always alters MS. *y* to *i.*
3. B. *iesu* (regularly) ; C. *Jesus* (always) ; M. *Jesu* (always) ; M. *Satan.*
4. M. *gan.* 5. M. *For to fette . . his.*
6. M. *And* (always) ; *parais.*
7. M. *michel.* 10. M. *Siþþen.* Varn *eve.*
15. M. *For.* 16. M. *leue.*
17. C. *sayd* ; M. *seid . . Abraham* ; last *a* in *habraham* above line.
18. M. *soþfast.* 19. B. *ant* ; H.M. *And.*
20. H. *onne.* 21. C.H. *the* ; M. *þe* ; *a* in *Iohan* above line ; C. *John the.*
23. B. *wyht* ; M. *wiht.* 24. C. *theme.*

DIGBY.

Til ihe*su* fader nom fles and blod
Of þe maiden marie god;
And suþþen was don ful muchel some,
Bou*n*de*n* and beten and maked ful lome
Tille þat gode friday at non;
þenne he was on rode idon,
His honden from his body wonden,
Mit here miȝte hoe him shenden.
To helle sone he nom gate
Adam and eve hout to take;
þo þe he to helle cam
Succhë wordes he bigan:

" Harde gates haui gon,
Serewes soffred moni hon,
þritti winter and half þritti ȝer
Haui ben wend alonde her;
Almest so muchel hit is agon
Suþþen þat i bicom furst mon;
Suþþen haui þoled and west
Boþe chele, hounger and þurst;
Men duden me so muchel same,
Wiþ wounde*n* stro*n*ge makede me lame;

15. Hal. *Till.* 17. Hal. *michel.*
18. Hal. *Bonden.* 22. Hal. *Nit.*
27. *Hardegates*: first *e* inserted from below.
29. First *i* in second *þritti* above line.

HARLEY.

ant to mony oþer holy mon
mo þen ich telle con,
þat weren alle in more wo
þen y con ou telle fro.
Ihe*su* c*ri*st arew hem sore
a*n*t seide he wolde vacche hem þore;
he lyhte of ys heȝe tour
into seinte Marie bour;
he wes bore for oure nede
in þis world in pore wede,
In þis world he wes ded
forte losen vs from þe qued;
þo ihe*su* heuede shed ys blod
for oure neode vpon þe rod,
In godhed tok*e* he þen way
þat to helle gates lay;
þe he com þere þo seide he,
asse y shal nouþe telle þe.

HArde gates hauy gon,
sorewen soffred mony on;
þritty wynter ant þridde half yer
hauy woned in londe her;
almost ys so muche agon
seþþe y bycom furst mon;
Ich haue seþþe þoled ant wyst
hot, cold, honger ant þurst;
Mon haþ do me shome ynoh
wyþ word ant dede in heore woh;

AUCHINLECK.

[1] **V**ntil crist loked þaim vnto, [leaf 36]
as man auȝt to prisouns do;
he liȝted out of his heiȝe tour
Into seynt mari bour;
he was born for our misdede
In þis world in pouer wede,
In þis world he suffred dede,
forto deliuer ous fram þe qued;
þan ihe*su* hadde spilt his blod
for our sinnes on þe rode,
he nam him þe riȝt way
vnto helle for soþe to say;
þan he com þer þan seyd he,
as y schal now telle þe.

dominus ait.

Hard gates haue y gon
[2]& suffred pines mani on;
þritti winter & þridde half ȝere
haue y wond in lond here;
almast is so michel gan
seþþen y bicom first man;
seþþen haue y fond & wist
hot & cold, hunger & þrest;
Man haþ don me schame & þouȝ
wiþ word, wiþ dede & michel wouȝ;

25. M. *mani* . . *man* (Mall often alters *o* before nasal of MS. to *a*, but he shows no consistency in making this change).
26. M. *þan*. 28. M. *þan I*; H. *i*.
29. M. *areu*. 30. M. *fette*.
31. C. *hege*; M. *his*.
33. M. *boren*. 34. M. *poure*.
36. M. *For to*; B. M. *lesen*; M. *ous*; Varn. *us*.
37. M. *his*. 38. M. *sinnes on*.
39. B. *tok*; M. reads line, *He nam him þe rihte wei*.
40. M. *Unto helle for soþe to sei*.
41. B. *þen*; M. *þo* . . *þer*.

[1] Initial letters of lines always touched with red.
[2] & is the contraction always used for *and*.

42. H. *Asse i*; M. *nou*; *Dominus ait* (B), and *Dominus* (M), not in version *L*.
43. M. *gon*. 44. C. *sorowen*; M. *sorewes suffred* . . *on*; Varn. *Serewen*. 45. M. *ȝer*.
46. M. *woned* . . *londe* (inconsistent).
47. M. *michel gan*.
48. M. *siþþen* . . *first*. 49. M. *siþþen*.
50. M. *hunger* . . *þrist*.
51. M. *don*. 52. M. *here*.

DIGBY.

Hi nomen me wiþouten sake,
Bounden min honden to mi bake,
Hi beten me þat I ran ablode,
And suþþen me duden one þe rode;
ffor adam sunful, Iwis,
Al haui þoled þis.

Adam, þu hauest about hit sore,
And I ne mai soffren hit na more;
Hit wille þe bringen of helle pine,
þe, adam, and alle þine."

"Wo is þat ich here þere?
Ne red ich him speken na more,
He may nou so muchel do,
þat he sal ous comen to
To ben houre fere
And witen hou we pleyeþ here."
þenne spak ih*es*u, þe king:
"Stille be þu, lording,
þat ich here greden þere;
Ich rede þat þou ne speke na more,
þou miȝt wel witen bi mi play
þat ich wile hauen mine away;
Wost þu neuere wat ich am?
More þen .xxx. vinter hit is agon
þat þu hauest fonded me

39. *þat* : *t* above line.
56. *o* in *þou* above line.

HARLEY.

bounden ant bueten yron of blode,
demeden me to deȝe on rode;
for Adames sunne fol ywis
Ich haue þoled al þis.
Adam, þou hauest aboht sore,
Inul soffre þat no more;
Adam, þou hast duere aboht,
þat þou leuedest me noht;
y shal þe bringe of helle pyne
ant wyþ þe alle myne.

Sathan ait.

Who ys þat ych here þore?
Ich him rede speke na more,
for he may so muche do
þat he shal vs come to
forte buen oure fere
ant fonden hou we pleyen here.

D*omin*u*s* ait.

þou miht wyten in þy lay
þat mine woll y haue away;
wost þou neuer whet ych am?
almost ys þritti wynter gan
þat þou hast fonded me

AUCHINLECK.

þai tok me wiþouten sake,
þai bond min honden bihi*n*de mi bac,
þai bete me til y ran on blode,
þai dempt me to hong on rode;
alle for adams sinne ywis,
þan haue y þoled þis.
adam, þus dere haue y bouȝt,
& þou no louedest me neu*er* nouȝt;
adam, y haue bouȝt ful sare
& y wil suffre it na mare;
to-day y schal bring of pine
adam, þe & alle þine.

satanas dixit.

Who is þat ich here þare?
y rede þat he spek na mare,
for he may so michel do
þat he schal comen ous vnto
forto ben our fere
& loke hou we playen here.

dominus ait.

þou may wele wite mi play
þat min wil y haue oway;
wele þou wost wat ich am,
More þan þritti winter is gan
þat þou hast frained me

53. Laing *toke*. 65. Varn. *Wo*. 75. Laing *framed*.

53. B.M. omit this line and interpolate three lines which are a patch-work partly from version O, partly from E: *He nomen me wiþ-outen sake / Bounden min honden to mi bake / He beten me, þat I ran on blode* (B. *þat y ron*); for consistency M. should have *namen* and *handen*.

54 (B.M. 56). M. *demden*; C. *dethe*.

55 (B.M. 57). H. *Fore*; M. *sinne, ful*.

57 (B. 59, M. 61). B. *aboht hit*; M. *it*.

58 (B. 60, M. 62). B. *Ant Inul*; M. *And I nil*; M. *suffre-na*.

59 (B. 57, M. 59). M. *hauest dere*.

65. M. (67) *michel*.

66. M. (68) *ous* (always).

67. M. (69) *to ben*.

68. C. *playen*; M. (70) *fonden*.

69. M. brackets this line and 70 (*i.e.* 71, 72), reading, *þou miht wel wite bi mi plei*; while B. transfers them almost to the end of this speech (77, 78 B.). B. reads for 69, *ant þou shalt wyte wel to-day*.

70. M. (72) *willi haue awei*; B. *wolle*.

71. M. (73) *what*.

72. M. (74) *almost þe þridde winter is gan*; B. *wynter ys*.

73. M. (75) *hauest fonded*.

DIGBY.

fforto witen wat I be;
Sunne ne foundest þou neuer non
In me as in anoþer mon;
þou miȝt wel witen þe bi þon
þat ich more þen ani mon;
þou salt wel witen þe to-day [leaf 119, bk.]
þat ich wyle hauen mine away;
þenne þou letest þe alone,
þenne þou miȝt gru*n*te*n* and grone."
þenne spak him satanas,
Maister-fend in helle he was:
"P*ar* ma fey! ich holde mine
Alle þo þat here ben hine;
Wiþ reisoun willy tellen þe,
þer aȝein ne miȝt þou nout be;

Adam þe hou*n*g*ri*e com me to,
Mani redes he gan me do;
ffor on appel þat ich ȝaf him
He is min and al is cun."

"Satanas, hit was min,
þe appel þat þou ȝeue him,
þe appel and þe appeltre,
Boþen veren maked þoru me;
Hou miȝtest þou in eni cu*n*nes wyse
Of oþer monnes þing maken marchau*n*dise?

63. *o* in *þou* above line.

HARLEY.

forte knowe wet y be;
Sunne fond þou neuer non
In me as in oþer mon;

ant þou shalt wyte wel to-day
þat mine wolle y haue away;
wen þou bileuest al þyn one,
þenne myht þou grede ant grone.

Sathan.
Par ma fey! ich holde myne
alle þo þat bueþ heryne;
resoun wol y telle þe
þer aȝeyn myht þou nouht be;

Whose buyþ any þyng, [leaf 56]
hit is hys ant hys ofspryng;
Adam hungry com me to,
Monrade dude y him me do;
ffor on appel ich ȝef hym
he is myn ant al hys kun.

Domin*us*.
Sathanas, hit wes myn,
þe appel þat þou ȝeue hym,
þe appel ant þe appeltre
boþe were maked þourh me;
hou myhstest þou on eny wyse
of oþer monnes þyng make marchan-[dise?

AUCHINLECK.

forto wite what y be;
seþþen fondestow neuer nan
wiþ me as wiþ anoþer man,
& þou wost wele for þan
þat ich am more þan ani man;
þou schalt wite þis ich day
þat y schal haue min oway,
& y schal þe leue here
In sorwe among þine fere.

satanas dixit.
Par ma fay! ich hald mine
al þat ben hereinne;
wiþ resoun wil y telle þe
þat þer ogain may þou nouȝt be,
þat me bihoueþ haue & hald
& wiþouten ende wald;
for whoso biggeþ aniþing,
It owe to ben his wiþouten lesing;
adam hungri come me to,
manred y made him me to do;
for an appel þat y ȝaf him
he is min & al his kin.

dominus ait.
Satanas, he seyd, it was min,
þe appel þat þou ȝaf him,
þe appel & þe appeltre,
boþe war maked þurch me;
hou may þou on ani wise
of oþer mennes þing mak marcha*n*dise?

74. B. *whet*; M. (76) *what*; M. *For to.*
75. M. (77) *sinne . . found.*
78. *haue, e* corrected from *a*; M. (80) *willi haue awei.*
79. B. *when*; M. (81) *whan . . one*; B. *alle.*
80. M. (82) *þanne-grete . . grone.*
82. C. *Alle so*; M. (84) *ben . . inne.*
83. C. *Resonn*; M. (85) *willi.*
84. C. *ageyn*; M. (86) *aȝen . . noht.*
85. C. *whoso*; M. (87) *whoso biggeþ.*
86. M. (88) *It.*
88. M. (90) *Manrede dide.*
89. C. *gef*; M. (91) *on . . ȝaf.*
90. C. *kinn*; M. (92) *kin.*
91. M. (93) *Satanas, it.*
92. C. geue; M. (94) *ȝaue.*
95. M. (97) *mihtest . . ani*; B. *myhtest.*

77. Laing, *foundestow.*
92. Laing *Nowe.* 94. *y*: Laing *I.*
95. *y*: Laing *I.*

DIGBY.

Seþþen þou bou*n*dest him wiþ min,
Wiþ reisoun wil ich hauen him."

" Ih*esu*, welcomen þou be,
þat ful sore reweþ me;
þou art louerd ouer al,
þou hauest þat þou habbe shal;
Heuene and erþe weldest þou þe,
þe soules in helle let þou be;
þat ich haue let me helde,
þat þou hauest wel mote þou welde."

" Stille, stille, satanas!
þe is fallen aunbesas.
Wendest þou i were ded for nout?
ffor mi deþ was monkun boust;
Hy þat habbeþ serued me
Sulen wiþ me in blisse be;
þo þat nolden on me bileuen
Sulen wiþ þe here bileuen;
þou salt hauen more pine
þen alle þo þat her ben ine."

" May mon me so worse do
þene I haue aved hiderto?
Ich aue þoled so muchel wo
þat I ne recche weder I go;
If þou bireuest me of mine,
I sal bireuen þe of þine;
I shal gon from mon to manne
And bireuen þe moni anne."

" God hit wot, I shal speken þe wiþ,
þat wel shaltou holde griþ;

92. *shal*; the *h* of *sh* appears to have been inserted by a later hand wherever it occurs in this MS.

100. Apparently an attempt was made to change *s* of *boust* to *h*.

HARLEY.

Seþþe he wes boht wyþ myn,
wyþ resoun wolle ich hauen hym.

Sath*an*.

Ihe*su*, wel y knowe þe,
þat ful sore reweþ me;
þou art louerd ouer al,
wo ys him þ*at* þe knowe ne shal!
heouene ant erþe tac to þe,
Soules in helle lef þou me;
Let me hauen hem ant helde,
þ*at* þou hauest wel mote þou welde.

Do*minus*.

Stille be þou, Sathanas!
þe ys fallen ambesaas.
Wendest þou ich were ded for noht?
þourh my deþ ys monkune boht;
þey þat haued serued me,
wyþ me he shulen in heuene be;

þou shalt buen in more pyne
þen eny þat þer is heryne.

Sath*an*.

Ne may non me worse do
þen ich haue had hiderto;
Ich haue had so muche wo
þat y ne recche whyder y go;
ȝef þou reuest me of myne,
y shal reue þe of þyne;
y shal gon from mon to mon
ant reue þe of mony on.

Do*minus*.

God wot y shal speke þe wyht
ant do þe to holde gryht;

AUCHINLECK.

seþþen þou bouȝtest him wiþ mine,
wiþ resoun schuld ichaue him.

satanas dixit.

Ihe*su*, wele y knawe þe,
þat ful sore reweþ me;
þou art lord ouer al,
& euer was & ay be schal;
heuen & erþe weld þou þe,
þe soules in helle lat þou be;
lat me haue þat ich halde, [1] [lf. 36, bk.]
[1]þat þou hast wele mot þou it wald.

dominus ait.

Sitte now stille, satanas!
þe is fallen amesas.
wenestow þat y dyed for nouȝt?
wiþ mi dede was mankin bouȝt;
þai þat haue serued me,
In blis schal þai euer be;
þai þat noþing serued me,
þai schal in helle be wiþ þe;
bot þou schalt ben in more pine
þan ani oþer þat is þereinne.

satanas dixit.

þer may me no man wers do
þan ichaue had hiderto;
Ich haue hadde so michel wo,
þat me no rek whider y go;
ȝif þou bireuest me of mine,
y schal bireue þe of þine;
y schal go fro man to man
& bireue þe mani an.

[d]ominus ait.

So y schal speke þe wiþ,
þat y schal do þe hold griþ;

115. Laing, *Wenestou.*

97. M. (99) *siþþen* (always).
98. C. *resonn*; M. (100) *wil.*
103. M. (105) *Heuene . . tak.*
104. M. (106) *þe soules.*
105. B.M. (107) substitute corrupt form of this line from E: *Let me hauen* (M. *haue*) *þat ich helde.* 108. M. *ambes as.*

110. M. (112) *For mi . . Mankin*; C. *kinne.*
111. B. *haueþ*; M. (113) *hauen.*
113. M. (115) *ben.* 114. M. (116) *þan ani . . inne.* 115. M. (117) *non . . werse.*
116. M. (118) *þan.* 117. M. (119) *michel.*
119. C. *Gef*; M. (121) *ȝif.* 121. M. (123) *go.*
123. M. (125) *wiþ.* 124. M. (126) *griþ.*

But Christ replies he will bind Satan so firmly that the latter will not be able to molest his servants till doomsday.

DIGBY.

So faste shal I binden þe,
þat fewe shalt þou bireuen me;
þou salt here ben bounden ay,
Tille þat comeþ domesday;

If þou were hou*n*bou*n*den among men,
Almest woldest þou bireu*en* me hem;
þe smale deuelen þat beþ hou*n*stro*n*ge,
Hoe sulen among moncun ȝonge
Forto hauen alle hem
þat hem ne willeþ stonden aȝein.
Helle ȝates ich come nou to,
Nou ich wille þat hy ben houndo;
Wer is nou þe ȝateward?
Ich holde him for a couard."

"Ich haue Iherd wordes harde,
Ne am ich na more ȝatewarde;
Ich haue Iherd wordes stronge, [leaf 120]
Ne dar ihc duellen er nout longe;
Loke hem nou, wose may,
Ich lete hem stonden and renne away."

"Helle ȝates her I falle
And suþþen go into helle;
Satanas, here I þe binde,
Ne salt þou neuere hene winde;
Ne salt þou neuere wenden away
Tille þat comeþ domesday.

134. *er* above line.
135. Varn. *mai*.

HARLEY.

so faste shal y bynde þe,
Lutel shalt þou reue me;
þou shalt buen in bondes ay
o þat come domesday;
þou shalt neuer out wende
monkunne forte shende;
for were þou among men,
þou woldest me reuen moni of hem;
þe smale fendes þat bueþ nout st*ro*nge,
he shulen among men yonge;
þilke þ*at* nulleþ aȝeyn hem stonde,
Ichulle he habben hem in honde.
helle gates y come nou to
ant y wole þat heo vndo;
wer ys nou þis ȝateward?
me þuncheþ he is a coward.

IAnitor.

Ich haue herd wordes stronge,
ne dar y her no lengore stonde;
kepe þe gates whose may,
y lete hem stonde ant renne away.

D*ominus*.

Helle gates wolle y falle
ant out taken myne alle;
Sathanas, y bynde þe, her shalt þou lay

o þat come domesday.

126. C. *Littel*; M. (128) *Litel*.
127–130. B.M. omit these four lines, and M. brackets 129–30. 130. C. *Monkinne*.
131. M. (129) omits *for*.
133. M. (131) *ben unstronge*.
134. M. (132) *ȝonge*. 135. C. *ageyn*; M. (133–134) *For to hauen alle hem / þat hem ne willen stonden aȝen*.
137. M. (135) *ȝates*. 138. M. *Ich wille . . he*.
139. B. (135) *wher*; M. (137) *where*; C. *gate*.
140. M. (138) *þinkeþ*. 143. M. (141) *ȝates whoso*. 144. M. (142) *stonde . . awei*.

AUCHINLECK.

so fast schal y binde þe,
þat fowe schaltow binim me;

were þou vnbounde among men,
al þou wost binim me hem;
þe smale deuels þat er vnstrang,
þai schal among mankin gang,
& al schul þai haue pain
þat wil nouȝt stond hem oȝain.
helle ȝates, y com ȝou to,
now ich wil þat ȝe vndo;
whare is he þat ȝateward?
Ich hold him for a coward.

Iannator ait.

Ich haue herd wordes hard
whi y no may be no steward;

y lete hem stond & ren oway,
lete hem ȝeme whoso may.

dominus ait.

Helle ȝates, here y ȝou felle,
& seþþen wil ich herwe helle;
lucifer, here y þe binde,
schaltow neuer heþen winde

vntil it com domesday.
fare þou seþþen whare þou may,

148. Laing *Let*.

---

145. M. (143) *ȝates her I felle / And siþþen wil ich herwe helle*.
147 (B. 143, M. 145). B.M. substitute three lines for this one, which are pure makeshifts of their own: *Satanas, her y þe bynde / Ne shalt þou neuer henne winde / þou shalt* (M. *Her shalt þou*) *buen* (M. *ben*) *in bondes ay* (M. *ai*) /.
148. M. *Til þat*.

DIGBY.

Fare so þou euere fare,
Ne salt þou neuere do mon kare."

"Uelcome, louerd god in londe,
Godes sone and godes sonde;
Welcome, louerd, wel þou be,
fful longe haueþ ous þout aft*er* þe;
fful welcomen art þou ous,
þou bring ous out of þis loþe hous.

Welcome, louerd, ich am adam
þat þou makedest of erþe mon;
Ihe*s*u crist, bide I þe
þat mine sunnen forȝef þou me."

"Welcome, louerd, ich am eve,
Adam and I þat weren so leve,
þou ȝeue ous leue to loken parais,
And we hit lokeden al amis;
We þi comaundement forleten
þo we of þen appel eten;
So longe hauen we ben herinne,

149. *h* before *ous* has been erased.
155. *louerd*: *d* above line.

HARLEY.

Adam.
Welcome, louerd god of londe,
godes sone ant godes sonde;
welcome, louerd, mote þou be,
þat þou wolt vs come & se,
Louerd, nou þou art come to ous,
bring ous of þis loþe hous;
bryng vs of þis loþe lond,
louerd, henne into þyn hond;
lou*er*d, wost þou whet ych am?
þou me shuptest of eorþe Adam;
for y þyn heste hueld noht,
duere ich habbe hit her aboht;

haue m*er*ci of vs, godes sone,
let ous no more her wone;
alle þat herynne be
ȝore haueþ ȝyrned after þe;
we hopeþ wel þourh þy comyng
of oure sunnes hauen froryng.

Eua.
Knou me, lou*er*d, ich am eue,
Ich ant Adam þe were so leoue;
þou laddest ous to parays, [leaf 56 bk.]
we hit forgulten ase vnwys;
we þin heste dude forleten,
þo we þen appel eten;
So longe we haueþ buen herynne,

AUCHINLECK.

fare þou seþþen ware þou fare,
no dostow neuer man care.

adam dixit.

Welcom, lord god of lond,
godes sone & godes sond,
welcom, lord, mot þou be,
long haues ous þouȝt after þe;
lord, seþþen þou art comen to ous,
þou bring ous out of þis hous;
lord, þou wost what ich am
þou me schope of erþe man,
& þou me madest formast man,
& þou me clepetest sone, adam;
& ȝif ich haue sinnes wrouȝt,
ful dere now here ichaue hem bouȝt;
whoso sinneþ ani wiȝt,
þe sinne is more þan þe pliȝt.
ȝa, leue lord, godes sone,
welcom be þou & worþ come;
al, lord, þat here be
haue ȝerned, lord, after þe;
we hope wele of þi coming
of our sinnes haue botening.

eua ait.

Knawe me, lord, ich am eue,
adam & ich ware þe so leue,
þou ȝaue ous to ȝeme paradis,
& we it ȝemed as vnwise
when we þi comandment forlete,
when we of þat appel ete;
so long haue we ben herinne,

149–150. M. often inconsistent in using *a* for *o*, here *londe—sonde.*
152. M. introduces a line patched together from other MSS.: *Longe haueþ ous þoht after þe.* 153. M. *comen*; H. *us.*
155–156. B.M. omit both these lines from the text.
157. M. *what.* 158. M. *shope of erþe.*
159. M. *held.* 160. M. *Dere . . haue it.*
161. M. *ous.*

160. *haues*: Varn. (176) *haves.*
165. A 2nd *me* marked for erasure in MS. Laing omits this line.

164. C. *Zore . . yyrned*; M. *hauen ȝerned.*
165. M. *hopen.* 166. M. *sinnes.*
168. M. *leue.*
169–170. M. *þou ȝaue ous to ȝeme parais / We it ȝemeden asse unwis!* 171. M. *dide.*
172. B.M. *of þen.* 173. M. *haue we ben.*

DIGBY.

þa fewe nou beþ oure sunne;
Leue louerd, ȝef ous leue,
Adam and I þat weren so leue,
To faren hof þis loþe lis
Into þe blisse of parais."

"Adam, adam, ich ȝaf mi lif
ffor þe and for eve, þi wif;
Wendest þou I were ded for nowt?
ffor mi deþ was monkun bout;
Adam, nou i sege hit þe,
To-day þou salt alesed be
And comen to paraises blisse,
þerof ne salt þou neuere misse."

"Louerd crist, ich hit am
þat þou clepedest abraam;
þou bihete þat of mire more
Sulde a god chil ben Ibore
þat sulde bringen of helle pine
Alle þat þou clepedest for þine;
þou art þat child, þou art þat mon
þat boren was of abraom!"

"Wel ich wot þat þou art abraam,
Of mine cunne þat þou cam,
More þe berewеþ þi riȝtwisnese
þene þe doþ þi sibnesse;
Abraam, I wot ful wel
þat hit is soþ, eueruch del,
þat mi suete moder was
Bigeten of þy suete fles;

162. M. (note, p. 32), Varn. *non.*
170. *s* in *was* above line.

HARLEY.	AUCHINLECK.
deore haue we aboht vr synne ;	þat wele haue we bet our sinne ;
Louerd god, ʒef vs leue,	leue lord, ʒiue ous leue,
Adam ant me, ys wyf eue,	adam & his wiif eue,
to faren of þis loþe wyke	to fare out of þis foule wike
to þe blisse of heueneryke.	Into þe blis of heuenrike.
Domi*nus*.	**dominus ait.**
Adam, ich haue ʒeue mi lyf	Adam, y haue ʒouen mi liif
for þe & for eue þi wyf ;	for þe & for eue þi wiif ;
wendest þou ich were ded for noht?	wenestow ichadde ben ded for nouʒt?
ffor my deþ wes monkune yboht.	for mi ded is mankin bouʒt. [leaf 37]
Habraha*m*.	**abraham ait.**
Lou*e*rd c*r*ist, ich am	Lord crist, ich it am
þat þou calledest habraham ;	þat þou cleptest abraham ;
þou me seidest þ*at* of me	
shulde such a child ybore be	
þat vs shulde brynge of pyne,	þou schust com to helle pine
Me ant wyþ me alle myne ;	forto haue ous, lord, for þin[e] ;
þou art þe child, þou art þe man	
þ*at* wes ybore of habraham ;	
do nou þat þou byhihstes me,	do astow bihet me,
bring me to heuene vp wiþ þe.	bring me lord to heuen wiþ[þe].
Domi*nus*.	**dominus dixit.**
Habraham, ych wot ful wel	Abraham, it was wel
wet þou seidest, eueruch del,	þat þou seydest, eueri del,
þ*at* mi leue moder wes	for mi swete moder wes
boren & shaped of þi fleyhs.	born & schapen of þi fles.

174. M. *Dere haue we bet oure sinne.*
175. C. *gef* ; M. *ʒif ous.* 176. M. *his.*
179. C. *geue* ; M. *ʒouen.*
182. C. *monkinne* ; M. *mankin boht.*
183. M. *ich it.* 184. M. *Abraham* ; last *a* in *habraham* above line.
186. M. *Shulde a god child boren be* ; H. *suche.*

187. Laing *foul.* 195. Laing *schult.*
196. Letters and words in brackets supplied by Laing ; a strip torn from leaf in MS.

190. M. *boren . . Abraham* ; last *a* in *habraham* above line. 191. M. *bihete.*
194. (B. 190). B. whet, M. *what . . . euerich.*
195. M. *suete* ; Varn. *leve* 196. M. *fles.*

DIGBY.

Abraam, I suge hit þe,
To-day þou sal alesed be
And comen to paradises blisse,
þerof ne salt þou neuere misse;
Bringen ich will out of pine
Abraam þe and alle þine."

"Louerd, ich am daui, þe king,
þat boren was of þin ofspring;
Do also þo me bihete [leaf 120, bk.]
þoru þe wordes of þe pr*o*phete;
Ih*es*u cr*i*st, godes sone,
Hou þou art hider Icome,
Let ous out of helle pine,
Alle þat þou holdest for þine."

"Daui, þou art bor*en* of mi kun,
ffor þi godnese art þou min,
More for þi godnesse
þen for þine sibnesse.
Daui, I suge hit þe,
To-day þou salt alesed be
And comen to p*ar*adises blisse,
þerof ne salt þou neuere misse."

"Louerd cr*i*st, ich am iohan
þat þe heuede of þe flim iordan;
Twelue winter hit is agon
þat ich þolede martirdom;
þou hete me to helle ware
And þat I sulde sugen þare
þat art þou cr*i*st, godes sone,
þat solde sone þider come
fforto lesen of helle pine,
Louerd, þat keneden for þine;

202. *Hou*: *H* scribal error for *N*; Varn. *Nou*.

HARLEY.

[1] Dauid
Louer*d*, ich am dauid þe kyng,
þat bore was of þyn ofsp*r*ing;
do me ase þou bihete
þourh þe lawe of þe p*ro*phete;
nou þou art come to ous,
bring vs from þis dredful hous.

Do*minus*
Dauid, þou were bore of my kyn,
for þi godnesse art þou myn,
More for þi godnesse
þen for eny sibnesse.

Ioh*annes*
Louerd c*ri*st, ich am Iohan
þat þe folewede in flum iordan;
Tuelf moneþ is agon, [col. 2]
þ*a*t y þolede martirdom;
þou sendest me þe ryhte wey
into helle forte sey
þat þou, c*ri*st, godes sone,
Sone shuldest to helle come
forto lesen of helle pyne
alle þat þou holdest þyne;

[1] *Dauid*: entered by later hand.
198. M. *boren wes.* 199. H. *as*; M. *also.*
201. M. *comen.* 203. M. *boren.*
206. M. *þan—ani.* 209. M. *Tuclue.*
212. M. *for soþe to sei.*

AUCHINLECK.

dauid dixit.
[1] **H**ord, ich am dauid þe king,
þat was born of þine of-s[pring]
also astow me bihet
þurch þe lore of þat p*r*ophete,
þou bring ous of þis foule [hous]
to þe blis of heuen ycore[n ous].

dominus ait.
Dauid, þou was born of mi [kin]
for þi godenes þou art m[in],
more for þi godenesse
þan for ani sibbenesse.

Ioh*anne*s dixit.
[1] **H**ord crist, ich am Iohan
þat þe hof in þe flom Iordan;
now a gode while is agon,
þat y suffred martirdom;
þou sentest me þe riȝt way
Into helle, for soþ to say,

þat þou schust deliuer of hell[e pine]
þat þou þerin fond, lord, of þi[ne];

[1] This initial is not an L as it should be.
207–208. *hous—ous* supplied from Varn.
219. Laing, *schult.*

214. B. (210), M. (212) *þider* for *to helle.*
215. C. *forte.*

DIGBY.

þou art comen, nou þou do
þat þu seidest me to."

"Iohan, iohan, ich hit wot
þat I seide þe þat,
þat þou salt comen me to,
þat I seide þe do."

"Louerd, ich am moises, þe p*r*ophete,
Ich dude þe lawen, þat þou hete,
Ich dude þe lawen þat þou astolde
Wor to ben oþin on wolde;
þou teitest me þene riȝte wey
Opone þe mounte of sinay,
þat me sulde comen to bote,
þe sune þat adam þoute suete."

"þou dedest wel wiþhouten delay
þe comaundement of þe lay;
þou mi comau*n*deme*n*t wel helde wiþ þe,
ffor þou nou salt in blisse be;
Hy þat habbeþ me serued treuliche
Comeþ wiþ me to heuene riche,
Hy sulen alle to heuene blysse,
þe curssede gostes sulen misse;
Hy þat nolde nout on me bileue,
Hy sulen in helle wiþ satanas bileue;
Long is O and long is ay
Tille þat comeþ domesday;
þou, satanas, and alle þine,
Wenden ȝe sulen to helle pine."

231. MS. possibly *astvlde.*
232. *oþin*; Varn. *opin.*
241. Varn. *treulich.*

HARLEY.

nou þou art come, nou þou do
þ*at* þou seidest fer ant þo.

Dom*inus*

Iohan, iohan, ich wot ful wel
whet þou seidest, eueruch del;
þou shalt seo whet y shal do
þat y seyde er þe to.

Moyses

Loue*r*d, þou knowest al wyþ skyl
þe lawe of Synay vpon þe hyl;
Ich am moyses, þe p*ro*phete
þat hueld þe lawes þ*at* þou byhete,
þat þou ih*esu*, godes sone,
woldest to þe helle come,
ant þ*at* þou woldest come to bete
þe sunnes þ*at* Ada*m* þohte suete.

Domi*nus*

Moyses, þ*at* ich hihte þe
In þe olde lawe þou dudest me;
& alle þe oþer þ*at* mine buen
shule to blisse wiþ me tuen;

þey þ*at* nolden on me leuen
shule wiþ Sathanas bileuen;
þer hue shulen wonen ay
o þ*at* come domesday.

AUCHINLECK.

now artow comen forto do
þat þou saidest me vnto.

dominus ait.

Iohan, Iohan, ich it wat
þat y sent þe þe gat;
þou schalt se þat y schal do
þat þou seydest me vnto.

moyses dixit.

Lord þou ȝaue me al wiþ skil
þe lay sinay on þe hil.

217. M. *comen.*
218. B. (219) *er ant þo*; M. (216) *me unto.*
219–220. B. (215–216), M. (217–218) substitute the two lines from *E.*, slightly changed; *Iohan, Iohan, ich it wat / þat I sende þe þe gat /*; C. *John.*
221. (B, 217, M. 219). M. *se*, B.M. *þat*, C. *what.*
223 (B. 219, M. 221). B. *ȝeue* (*M. ȝaue*) *me* (for *knowest*).
226. (B. 222, M. 224). B.M. *Ich*; M. *held;* B.M. *hete.*

227–228. B.M. omit these lines from the text.
229. (B. 223, M. 225). B.M. *þat men shulde come, etc.*
230. (B. 224, M. 226). B. *Sunne*, M. *sinne.*
232. M. *didest.* 233. M. *ben.*
234. M. *Shulen . . ten.*
236. M. *Shulen.*
237. C. *There*; M. *he.*
238. M. *Til þat.*

DIGBY.

Heueriche is redy to mon,
Gou we þider, gou we anon;
Louerd, ȝef ous þat ilke blisse
þat þou wonest ine iwisse,
þat we moten comen þe to
And hauen wiþ þe reste and ro. amen.

254. Varn. *inne.*
256. Varn. *a* for *amen.*

The Gospel of Nicodemus.

Galba MS. TEXT G.

Hic incipit eu*a*ngeliu*m* Nichodemi.

(1)

BItid þe time Tiberius [leaf 57 bk.]
rewled Rome wit*h* realte,
þat same tyme Theodosius
was p*ro*ued prince in Galile,
þis stori wrate Nichodemus
in ebreu for ful grete dainte;
seþin þe emp*er*oure Theodosius
gert it þus translated be
þat men may vnderstand,
both lered and lawed in ledes;
a clerk of ingland
in his remail þus redes:

Harley MS. TEXT H.

Hic incipit eu*a*ngeliu*m* Nichodemi.

(1)

Bytyd þe tyme Tyberius [leaf 206]
Rewled rome wit*h* realte,
þe same tyme theodosius
was proued prynce in galile,
þis story wrote Nichodemus
In ebrew for full gret daynte;
Sythen þe Emp*er*oure Theodosius
Gert it þus t*ra*nslate be
þat men may understand,
Both lered & lawed in ledes;
A clerk of yngland
In his remaile þ*us* redes:

HARLEY.

god, for is moder loue,
let vs neuer þider come !
louerd, for þi muchele *grace*,
*gra*unte vs in heouene one place ;
let vs neu*er* be forloren
for no sunne, *cri*st ycoren ;
ah bring vs out of helle pyne,
louerd, ous & alle þyne,
ant ȝef vs *grace* to libbe & ende
In þi seruice ant to heuene wende.
ame*n*.

239. M. *his* ; C. *lone*. 241. M. *michele*. 242. M. *heuene*. 244. M. *sinne*. 247. C. *gef* ; M. *ȝif . . . liue*.

It should be said in conclusion, that in those lines and passages where Mall (generally followed by Boeddeker) makes alterations of and interpolations into the text as given in the Harleian MS., he generally gives the correct readings in his footnotes.

The Gospel of Nicodemus.

Sion MS. TEXT S.

Of þe passioun of Crist, als wittenes Nichodeme.

(1)

BItid*e* þe tyme þat Tiberius [leaf 13]
Reweled rome with realte,
þe same tyme theodosius
was halden prynce in Galile,
þis stori wrate Nechodem*us*
In Ebru for grette daynte ;
Sythen þe empe*r*oure theodosius
gert itte al translated bee ;
and sithen fra hand*e* to hand*e*,
ffor þere vnletterd*e* ledes
A clerk of Inglande
In his rymaly þus redes :

9. *and* : as no instance of *ande* occurs in the MS., it may be considered very doubtful whether the scribe intended the flourish at the end of the *d* to be an abbreviation for *e* ; Horst's *e* is accordingly always omitted.

Additional MS. TEXT A.

(1)

[1]It betide þat tyme þat tybe*r*yus
Ruled all Rome *with* ryalte,
And also theodosius [1] [leaf 116, bk
Was p*r*ince in þe lande of galilee,
þis story wrot nycodem*us*
In ebrewe for gret daynte ;
Sithen þe Empe*r*oure teodocius
Gart it t*ra*nslated be ;
And sithen fro land to lande,
For þes vnlettred ledes,
To make þai*me* vndrestande,
In Englische þus he redis :

GALBA.

(2)

Simon, Zayrus and Caiphas,
datan and Gamaliell,
Neptalim, Leui and Iudas,
With þaire accusinges fals and fell,
Alexander and als annas,
Ogaines Ih*esu* þai speke and spell;
bifore sir pilate gan þai pas,
þaire tales vntill him gan þai tell:
"þis mopp þat merres oure men,
kalles him god sun of heuyn,
his sire, his dam we ken,
bi name we kan þam neuyn;

(3)

We wate wele Ioseph was a wright,
suthly he was his sire,
and mari vs menes his moder hight,
we, whatkin goddes er þise?
he es þaire sun, þis weried wight,
þat egges vs all till ire;
oure lawes to breke both day & night,
þat es his moste desire."
Sir pilate answerd þan:
"sais me whilk er his sawes,
on what maner þis man
aleges ogaines oure lawes."

(4)

"Oure law vs leres," þan said a Iew,
"þe sabot to do no thing;
þan wirkes he wonder werkes new,
heles al þat askes heleing,
þe croked cripilles þat we knew,
þis es a wonder thing;

HARLEY.

(2)

Symon, Zayrus & Cayphas,
Datan & Gamaliel,
Neptalim, Leui a*n*d Iudas,
w*ith* þair accusynges fals & fell,
Alexander and als Annas,
Ogayns Ih*esu* þai speke & spell;
Bifor sir Pilate gan þai pass,
þair tales vntyll him gan þai tell:
"þis mopp þ*at* merres our men,
Calles him god son of heuen,
His syre, his dam we ken,
Be name we kan þam neuen;

(3)

We wate wele Ioseph was a wryght,
Sothly he was his syre,
And mary vs menes his mod*er* hight,
we, whatkyn godes er þire?
He es þair son, þis weryed wight,
þat egges vs all tyll ire;
Our lawes to brek both day & nyght,
þ*at* es his most desyre."
Sir Pilate answerd þan:
"Says me whilk er his sawes,
On what man*er*e þis man
Alegges ogayne our lawes."

(4)

"Our law vs leres," þan said a Iew,
"þe sabot day to do no thing;
þan wirkes he wond*er* werkes new,
Heles all þ*at* askes heleyng,
þe croked crypels þat we knew,
þis es a wonder thing;

20. *trew* marked for erasure between *vn* and *tyll*.

SION.

(2)

Symeon, zairus and cayphas,
  Datan and Gamaliele,
Neptalym, leuy, Iudas,
  with þaire accusynges felle,
Alexander and annas,
  Ogayne Ih*es*u gun spelle ;
Byfore sire Pylate gun þai pas,
  þaire tales þus forto telle :
" þis moppe þat merres þe men,
  Calles hym Goddes sonne of heuen,
Hijs sire, hijs dame we wele ken,
  By name we kan þayme neuen ;

(3)

Welle wate we Ioseph was a wright*e*,
  Sothely he was hijs sire,
Hijs modir vs menes mary hight*e*,
  We, whakyns goddes er þere ?
Mare sary er we for a sight*e*
  þat egges vs alle tille Ire ;
Oure lawes he brekes at alle hys mÿghte,
  þat egges vs alle tille Ire." [leaf 13 bk]
Pilate says til þam þan :
  " Say me what er his saghe,
On what manere þat man
  Alleges ogayne yhoure lawes."

(4)

" Oure lawes vs Iuges," quod*e* a Iowe,
  " þe sabbott*e*day to do na thyng*e* ;
þan wirkes he wonder werkes Inoghe,
  Heles alle þat askes helynge
Of criples and cruked þat we knowe,
  It es to here a grette wonderynge ;

27. *vs*: above *we*, which is marked for erasure ; *menes* : *s* above line.
38. Horst. *sabbot-day*.
42. MS. *to he here*.

ADDITIONAL.

(2)

Symeon, Cesar & Kayfas,
  Dathan & gamaliell,
Neptalem, Leui and Iudas,
  þat were halden fals & felle,
Alexandir*e* and Annas,
  Agayne ih*es*u gan þai spelle ;
Befor sir pilat gan þai passe
  And on þis wyse þai gan hym telle :
" Ih*es*u þat marres alle oure mene,
  Calles hym gods sone of heuene,
His syre, his dame ryght wele we kene,
  þair*e* ryght names wele gan we neuene ;

(3)

We wot wele Iosep was a wryght,
  And for sothe he was his sire,
And Mary was his modir*e* ryght,
  And what maner*e* of goddes ar*e* þere ?
We are full sory of his syght,
  ffor it egges vs ay till ire ;
Oure lawes he brekys *with* all his myght
  And þat is his most desyre."
Pilat sayde to þai*me* þan :
  " Say me what ar*e* ȝowr*e* sawes,
In what wyse at þ*at* man
  Allegges agayne ȝour*e* lawes."

(4)

[1] " Vs oghe noȝt be our*e* lawe," q*uod* a Iuwe, [[1] leaf 117]
  " On our*e* sabot to do no thynge ;
þen wyrkes he warkes wondr*e* newe,
  Helys alle þat aske helynge,
Bothe blynde & lame þ*at* we wele knewe,
  And þat vs thynk a wondr*e* thynge;

38. *to* : above line in MS.

GALBA.

he makes þam hale of hide & hew
 thurgh his fals charmeing."
to pilat said þai all:
 "for soth slike er his dedes,
slike fare he fares withall,
 with fendes craft he him fedes."

(5)

Þan said pilat: "ȝe have no right
 to blame him by no way;
his miracles musters his might,
 it es noght als ȝe say;
sen he to blind has gifen þe sight
 and raised þat beried lay,
whi suld he vnto ded be dight
 þat mendes all þat he may?"
þan all þe iewes cride:
 "sir pelate, we þe pray,
bring him to bar þis tide
 þat makes vs all þis dray."

(6)

A bedell to bring him gan he bid,
 Romayne he hight, we rede,
and he þat was for curtais kid
 did it sone in dede;
a wonden wrethe þat his heuid hid
 spred he all furth on brede:
"lord, þe to call domesman me did,
 bot walk in on þis wede."
þe iewes all of þat gate
 wex all ful gul and grene
and said to sir pilate:
 "a deuil, what may þis mene?

(7)

Þe bedel suld to þe be trew [leaf 58]
 and do þi comandment;

HARLEY.

He makes þam hale of hyde & hew
 Thurgh his fals charmyng."
To Pilate said þai all:
 "for soth slyke er his dedes,
Slyke fare he fars w*ith*all,
 W*ith* fendes craft he him fedes."

(5)

Þan said Pilate: "yhe haue no ryght
 To blame him bi no way;
His miracles muste*r*s his myght,
 It es noght als yhe say;
Sen he to blynd has gyfen þe syght
 And raysed þ*at* byried lay,
whi suld he vnto ded be dyght
 þat mendes all þat he may?"
þan all þe Iewes cryde:
 "Sir Pilate, we þe pray,
Bryng him to barr þis tyde
 þat makes vs all þis dray."

(6)

A bedell to bryng him gan he byd,
 Romayne he hight, we rede,
And he þat was for curtays kyd
 Dyd it sone in dede;
A wonden wrethe þ*at* his heued hyd
 Spred he all furth on brede:
"Lord, þe to call domesman me dyd,
 Bot walk in on þis wede."
þe Iewes all of þ*at* gate
 wex all full gull & grene
And said to sir Pilate:
 "A deuell, what may þis mene?

(7)

Þe bedell suld to þe be trew
 And do þi comandment;

SION.

Wilde and wode to his bydynge gun [bowe,
And alle thurgh his fals charmynge."
  Pilate sayde tille þayme alle:
"how may yhe blame his dedes?"
  "With crafte he wirkes withalle,
With fendes crafte he hym fedes."

(5)

þan sayd pilate: "yhe haue na righte
  To blame hym by nanekyn way,
His miracles mustres his myghte,
  It es noght als ye say;
Sythen he þus þe blynde has sent þe [sight
  And raysed þat byriede lay,
Wa suld deme hym to deede be dighte
  þat mendes men als he may?"
"Sire pilate, we þe praye,"
  Quod alle þere Iewes þan,
"Brynge hym till barre þis day
  To coupe hym þare if we kan."

(6)

A bedel he bad buske hym to bidde,
  Romayne he highte, we rede,
And he, als curtayse þat was kidde,
  þat erand did in dede;
Of wonden wrethes his heued vnhid,
  In space he gun it sprede: [leaf 11.]
"Louerd, þe to kalle þe domesman me [didde,
  Botte walk yn on þis wede."
þire Iewes þare þai satte
  ffor gram wex gulle and grene
And sayde to sire Pilate:
  "Ey dieux, what may þis mene?

(7)

Bedels suld tille þi bidynge bowe
  And cry þi comandment;

51. MS. *my myght.* 56. *kan* between *he may* marked for erasure.
62. *we*: before *he* marked for erasure.

ADDITIONAL.

Wylde & wode till his biddynge bowe
  All thurgh his fals charmyngo."
Pilat sayde to þaime alle:
  "Howe may ȝhe blame his dedys?"
þai answerd gret & smalle:
  "With wychecrafte he þaime ledes."

(5)

"Nay," sayde Pilat, "ȝhe haue no [ryght
  To blame hym be no manere of way;
þos myracles he dos by myght,
  It is no thynge als ȝhe say;
Sen he to þe blynd has sent his sight
  And puttyd to lyfe þat ded lay,
Who suld hym deme to ded be dyght
  þat dos þe gud all þat he may?"
"Sire Pilat, we þe pray,"
  Sayd alle þe Iuwes þan,
"Brynge hym to barre þis day,
  Accuse hym gif we kan."

(6)

A Messagere he gart go bidde
  Ihesu come vnto þat place;
Romayne he hyght þat wele was kydde,
  And after ihesu forthe he gace
Withoutyn malice, with heued vn- [hidde,
  his speche he gan to sprede:
"Lorde, þe to calle pilat me didde,
  I durst not ellis for drede."
þe Iuwes þere þai satte
  ffor angre wex all grene
And sayd to sir pilat:
  "O, what may þis mene?

(7)

[1] Bedels sulde to þi biddynge bowe
  And smertly do þi commandment;
[[1] lf. 117 bk.]

64. *gace*: *s* written above *c* in later hand.

GALBA.

on knese here knelid he to ih*esu*
right in þine auwen present;
vs noyes gretly þir notes new,
we toke þarto gude tent,
slike curtaisy vnto him he knew,
right on his wreth he went."
þai asked him whi he kid
ih*esu* slike curtaysy;
and he said: "þat I did
I had encheson whi;

(8)

Til Alisander, wele ȝe wate,
in message was I made,
to Ierusalem I come so late
þat till þe morn I bade;
þis ih*esus* on ane Ass þare sate
and thurgh þe toun he rade;
childer byfore him in þe gate
spred þaire clothes obrade,
to him all gan þai bow;
'Osanna,' was þaire sang,
'blisced be he þat cumes now
in goddes name vs omang.'"

(9)

þan said þe iews: "traytur vntrew,
with lies þou has vs led,
þaire carping þare no thing þou knew,
we lay oure heuiddes in wed;
iherusalem langage es ebrew,
ful fer þeþin was þou fed."
he said: "I spirde at me*n* inowe
þat in þat burgh war bred."
"Osanna," quod pilate,
"what es þat forto say?"
þai said: "it menes algate,
'Lord, saue vs, we þe pray.'"

HARLEY.

On knese here kneled he to Ih*esu*
Right in þine awen p*re*sent;
vs noyes gretely þir notes new,
we toke þarto gud tent,
Slyke curtasy vnto him he knew,
Ryght on his wreth he went."
þai asked him whi he kyd
Ih*esu* slyke curtasy;
And he said: "þ*at* I did
I had encheson why;

(8)

Tyll alexander, wele yhe wate,
In message was I made,
To Ierusalem I come so late
þ*at* tyll þe morn I bade;
þis Ih*esus* on ane Ass þare sate
And thurgh þe toune he rade;
Childer bifor him in þe gate
Spred þair clothes on brade,
Tyll him all gan þai bow;
'Osanna,' was þair sang,
'Blyssed be he þ*at* comes now [lf. 206, bk.]
In godes name vs omang.'"

(9)

þan said þe Iewes: "t*ra*ytour vntrew,
w*ith* lyes þou has vs led,
þare carpyng þare no thing þou knew,
we lay our heuedes in wed;
Ierusalem langage es hebrew,
ffull fer þethen was þou fed."
He said: "I spyrd at men Inoghe
þ*at* in þat burgh war bred."
"Osanna," q*ua*d Pilate,
"what es þat forto say?"
þai said: "it menes allgate
'Lord, saue vs, we þe pray.'"

SION.

On knese he knelede to Ihe*s*u
Righte in þine awen present;
Nedelynges us noyes þire notes newe,
We toke þareto fulle gude tente,
Swilk*e* curtasy neuer yit we knewe,
Vppon his wrethe he wente."
Pilate asked why he kidde
Ihe*s*u swilk*e* curtasy;
And he sayd: "þat þat I didde
I had*e* enchesoun why;

(8)

Tille Alexander, wele ye wate,
Messagere was I made,
Bott*e* to Ieru*sa*lem come I late,
vnto þe morn I habade;
þisse Ihe*s*u on ane asse satte
And thurgh þe toun he rade;
Childer byfor his fete algate
Spredde þaire clathes on brade,
Swilke wirchippe þare had he;
'Osanna,' was þaire sauge,
'þat comes blissed mot he be
In goddes name vs omang.'"

(9)

þire Iewes sayde þan: "traytoure vn-[trwe,
[1]With leghes þou haues vs ledde,
þayr carpyng þare nathyng þou knewe,
We welle lay our lyfe to wedde;
Ieru*sa*lem langage es Ebru,
ffulle ferre þethen was þou fedde."
He sayde: "I spird at men Inowe
þat in þat burgh was bredde."
"Osanna," quod Pilate, [1 leaf 14, bk.]
"What es it forto say?"
Quod þe Iewes: "it menes þusgate,
'Lord, saue vs, we þe pray.'"

97. First *e* in *Iewes* above line; Horst. *þir*.
102. *fendde* with *n* marked for erasure.

ADDITIONAL.

And he nowe knelis to ihe*s*u
Whiles þou þiselue es in p*re*sent;
Bot eue*r*e vs newes noyes newe,
We toke þe*r*eto full gud entent,
Siche curtaysye neue*r*e ere we knewe,
W*it*h reue*r*ence he to ihe*s*u went."
Pilat sayde: "whi did þou soo
Vnto ihe*s*u siche curtaysy?"
Romayne sayde: "þat I haue doo
I hade gud enchesone*s* whi;

(8)

To alexandre, wele ȝhe wate,
A messager*e* þen was I made,
Vnto Ieru*sa*lem come I late
And to þe morne þe*r*ein I bade;
And thurghe þe toune als ihe*s*u rode,
ffolke before his fete all þe gate
Riche clothes spradde on brode,
Siche reue*r*ence þe*r*e he hade,
Siche reue*r*ence þe*r*e hade he;
'Osanna,' was þair*e* songe,
'þat nowe comes blessed mot be
In gods name vs amonge.'"

(9)

þe Iuwes sayde: "Trayto*ur* vntrewe,
W*it*h lesynges here has þo*u* vs ledde,
þaire langage neue*r*e ȝit þou knewe,
þat durst we lay oure life in wedde;
Ie*rusa*lem langage is Ebrewe,
And þou full farre þethen was fedde."
He sayde: "I spyrde at men ynewe
þat in þis same Cyte was bredde."
"Osanna," quod pilatt,
"What is þat forto say?"
"We construe it þusgate:
'Lorde, saue vs, we þe p*r*ay.'"

GALBA.

(10)

þan said pilate: "me think in thoght
þe bedell wrang ȝe blame;
ȝowre childer sawes forsake ȝe noght,
ȝowreseluen sais þe same;
bot, bedell, to bar sen þou him broght
to schilde þiself fro schame,
haue him furth þat þou wirschip wroght
and call him in by name."
Out of þat rout romayne
oure lord Ihe*s*u he ledes,
and calles him in ogayn,
als he þat domesman dredes.

(11)

Of Empe*r*oures þat are had bene
þis was used in þat land,
for folk suld on þair menskes mene,
men suld hald in þaire hand
þaire armes set on schaftes schene,
graythed of gold gleterand;
so did þai þare þat day bidene,
and stabilly gan þai stand;
when he þat all sall welde
was led into þe hall,
þe heuides haly gan helde
and did him honors all.

(12)

þan þe iews ful sterne and stout
said: "þis es hard hething,
þir lurdans lattes þaire schaftes lout
and wroght him wirschiping."

HARLEY.

(10)

þan said Pilate: "me think in thoght
þe bedell wrang yhe blame;
yho*ur* childer sawes forsake yhe noght,
yh*our*seluen says þe same;
Bot, bedell, to barr sen þou him broght
To scheld þiself fro schame,
Haue him furth *þat* þou wirschip wroght
& call him in by name."
Out of *þat* rout Romayne
Our lord Ihe*s*u he ledes,
And calles him in ogayne,
Als he *þat* domesman dredes.

(11)

Of Empe*r*ours *þat* are had bene
þis was vsed in þat land,
ffor folk suld on þair menskes mene,
Men suld hald in þair hand
þair armes sett on schaftes sene,
G*ra*ythed of gold gleterand;
So did þai þare *þat* day bidene,
And stabilly gan þai stand;
when he þat all sall weld
was led into þe hall,
þe heuedes halely gan held
A*n*d did him honoure all.

(12)

þan þe Iewes full sterne & stout
Said: "þis es hard hethyng,
þir lurdans lattes þair schaftes lout
And wroght him wirschipyng."

SION.

(10)

“Me thynk,” quod pilat, “in my thoght,
With wrange þe bedel yhe blame;
Yhour childer saghes forsak yhe noght,
Yhourseluen says þe same;
Bot, bedel, tille barre sithen þou hy*m* broght
At scheld þiself fra schame,
Led hym forthe þat þou worschepe wroght,
Calle hym eft in by name.”
Oute of þat route Romayne
Our lorde Ihe*s*u he ledes,
And calles hym ogayne,
Als he þat domesman dredes.

(11)

Of empe*r*ours þat þar had bene
þis was þe lawe in lande,
ffor men suld of þair menskes mene,
Men suld hald itte in þair hande
Men heuedes sette on schaftes schene,
Graythed of golde gliterande;
[1] Saunz doute swa did*e* þai alle bydene,
Stille stably gun þai stande;
When he þat alle salle welde [[1] leaf 15]
Was had intil þat halle,
þhe heuedes haaly gun helde
At wirchipe hym withalle.

(12)

þan saide þere Iewes steren and stoute:
“þis hald we hard hethynge,
þire Iewes lete þaire schaftes loute
At wirk hym worschipyng.”

130. *halden* has been marked for erasure before *had*.
135. *lele* marked for erasure before *lete*.

ADDITIONAL.

(10)

“Me thynke,” q*uo*d pilat, “in my thoght,
þat ȝhe *with* wrange þe bedel blame;
Sen he sawe þ*er*e siche wyrschippes wroght,
I wote hym thynke he suld do þe same;
[1] Bot, bedell, to barr*e* sen þ*o*u hym broght [[1] leaf 118]
þiselue forto schilde fro schame,
ffott forthe hym þat þ*o*u wyrschipp wroght,
And loke þ*o*u calle hym in þe name.”
Out of þat route Romayne
Ihe*s*u, our*e* lorde, he ledes,
And calles hym agayne,
als man þat pilat dredes.

(11)

Of Empe*r*ours þ*at* before had bene
þis was eu*er*emore þe lawȝ i*n* landes:
þat foure men at siche a Iugeme*n*t kene
Suld at þe barr*e* halde in þair*e* handes
Mens heuedes sett on stakes schene,
All of fyne golde blasand as brande;
And so þe Iuwes did þen, I wene,
ffour*e* men *with* siche iiij heuedes gan stande;
Bot when he þat all sall welde
Was broght into þe halle,
þos heuedes of gold gan helde
To wyrschippe c*ri*st *with*alle.

(12)

þen sayde þe Iuwes sturne & stoute:
“þis is a skorne till our*e* semynge,
þes boyes lat þair*e* schaftes lowte
To do till ihe*s*u wyrschippynge.”

126. *as*: possibly *cs* in MS.

GALBA.

þan pilat asked þam all obout:
"Whi did ȝe swilk a thing?"
þai said: "we do ȝow out of dout,
it was noght oure witing,
we toke no tent him till,
þe baners gan him bow;
it was ogains oure will,
þat sall ȝe trewly trow."

(13)

Þai said þat it was weterly
ogains·þaire will algate;
þe iews þan ful loud gan cry
and pleinde þam to pilate;
he bad þam tak men more mighty,
strang and stabill of state,
and lat þam hald þe schaftes in hy,
þaire baret to abate.
In þaire iewry aiwhare
on ilk side haue þai soght,
of men þat mighty ware
þe boldest haue þay broght.

(14)

Sir pilat to þase iews þan sware,
suld hald þo schaftes in hand:
"if þai lout vnto ihesu mare,
ȝe sall lose life and land."
þe men þat wight and willy ware
said: "to þi steuin we stand;
whas heuid so heldes brede of ane hare,
hardily hag of his hand."
"haue ihesus out of þe hall,"
said pelat þe bedell vntill,
"and eft in þou him call,
on what wise so þou will."

HARLEY.

þan Pilate asked þam all obout:
"whi did yhe swilk a thing?"
þai sad: "we do yhow out of dout,
It was noght our wyttyng,
we toke no tent him tyll,
þe baners gan him bow;
It was ogayns our will,
þat sall yhe trewly trow."

(13)

Þai said *þat* it was witerly
Ogayns þair will allgate;
þe Iewes þan full loud gan cry
And pleyned þam to Pilate;
He bad þam tak men more myghty,
Strang & stabyll of state,
And lat þam hald þe schaftes in hy,
þair barett to abate.
In þair iewry aywhare
On ilk syde haue þai soght,
Of men *þat* myghty ware
þe boldest haue þai broght.

(14)

Sir Pilate to þase Iewes þan sware,
Suld hold þa schaftes in hand:
"If þai lout vnto Ihesu mare,
yhe sall lose lyfe and land."
þe men *þat* wyght & willy ware
Said: "to þi steuen we stand;
Whase heued so heldes brede of ane hare,
Hardily hag of his hand."
"Haue Ihesus out of þe hall,"
Said Pilate þe bedell vntyll,
"And eft in þou him call,
On what wise so þou will."

139. Horst. *sa(i)d.* 140. Horst. *wytting.*

SION.

And pilate asked þam alle aboute:
" Why did yhe swylk a thyng?"
þai sayde: "we do yhow oute of
It was noght oure wittynge, [doute,
We toke na tent þareto, 141
þe baners gun hym bowe;
What had we forto do
To make reuerence to Ih*esu*?" 144

(13)

" Lowte hym we sawe þam sykerly,"
þe Iewes swore to pilate.
Quod pilate: " þai say oppenly
It was noght swa nanegate; 148
Bot take vs men mare myghty,
Strang and stabil of state,
To hald yhour schaftes tentifly,
þis barete alle to habate." 152
Thurghout alle þe Iewery
Sykyr men haf þai soght
At stere þam strenghefully,
þe best þan haf þai broght. 156

(14)

Syr Pilate tille þa Iewes sware
þat suld halde þa heuedes in hande:
"And louted Ih*esu* any mar, [leaf 15, bk.]
yhe sal loose bathe lyfe and lande."
And þai þat wight and willy ware 161
Sayd: "to þi dome wille we
stande;
What heued helded þe bred of anne
hardly hagge of his hand." [hare,
" Late haue hym out of halle," 165
Quod pilate þe bedel tille,
"and eft in þou hym calle,
On what wyse swa þou wylle." 168

152. *barete* corrected from *basete* (?)
159. Horst. *and* (*þai*).

ADDITIONAL.

And pilat asked þai*m*e alle abowte
Whi þe schaftes made siche stoup-
ynge, 138
þai saide: "we dou ȝowe out of dowte,
þai lowtyd noȝt at our*e* wyttynge,
We toke no hede þ*er*eto,
þat þes baners gan stoupe;
What haue we forto do
vnto ih*esu* to lowte?" 144

(13)

"We sawe þes baners stoupe wyt*er*ly,"
þe Iuwes sware to pilate.
Q*uo*d pilat: "þai say apertely
It was noȝt so nogate; 148
Bot take vs men more myghty,
Stronge & stable of estate,
To halde þes baners sikirly,
þis stryfe þus sall we bate." 152
And þen thurgh all Iury [leaf 118, bk.]
Stronge men haue þai soght
To halde þai*m*e myghtily,
ffour*e* me*n* þ*er*eto þai broght. 156

(14)

þen saide pilat vnto þai*m*e þore
þat þe baners suld halde in hande:
"If þai lowte ih*esu* any more, 159
ȝhe sall þ*er*efore lose life & lande."
And þai þat stronge & myghty wore
Sayde: "To þi dome, sir, will we
stande;
Whas baner*e* bowes for gods hore,
Lat sle hym sone w*ith* hyngman
hande." 164
" Lat haue hym out of þe halle,"
Sayde pilat for þis skille,
" And eftesones in hym calle,
On what wyse so ȝhe wille." 168

GALBA.

(15) [[1] lf. 58, bk.]

[1]His heuid vnhild on knese he knelid,
his clathes on brede he spred,
with all wirschip þat he kouth welde
oure lord eft in he led;
þe heuides on heght halely gan helde
and bowing to him þai bed;
þe men when þai þam failand feld
drowpid and war adred.
when pilat saw in sight
how þe baners gan bow,
for drede he rase vpright
ogans oure lord ihesu.

(16)

Broght was he þus to bar ogain,
þe king of all mankin;
þe fende þan thoght: "if he war slayn,
he suld saue men of sin,
and sawlès þat he had tane with traine
fro him þat tyme suld twin."
forþi he dose his might & mayn
to ger þat bargan blin;
on þe night als ane angell
he appered to pilates wife:
"vnto þi lord þou tell
he lett noght ihesus life."

(17)

Sir pilates wife, dame p*r*ocula,
till hir lord þus gan say:
"deme ȝe noght ih*esus* till ne fra,
bot mensk him þat ȝe may,
I haue bene drechid with dremis swa
þis ilk night als I lay;
if ȝe him deme to ded at ga,
oure welth mu*n* wend oway."

HARLEY.

(15)

His heued vnhyld on knese he kneled,
His clathes on bred he spred,
w*ith* all wirschip þ*at* he couth weld
Our lord eft in he led;
þe heuedes on heght halely gan held
And bowyng to him þai bed;
þe men when þai þam fayland feld
Drowped & war adred.
when Pilate saw in syght
How þe baners gan bow,
ffor dred he rayse vpryght
Ogayns our lord Ih*esu*.

(16)

Broght was he þus to barr ogayne,
þe kyng of all mankyn;
þe fende þan thoght: "if he war slayne,
He suld saue men of syn,
And sawles þ*at* he had tane w*ith* trayne
ffro him þ*at* tyme suld twyne."
fforþi he dose his myght & mayne
To ger þat bargan blyn;
On þe nyght als ane aungell
He appered to Pilates wyfe:
"vnto þi lord þou tell [leaf 207]
He lett noght ih*esus* lyf."

(17)

Sir Pilates wife, dame p*r*ocula,
Till hir lord þus gan say:
"Deme noght ih*esus* tyll ne fra,
Bot mensk him þ*at* yhe may,
I haue bene dreched w*ith* dremes swa
þis ilk nyght als I lay;
If ȝe him deme to ded at ga,
Our welth mon wend oway."

187. *fforþi*: Horst. *þe*.

SION.

(15)

His heued vnhild on knese he kneled,
His clathes byfor hym sprede,[welde
With alle þe worschepe þat he couthe
In eft our lourd he ledde ; [helde,
þair heuedes on heghe haalely gun
Bowyng tille Ih*esu* þai bedde ;
þere Iewes þat þam in handes helde
Ware drowpand and fordredde.
When Pilate sawe þat sighte,
How þa baners gun bowe,
ffor drede he ras vpryght
Ogayne our*e* lorde Ih*esu*.

ADDITIONAL.

(15)

þis messager*e* to ih*esu* knelid [spradde
And clothes before his fete he
Wit*h* alle þe wyrschippes þat he couth welde,
And ih*esu* efte to pilat ladde ;
þes baners sone gan helde
And bowed to ih*esu* vnbedde ;
þe Iuwes þat þai*m*e behelde
ffor þat sight were all dredde.
When pilat sawe þis sight,
howe þos baners gan bowe,
ffor drede he ros vpryght
Agayne our*e* lorde ih*esu*.

SION.

(17)

Sir*e* Pilate wyfe, dam p*ro*cula,
Sent hir*e* lorde forto say :
" Deme nouther Ih*esu* til na fra,
Bot menske hym þat yhe may,
I haue bene dreched with dremes swa
þis ilk nyght als I lay ;
If he thurgh dome tille deede ga,
Our welthe sal wende oway."

ADDITIONAL.

(17)

Sir pilat wife, so mot I go,
Sent to pilat þus to say :
" Deme ih*esu* nouthir*e* to ne fro,
Bot wyrschip hym all þat þou may,
I haue ben dreched wit*h* dremes so
all þis nyght, þe sothe to say ;
If þou hym deme to ded to go,
Our*e* wele I wot sall wast away."

GALBA.

pilat als man amayde
  stode in a grete stody,
seþin to þe iewes he sayd:
  "ȝe wrigh him wrangwisly;

(18)

My wife, ȝe wate wele, es no iew,
  scho es a sarizene;
mynsters has scho made ȝow new
  and done gude dedis bidene;
scho sais Ih*esus* es gude and trew,
  slepand þus has scho sene;
if we him reyne, it mu*n* vs rew
  euermore þaron to mene."
þai said: "þis wist we are,
  ilk man þe suth may se;
he fares with fendes fare,
  witched þi wife has he."

(19)

Sir pilat said: "it meruailes me
  þat þou standes so still,
sen þat þiself þe suth may se
  what þai tell þe vntill."
crist said: "ilk man a mowth has fre
  to welde at his awin will;
þaire wordes ful wide sall witen be
  wheþer þai be gude or ill."
"Ih*esus*, lat be þi dyn!"
  said all þe iews on raw,
"a horcop born in syn
  ilkane wele we þe knaw;

(20)

We wate wele for þi sake was slayne
  all þe barnes in Bedlem born;
to fle with þe þi frendes war fayn,
  and els had þi life bene forlorn;

HARLEY.

Pilate als man amayde
  Stode in a gret stody,
Syth'en to þe Iewes he said:
  "yhe wregh him wrangwisly;

(18)

My wife, yhe wate wele, es no Iew,
  Scho es a sarizene;
Mynsters has scho made yhow new
  And done gud dedes bydene;
Scho sais es gud & trew,
  Slepand þ*us* has scho sene;
If we him reyne, it mon vs rew
  Euermore þaron to mene."
þai said: "þis wist we are,
  Ilk man þe soth may se;
He fars wi*th* fendes fare,
  wyched þi wyf has he."

(19)

Sir Pilate said: "it me*r*uayles me
  þat þou standes so styll,
Sen þ*at* þiself þe soth may se
  what þai tell þe vntyll."
Crist said: "ilk man a mowth has fre
  To weld at his awen will;
þare wordes full wyde sall wyten be
  whether þai be gud or ill."
"Ih*esus*, lat be þi dyn!"
  Said all þe Iewes on raw,
"A horcop born in syn
  Ilkane wele we þe knaw;

(20)

We wate wele for þi sake was slayne
  All þe barnes in bethleem born;
To fle wi*th* þe þi frendes war fayne,
  And els had þi lyfe bene lorn;

SION.

Pilate als man amayed [leaf 16]
Stude in a greete study,
He sayde : "I am noght payde,
Yhe wreghe hym wrangwisly ;

(18)

My wyf, yhe wate wele, es na Iewe,
Scho es a sarzine ;
Many mynsters has scho made yhow
And done in gode dedis bydene ;
þai say Ihesu of trouthe es trewe,
Slepand þus has scho sene ;
If we hym reyne, it sal vs rewe
Euer þareof to mene."
þai sayde : " þis sayde we are,
Yhe may see suthe es þis,
he fares with fendes fare,
he has witched þi wif, Iwyse."

(19)

þan sayd pilate : "me thynk selcouthe
þat þou standes so stille ;
Tille þaire accusyngs aswer þou couthe
[1]
Ihesu sayde : " ilk man has a mouthe
At weld it at his wille ;
þair sawes mon be knawen and couthe
Whethir þai be gode or ille."
" Ihesu, lat be þi dyn ! "
Sayde alle þere Iewes on rawe,
" Ane horcop born in synne
ffulle couthely we þe knawe ;

(20)

We wate wele for þi sake was slayne
Alle þe barnes in betheleem born ;
At fle with þe þi frendes ware fayne,
[2] Elles had þi lyfe bene lorne ;

208. Horst. omits *in*. [[2] lf. 16, bk.]

[1] Horst. says (*Archiv* 68, 209) : *Nach* 218 *fehlt ein Verspaar*, whereas there is only one line missing.

ADDITIONAL.

Pilat was all amayde
And saide to þe Iuwes in hye :
" I am noȝt wele apayde,
ȝhe blame hym wrangwisly ;

(18)

[3] My wife, ȝhe wote, scho is no Iuwe,
ȝhe knawe sho is a sarasyne ; [[3] lf. 119]
Scho biddis þat I no bargayne brewe
To put ihesu to ded, ne pyne ;
Sho says ihesu of treuth is trewe,
Slepand scho sawe þis with hyre yne ;
If we hym deme, it sall vs rewe,
ffor he of fayth is gud & fyne."
þen sayde þe Iuwes belyue :
" þe sothe þou may wele see,
he has bewyched þi wyfe,
It may non outhire be."

(19)

Pilat saide : " me thynk selcouthe,
Ihesu, whi þou standes so stille ;
To þis accusynge answere þou couthe
þat þe Iuwes put þe vntille."
Ihesu saide : " ilke man has mouthe
fforto welde it at his wille ;
þaire sawes to þe are knawen & kouthe
Whethire þat þai speke gud or ille."
" Ihesu, lat be þi dynne !"
Saide alle þe Iuwes on rawe,
" A horcoppe borne in synne
ffor sothe alle we þe knawe ;

(20)

We wot wele for þi sake was slayne
Alle þe childre in bedlem borne ;
To fle with þe þi frendes were fayne,
And ellis þi life had bene forlorne ;

GALBA.

when herod died, es noght at layn,
  þat þi ded hertly had sworn,
till ȝowre cuntre ȝe come ogayn
  þat ȝe war fled fro byforn."
pilat said: "es þis he
  þat herod soght to sla?"
þai said: "sir, ȝa parde,
  bot þus he passed him fra."

(21)

Pilat when he herd how it was,
  he dred mekill þe mare;
he chesed a quest on him to pas
  and by þaire law þai sware,
þai said to pilat and to Cayfas:
  "þe soth we will noght spare,
mary with ioseph wedid was,
  at þaire weding we ware."
pilat said to þam þan
  þat had blamed him biforn:
"with wrang ȝe wrigh þis man,
  in wedlayk was he born."

(22)

Þan stirt vp iews bitter and bald
  and said to sir pilate:
"þe tales þat we haue of him talde
  will we avow algate;
at þir men es ful litell halde,
  sir, þai say als þai wate,
þai er bot barnes, sir, be ȝe balde,
  cumen till oure law now late."
þis quest stedfast als stele
  said to þase oþer twelue:
"we er Iews, wit ȝe wele,
  born frely als ȝowreselue."

HARLEY.

when Herode dyed, es noght at layn,
  þat þi ded hertly had sworn,
Till yh*our* contre yhe come ogayn
  þat yhe war fled fro byforn."
Pilate said: "es þis he
  þ*at* Herode soght to sla?"
[1] þai said: "sir, yha parde,
  Bot þus he passed him fra."

(21)

Pilate when he herd how it was,
  He dred mykell þe mare;
He chesed a quest on him to pas
  And bi þair law þai sware,
þai said to Pilate & to Cayphas:
  "þe soth we will noght spare,
Mary *with* Ioseph wedded was,
  At þair wedyng we ware."
Pilate said to þam þan
  þ*at* had blamed him biforne:
"with wrang yhe wregh þis man,
  In wedlake was he borne."

(22)

Þan styrt vp Iewes bytt*er* & bald
  And said to sir Pilate:
"þe tales þ*at* we haue of him tald
  will we avow allgate;
At þir men es full lytell hald,
  Sir, þai say als þai wate,
þai er bot barnes, sir, be yhe bald,
  Comen tyll our law now late."
þis quest stedfast als stele
  Said to þase other twelue:
"we er Iewes, witt yhe wele,
  Born frely als yh*our*selue."

[1] Þ very large and ornamental.

SION.

Aftir herodes, es noght to layne,
  þat had þi deede sworne,
Tille yhoure contre yhe come agayne
  þat ye fore fra beforne." 236
Sayde Pilate: "es þis he
  þat herode p*ur*sued swa?"
þai sayde: "syre, ya, p*ar*de,
  Bott*e* yite he schape hym fra." 240

(21)

When Pilate hard þat it was he,
  He dred hym mykil mare;
He chees a queste on hym to pas
  Of Iewes þat suthefaste ware, 244
þai saide tille pilate and cayfas:
  "þe suthe botte we wille spare,
Mary with Ioseph weddyd*e* was,
  And at þaire weddynge we ware."
Pilate sayde to þayme þan 249
  þat couped hym byforne:
"yhe putte wrange on þis man,
  In wedlayk*e* was he borne." 252

(22)

Vppe stirte a Iewe bittir and bald*e*
  And sayd to sire Pilate:
"þe tales þat we haue on hym talde
  we wille avowe algate; 256
At þayme es littille helpe or hald*e*,
  Sire, þai say als þai wa,
þai comlyngs of cu*n*nynge calde
  Comen tille oure lawe nowe late."
þis queste stedfast als stele 261
  Sayde tille þe othir twelf*e*:
"we er Iewes, witte yhe wele,
  Borne frely als yhoureseluen." 264

ADDITIONAL.

When herode was ded, is noȝt to layne,
  þat bitt*er*ly þi ded had sworne,
Into þi contre þou come agayne,
  ffro þen as þou was fled beforne."
Pilate saide: "is þis he 237
  þat herode pursewed soo?"
"ȝha," þai saide, "p*ar*dye,
  and ȝit he skappid hym fro." 240

(21)

When pilat wist þat he it was,
  Hit deryd hym þen mykill þe more;
he chese a quest on hym to passe
  Of men þat trewe & sothfast wore,
þai saide to pilat & cayphas: [lf. 119, bk.]
  "þe c*er*tayne sothe we will noȝt spare,
Mary to Ioseph weddid was,
  ffor at þai*r*e weddynge for sothe we [ware."
Pilat saide to þai*me* þanne 249
  þat blamed hade hym beforne:
"To wrange ȝe put þis man,
  In wedloyke was he borne." 252

(22)

Vp styrte a Iuwe bitt*er* & bolde
  And þus he sayde to sir*e* pilat:
"þe tales þat we of hym haue tolde
  We will avowe erly & late; 256
By þis enquest no prisse I holde,
  þos caytifes sayne bot as þi wate,
þai are comylnges, & fayne þai wolde
  Mayntene ihe*su* & his estate." 260
þis quest was trewe als stele
  And sayde: "takes outhir*e* twelue,
We are Iuwes, wit hit wele,
  Als trewe als ȝowreselue." 264

256. *we* marked for erasure between *a* and *vowe*.
258. Horst. *wa(te)*.
264. *h* above line.

GALBA.

(23)

[1] Sir pilat to bar a boke has broght
  þir two questes to twin ; [1 leaf 59]
with swering sal þe suth be soght,
  first quest he biddes bigin ;
and þai say : "nay, þat falles vs noght,
  we say swering es syn ;
lat þam swere þat þis wrang has wroght,
  all knew we ihesus kyin ;
if we be fun gilty
  in þis thing þat we say,
we oblis vs forto dy
  bifor domesmen þis day."

(24)

Þan spac annas and Cayfas
  and said to sir pilate :
"we trow wele mari wedded was
  and þat ioseph him gate ;
bot till anoþer point we pas
  þat sall hald him ful hate :
we say a spirit enclosed he has,
  wharthurth all thinges he wate."
pilat gert haue out all
  þat þan war in þat hows,
and þat quest gert he call
  þat p*ro*ued him born in spowse ;

(25)

He said : "I fand ȝow trew langare,
  telles me now ȝowre rede,
whi hate þir iews ih*es*u so sare
  and will þus haue him ded ?"

HARLEY.

(23)

Sir Pilate to bar a boke has broght
  þir two questes to twyn ;
with sweryng sall þe soth be soght,
  ffyrst quest he bydes bygyn ;
And þai say : "nay, þ*a*t falles vs [noght,
  we say sweryng es syn ;
Lat þam swere þat þis wrang has wroght,
  All knew we Ih*esus* kyn ;
If we be fon gylty
  In þis thing that we say,
we oblysch vs forto dy
  Bifor domesmen þis day."

(24)

Þan spak Annas & Cayphas
  And said to sir Pilate :
"we trow wele Mary wedded was
  And þ*a*t Ioseph him gate ;
Bot tyll aneother poynt we pas
  þ*a*t sall hald him full hate :
we say a spyrit enclosed he has,
  wharethurgh all thynges he wate."
Pilate gert haue out all
  þat þan war in þ*a*t hows,
And þ*a*t quest gert he call [leaf 207, bk.]
  þ*a*t proued him born in spowse ;

(25)

He said : "I fand yhow trew langare,
  Telles me now yho*ur* rede,
whi hate þir Iewes Ih*es*u so sare
  And will þus haue him dede ?"

269. *falles* : *s* above line.
271. *has* : *s* above line.

SION.

(23)

Pilate tille barre a buke had broghte
þe twa questes to twynne;
withe sweryng*e* sal þe suthe by soght*e*,
He bydes þe trewe bygynne;
[1]And þai say þan: "þat falles vs noght*e*,
We sai sweryng*e* es synne; [[1] leaf 17]
Latte þaime swere þat þis wrangh has wroghte,
Alle knawe þai Ih*esu* kyn;
Yff we be funden gilty
Yn þis thyng*e* þat we say,
We oblesse vs forto dye
Byfore domesman to-day."

(24)

þan spacke Annas and Cayphas
And sayd to sire Pilate:
"We trowe wele mary weddid*e* was
Tille Ioseph þat hym gatte;
Botte tille anothir poynte we pas
þat hym halde ful hate:
We say spirite inclosed he has,
Wharethurgh*e* alle thynges he watte."
Pilate gartte haf oute alle
þat was within þat house,
And þat queste gertte he calle
þat proued hym borne in spouse;

(25)

He sayde: "I fande yhow trowe langare,
Say me qwate es yhowre rede,
Whi hates þire Iewes Ih*esu* swa sare,
Whi wille þai haue hym deede?"

274. *Yn:* Horst. *in.* 282. Horst. *þat(sall).*
283. Horst. *(a) spirite.*
284. MS. *thynges* with *es* marked for erasure. Horst. *thyng.*
287. *gan* marked for erasure before *gertte.*

ADDITIONAL.

(23)

Pilat a boke to barre has broght
þos two enquest*es* forto twynne:
W*ith* sweryng*e* sall þe sothe be soght,
And badde þe trewe quest suld begyn*ne*;
And þai saide þan: "it falles vs noȝt
To swere, for sweryng*e* is a syn*ne*;
Lat þai*me* swere þat wrange has wroght,
ffor alle þai knewe wele ih*esu* kyn*ne*;
Gif we be fonden gilty
In þes sawes þat we say,
We obblische vs to dye
Befor ȝowe here þis day."

(24)

þen spak annas & cayphas
And þus þai saide to sir*e* pilate:
"We trowe wele mary weddid wase
Vnto Ioseph þat so hym gate;
Bot to anothir*e* poynt we passe:
Mawgr*e* alle þat mayntens his state
We say a spirit inclose he hase, [leaf 120]
þat tellis hym all thynge erly & late."
Pilat gart voyde þame alle
þat were w*ith*in þat house,
And þat quest gart in calle
Sayde ih*esu* was borne i*n* spouse;

(25)

he saide: "I fonde ȝowe trewe langeore,
And þ*er*efore telle me nowe ȝour*e* rede,
Whi hate þes Iuwes ih*esu* so sore,
Be what skille walde þai haue hym dede?"

269. *it* above line, *vs* erased beneath *it.*

GALBA.

þai say: "his lessons passes þaire lare,
þarfore þai haue hatred,
and als his miracles moues þam mare,
þat standes þam mekill in stede."
wrath es sir pilat þan
and sais: "þis es enuy;
will þai þus deme a man
for his gude dedes to dy?"

(26)

Sir pilat highed out of þe hall
and said þe iews vntill:
"I witnes here byfor ȝow all
I find in him none ill."
and þai answerd both grete & small:
"syr, ift it war þi will,
we gert him noght bifor þe call
to deme withowten skill."
he sais: "þan bus him dy,
I se wele by ȝowre saws;
takes him to ȝow forþi
and demes him by ȝowre laws."

(27)

þan said þe iews: "syr, wele þou wate,
god biddes vs sla no man."
vnto þam þus answerd pilate:
"biddes god me sla men þan?
I haue wele herd whi ȝe him hate
and whi ȝowre grefe bigan;
with my will bese he ded nonegate
by no craft þat ȝe can;
it sall noght stand in stede,
for sertes it war no reson
at deme a man to ded,
bot ȝe had more encheson."

HARLEY.

þai say: "his lessons passes þair lare,
þarfore þai haue hatred,
A*nd* als his miracles moues þam mare,
þ*at* standes þam mykell in stede."
wrathe es sir Pilate þan
And sais: "þis es envy;
will þai þus deme a man
ffor his gud dedes to dy?"

(26)

Sir Pilate hyghed out of þe hall
And said þe Iewes vntyll:
"I witnes here bifor yhow all
I fynd in him none ill."
And þai answerd both gret & small:
"Sir, if it war þi will,
we gert him noght befor þe call
To deme w*ith*outen skyll."
He says: "þan bus him dy,
I se wele be yho*ur* sawes;
Takes him to yhow forþi
And demes him be yho*ur* lawes."

(27)

þan said þe Iewes: "sir, wele þou wate,
God byddes vs sla no man."
vnto þam þus answerd Pilate:
"Byddes god me sla men þan?
I haue wele herd why yhe him hate
And whi yho*ur* grefe bigan;
w*ith* my will bese he ded nonegate
Bi no craft þ*at* yhe kan;
It sall noght stand in stede,
ffor certes it war no resoune
At deme a man to ded,
Bot yhe had more enchesoune."

SION.

þai say: "hys lerynge passes þaire
lare,
þat gers þaime haue hattrede;
His myrecles merres þaime mare,
þat standes mykel in stedde." 296
Wrathe es Pilate þan,
He says: "þis es envy;
Wille þai þus deme a man
ffor his godde dedes to dye?" 300

(26)

Pilate hym hyed oute of þe halle
And sayde þe Iewes vntille:
"Loo here wittnes byfore yhowe alle,
In hym es funden nane ille." 304
þan þai answerde bathe grette and
"Sire, if it be þi wille, [smalle:
[1] We gert hym noght come to þi calle
To coupe hym withouten skylle."
Pilate sayd: "hym byhoues dye,
I see wele be yhoure saghes;
Take hym tille yhow alle forþi 311
And deme hym be yowre laghes."
[[1] leaf 17, bk.]

(27)

þan said þire Iewes: "wele þou wate,
God biddes vs sla na man."
Vntil þire Iewes answerd Pilate:
"Biddes god me slaa men þan? 316
I haue wele hard whi yhe hym hate
And how yhoure hatred bygan;
With my wille he bes deede nanagate
ffor na craft þat yhe can; 320
It es noght botte hatrede,
þat ware ful lyttell resoune
fforto deme a man to deede, 323
Botte þare ware mare enchesoun."

301. MS. *hym hym*; Horst. *hyld* for *hyed*.
312. *law* marked for erasure before *laghes*.
319. Horst. *nanegate*. 322. Horst. *lyttelle*.

ADDITIONAL.

þai saide: "his wittes passes þaire
lore,
fforþi to hym þai haue hatrede,
And his myracles greues þai*m*e sore,
And ȝit þai stande þai*m*e ofte in
"ffor sothe," saide pilat þan, [stede."
"Me thynke þis is envye;
Walde þai þus deme a man
ffor his gude dedys to dye?" 300

(26)

Pilat hym hyede oute of þe halle
And sadly saide þe Iuwes vntille:
"Lo here wytnes befor ȝowe alle
þat in hym can I fynde non ille."
And þai answerde bothe gret & smalle
And saide: "sir pilat, be þi wille,
We gart hym noȝt come to þi calle,
Wyt it wele wythoutyn skille." 308
Pilat saide: "he mon dye,
I seȝ wele be ȝour*e* sawes;
Takes hym to ȝowe forþi 311
And deme hym be ȝour*e* lawes."

(27)

þen saide þes Iuwes: "sir, wele ȝhe
wate
þat god biddes vs we sle no man."
To þai*m*e agayne saide sir pilate:
"Biddes god þat I suld sle men þan?
I wote full wele whi ȝhe hym hate
And howe ȝour*e* wrathe till hym
began;
Be my wille sall he dye nogate
ffor no crafte þ*at* ȝhe alle cane; 320
It is alle for hatrede, [leaf 120, back]
And þis were litill resone
To deme a man to þe ded,
Bot þ*er*e were more encheson." 324

GALBA.

(28)

He led ihesus þe iewes fra
  þat bifore stode him by
and said till him bitwix þam twa:
  "þou es king of iewry?"
Ih*esus* sais: "oiþer was it tald þe swa,
  or þou red rightwisly?"
þan said pilat: "me war full wa
  þi folk suld ger þe dy;
þou ert bytane to me
  forto be demid þis day;
king of iews if þou be
  answer to þat, I say."

(29)

Ih*esus* sayd þan to him ogayne:
  "my kingdom es noght here;
if my kingdom, es noght at layn,
  within þis werld now were,
or I omang þir iews war slaine,
  my men þat er me dere
wald put þam fro þaire purpos playn
  with ful grete powere."
"þan ertou king algate,"
  says pelate, "sikerly?"
Ihesus said to pilate:
  "þou sais it and noght I;

(30)

Cumen I am to þis cuntre
  and þarto was I born,
of suthfastnes witnes to be
  þat was noght sene biforn;
al þat suthfast lithes me
  lely both euyn and morn;
þai sal be demed in þaire degre
  þat suthfastnes has lorn."

HARLEY.

(28)

He led Ih*esus* þe Iewes fra
  þ*a*t bifore stode him by
And said tyll him bitwix þam twa:
  "þou es kyng of Iewry?"
Ih*esus* sais: "owth*er* was it tald þe [swa,
  Or þou red ryghtwisly?"
þan said Pilate: "me war full wa
  þi folk suld ger þe dy;
þou ert bitane to me
  fforto be demed þis day;
Kyng of Iewes if þou be
  Answer to þat, I say."

(29)

Ih*esus* said þan to him ogayne:
  "My kyngdom es noght here;
If my kyngdom, es noght at layne,
  wit*h*in þis world now were,
Or I omang þir Iewes war slayne,
  My men þat war me dere
wald putt þam fro þair p*ur*pose playne
  wit*h* full gret powere."
"þan ertow kyng allgate,"
  says Pilate, "sykerly?"
Ih*esus* said to Pilate:
  "þou sais it & noght I;

(30)

Comen I am to þis contre
  And þareto was I born,
Of sothfastnes wytnes to be
  þ*a*t was noght sene biforn;
All þ*a*t sothfast lythes me
  Lely both euen & morn;
þai sall be demed in þair degre
  þ*a*t sothfastnes has lorn."

325. Horst. *Ihu.*

SION.

(28)

Pilate ledde Ihesu þe Iewes fra
þat stode byfore hym by
And saydetil hym bytwyx þaime twa:
"þou ert kynge of Iewery?" 328
Ihesu sayde: "outhir it was sayde þe
Or þou redde righwisly?" [swa,
And Pilate sayde: "me ware full wa
þi folke suld gar þe dye; 332
þi folke haues taght þe me
fforto be damned to-day;
Kynge of Iewes if þou be
Answer to þat, I say." 336

(29)

Ihesu answard tille hym agayne:
"My kyngdome es noght here;
If my kyndome, sothely to sayne,
Within þaire grethe were, [tane,
[1] Are I omange þire Iewes ware here
My men þat ware me dere [1 leaf 18]
Wald stande and stryfe fulle faste
agayne 344
With fulle grette powere."
"þan ert þou kynge algate,"
Quod Pilate, "sykerly?"
Ihesu sayde tille Pilate:
"þou says for kynge am I; 348

(30)

And I am comen to þis contre
And þarto was I borne,
Witnes of sothefastnes to be
þat was noght sene byforne; 352
Alle þat es sothefast lys in me,
Leely bathe euen and morne;
In erthe suthefastnes dampned by-
Of þam þat has it lorne." [houes be

330. Horst. *righ(t)wisly.*

ADDITIONAL.

(28)

Pilat ladde ihesu þe Iewes fro
þat to hym had grete envye
And saide till hym betwyx þaime two:
"Ihesu, þou art kynge of Iury?" 328
Ihesu saide: "whethire was it saide
Or of þin awen outorytye?" [þe soo,
Pilat said: "me were full wo
þi folke suld þus deme þe to dye;
þi folke has taght þe to me 333
fforto be dampned þis day;
Kynge of Iuwes if þou be
Answere to þis, I þe say." 336

(29)

Ihesu answerd mekly agayne:
"Iwisse, my kyngdome is noȝt here;
ffor if my kyngdome, sothe to sayne,
Within þis wankill worlde nowe
were, 340
Or I amonge þes Iuwes were slayne,
My men þat are me leef & dere
Wald stand & fyght with mode &
mayne [powere."
And brynge with þaime full grete
"þen art þou kynge allgate?" 345
Pilat saide sikirly.
Ihesu sayde to pilate:
"þowe says þat kynge am I; 348

(30)

I am come to þis contre
And for þis skill þen was I borne,
witnes of sothefastnes to be
þat has bene saide full lange beforne,
And forto make þe peple fre 353
þat suld haue bene with syne for-
All þat is sothfaste likes me [lorne;
And pleses me both euene & morne."

GALBA.	HARLEY.
pilat þan asked him eft:	Pilate þan asked him eft:
"what thing es suthfastnes?"	"what thing es sothfastnes?"
with þat Ihesus he left	with þ*at* Ihe*sus* he left
als man þat stonayd es.	Als man þ*at* stonayd es.
(31)	(31)
[1] He said vnto þe iewes al þus:	He said vnto þe Iewes all þus:
"sirs, if it war ȝowre will, [[1] lf. 59, bk.]	"Sirs, if it war yho*ur* wyll,
I haue enquered more of ihesus,	I haue enquered more of Ihe*sus*,
I find in hym none ill."	I fynd in him none ill."
þai sayd: "he was noght wrighed for	þai said: "he was noght wreghed for
withowen sertayn skill." [vs	W*ith*outen certayne skyll." [vs
sir pilat said: "dy sen him bus,	Sir Pilate said: "dy sen him bus,
I consent noght þartill,	I consent noght þaretyll,
I am withowten gilt,	I am withouten gylt,
to proue in ȝowre present;	To proue in yhoure p*re*sent;
his blude sal noght be spilt	His blode sall noght be spylt
forsoth by myne assent."	fforsoth be myne assent."
(32)	(32)
To þis answerd þe iewes all	To þis answerd þe Iewes all
and made þam wonder wrath,	And made þam wonder wrathe,
þai say: "his blude mot on vs fall	þai say: "his blode mot on vs fall
and on oure childer bath."	And on our childer bathe."
sir pilat said: "parchance so sall,	Sir Pilate said: "p*ar*chaunce so sall,
þat es ful mekill wath;	þat es full mykell wathe;
þarfore lat haue him out of hall	þarfor lat haue him out of hall
and skape withowten skath."	A*n*d schape w*ith*outen skathe."
þai say: "sir, wele þou wate,	þai say: "sir, wele þou wate,
we say bot lawfully;	we say bot lawfully;
wha blemis Kinges astate	Wha blemys kynges astate [leaf 208]
es wele worth forto dy;	Es wele worth forto dy;
(33)	(33)
And whoso sklandres þe godhede	And whoso sklaunders þe godhede
es more syn þan swilk seuyn;	Es more syn þan swilk seuen;

361. Horst. *al.*

SION.

Pilate asked hym eft:
" What es suthefastnes ? "
With þat Ihesu he left
Als man þan stonayd es.

ADDITIONAL.

And pilat asked efte:
" Say, what is sothefastnes ? "
With þat ihesu he lefte
Als man þat stonyed wasse.

(31)

Pilate sayde tille þire Iewes þus:
" Syrs, if it be yhoure wille,
I haf enquered mare of Ihesus,
In hym es funden nane ille."
þai sayde: "we wald noght coup hym
Nanegates withouten skille." [þus
Quod pilate: "algate dye him byhoues,
I consent noght þaretille,
I am withouten gilt,
Clene als anne Innocent;
His blode sal neuere be spilt
Nanegates thurgh myne assent."

(31)

Pilat saide to þe Iuwes yfere: [leaf 121]
" Lordynges, if it be ȝoure wille,
I haue enquerd of ihesu here,
And in hym can I fynde no ille."
And þai answerde with herdy chere:
" we blame hym noȝt withoutyn
Pilat saide withoutyn were: [skille."
" ȝhe will hym sle with paynes
Bot I am oute of gilte, [grille,
Als clene as Innocent;
His bloude sall noȝt be spilte,
Noȝt als be myn assent."

(32)

And þan answerd þire Iewes alle
[1]And made þam wondir wrathe,
þai sayde: " hys blode mot vs falle
And on our childer bathe." [[1] lf. 18, bk.]
And pilate sayde: " perchaunce it salle,
And þat es mekel wathe;
þarefore lat haf hym oute of halle
And late hym haf na scathe."
þai sayde: " syre, wele þou wate,
We say bot lawefully;
Whaso blemysshe þe kyng state
Es worthy forto dye;

(32)

þen answerd þe Iuwes alle [wrothe,
and made þaime wondre kene &
þai saide: " is bloude mot on vs falle
and on alle oure chyldre bothe."
And pilat saide: " perchaunche it schalle,
[lothe;
And þat me walde ȝit thynk full
þerefore haue hym out of þe halle
And do hym nouthire harme ne brothe."
þe Iuwes saide: " wele ȝhe wate,
we say bot skilfully;
who presentes þe kynges estate,
he is worthy to dye;

(33)

And whaswa sclaunders þe godhede
Es mare syn þan swylk seuen;

(33)

And he þat sklaundres þe godhede
More syne it is þen siche seuene

375. Horst. (*on*) *vs*.

GALBA.

he þat es man withowten drede
als god sun will him neuyn,
he hetes to sit, whoso tase hede,
on goddes right hand in heuyn,
to deme ilk man efter his dede
at his awin ordinance euyn."
out of þat company
pilat went Ihesu vnto
and said: "syr, sekerly,
I ne wate what es to do."

(34)

Crist said: "als gifen þe and me,
so bus be done alwise."
pilat sais: "how?" and þan sais he:
"als proues þe prophecise,
Moyses, dauid and Iosue,
and oþer mo þan þise;
als þai said, bese fulfild in me
to suffer and dye and rise."
þan pilat went to hall
als man þat was amayd
and tald to þe iews all
how þat Ihesus had sayd.

(35)

þan said þe iews to pilat: "lo,
in swilk errowre he dwelles,
with more witnes what suld we do?
himself ful trewly telles."
pilat said: "takes him ȝow vnto,
sen ilk man þus him melles,
and demes als ȝe bigan þis bro,
for I will say noght els."
þai say: "wha melling makes
to man, þis find we wretyn,
'ane wane of fourty strakes
with ȝerde he sal be smeten;'

HARLEY.

He þat es man w*ith*oute*n* dred
Als god son will him neuen,
He hetes to sytt, who takes hede,
On ryght hand in heuen,
To deme ilk man aft*er* his awen dede
At his awen ordenance euen."
Out of þ*at* company
Pilate went Ihe*su* vnto
And said: "sir, sykerly,
I ne wayte what es to do."

(34)

Crist said: "als gyfen þe & me,
So bus be done allwyse."
Pilate sais: "how?" & þan says he:
"Als p*ro*ues þe p*ro*phecyse,
Moyses, Dauid & Iosue,
And other mo þan þese;
Als þai said, bese fullfyld in me,
To suffer & degh & ryse."
þan Pilate went to hall
Als man þ*at* was amayd
And tald to þe Iewes all
How þ*at* Ihes*us* had said.

(35)

þan said þe Iewes to Pilate: "lo,
In swilk erroure he dwelles,
w*ith* more witnes what suld we do?
Himself full trewly telles."
Pilate said: "takes him yhow vnto,
Sen ilk man þus him melles,
And demes als yhe bygan þis bro,
ffor I will say noght elles."
þai say: "wha mellyng makes
To man, þis fynd we wryten,
'Ane wane of fourty strakes
w*ith* yherd he sall be smyten;'

SION.

He þat es made of pure manhed
  Goddes son he wille hym neuen,
He says he has his sittyngestede
  On goddes right hand in heuen,
And says he sal deme bath quyk and
  After oure dedes fulle euen." [deede
Out of þat company
  Pilate yhede Ihesu vnto
And sayde: "sire, sykerly,
  I ne wate what I sal do."

ADDITIONAL.

He þat is made of pure manhede,
  þat he gods sone so walde hym neuene,
Says he sall haue his sittyngstede
  On gods ryght hand þat is in heuene,
fforto deme both quike & dede
  After þat þaire dedes are euene."
Out of þat company
  Pilat ȝhede ihesu to
And saide: "sir, sikirly,
  I ne wote what I sall do."

(34)

SION.

"Als it es gyfen tille þe and me,"
  Quod Ihesu, "bes done allewyse."
Pilate askes: "how?" and þan says
  "Als telles þe prophecyse, [he:
Moyses, Dauid and Iosue,
  And othir many þan þise;
þat þai say byhoues be fulfild in me
  T[o] suffir deede and ryse."
Pilate went oute of halle
  Als man þat was amayed
And talde þire Iewes alle [leaf 19]
  How þat Ihesu had sayde.

ADDITIONAL.

"Als it is gyfen to þe & me,"
  Quod ihesu, "be it on alle wise."
Pilat saide: "what?" & þen saide he:
  "Als trewely tellen þe prophecyes,
Moyses, dauid & Iosue, [leaf 121, bk.]
  and mony outhire mo þen þes;
þat þai saide most fulfilled be
  In me, for I sall dye & Ryse."
Pilat went out of þe halle
  Als man þat was amayde
And tolde þe Iuwes alle
  how þat ihesu hade sayde.

(35)

SION.

þire Iewes sayde alle tille syre Pilate:
  In what erroure he dwelles, ["loo
With mare wittenes what suld yhe do
  Bot als hymseluen telles?"
Pilate sayde: "tak yhow vnto,
  Sithe ilk man þus hym melles,
Deme forthe als yhe bygan þis bro,
  ffor I will say noght elles."
þai say: "whaswa mellynge makes
  Tille man, þis fynde we written,
'Ane wane of fourty strakes [smyten;'
  With yherde falles hym be

ADDITIONAL.

þe Iuwes saide to pilat: "loo,
  Siche an errore þat he in dwelles,
what suld we with more witness doo
  Bot ryghtals hisawen tonge telles?"
Pilat sayde: "take hym ȝowe too,
  Sen it is so iche man hym mellis,
Deme forth als ȝhe began þis broo,
  ffor I can say to ȝowe noȝt elles."
þai sayde: "who mellynge makys
  To man, þis fynde we wryten,
'No lesse þen fourty strakys
  Hym falles forto be strikyn;'

413. Horst. *tak* (*him*); *yhow*, *o* above line.

GALBA.

(36)

Wha sklanders god, ȝe wate he mon
be staned to ded for syn;
he telles ȝow þat he es god son,
and we knaw all his kyn;
he sais þat he sall sit in trone,
þarfore or euer we blin,
we will þat he on cros be done
and ded for all his dyn;
if he regne sekerly,
all sall turn to his lare;
and better es þat a man dy
þan all þe folk forfare."

(37)

In come sir nicodeme by þan,
was prince of þe iewry,
he said: "I rede ȝe do þis man
no maner of velany;
slike sotell talkinges als he can
and schewes vs opinly
was neuer ȝit sene þe werld bigan
sene in prophecy;
and if his fare war fals,
it suld be sene ful sone;
his sawes and his dedes als
suld dy and be vndone.

(38)

When signes war schewed thurgh [Moises
vntill pharao þe kyng,
two witnes, Iamnes and mambres,
did him ful grete hething;
signes þat he schewed made þai lese
with þaire fals enchaunting,
als goddes þam held all hathenes;
bot lithes þe last ending;

HARLEY.

(36)

Wha sklaund*er*s god, yhe wate he mon
Be staned to ded for syn;
He telles yhow þat he es god son,
And we knaw all his kyn;
He says þ*at* he sall sytt in trone,
þarfore or euer we blyn,
we will þ*at* he on cross be done
And ded for all his dyn;
If he regne sykerly,
All sall turne tyll his lare;
And bett*er* es þ*at* a man dy
þan all þe folk forfare."

(37)

[1] In come syr Nichodeme by þan,
was prynce of þe Iewry,
He said: "I red yhe do þis man
No man*er*e of vylany;
Slyke sotell talkyng*es* als yhe can
And schewes vs openly
was neu*er* yhit sen þe world bygan
Sene in prophecy;
And if his fare war fals,
It suld be sene full sone;
His sawes & his dedes als
Suld dy and be vndone.

(38)

When sygnes war schewed thurgh [Moyses
Vntyll Pharao þe kyng,
Two witnes, Iamnes & mambres,
Did him full gret hethyng;
Signes þ*at* he schewed made þai lese
w*ith* þair fals enchauntyng,
Als godes þam held all hathenes;
Bot lythes þe last endyng;

[1] *I*: very large ornamental.
445. *Moyses*: last *s* above line.

SION.

(36)

And he þat trespas god, alsone
Hym falles be staned to deede;
Sithen he says he es goddes sone,
And we knawe hys kynrede, 424
And says þat he salle sitte in trone,
þarefore gyf we þis rede:
We wille þat he on cros be done
Are we passe of þis stede; 428
ffor if he regne sykerly,
Alle sal trowe on his lare;
Better it es þat a man dye
þan alle þe folke forfare." 432

(37)

In come sire Nichodeme be þan,
þat was Prince of þe Iewery,
He sayd: "I rede yhow do þis man
Na mare of vilany; 436
Swilke takyngs als he do kan
And has schewed vs oppenly
Was neuer sene sithen þis warlde [bygan
[1]In alle our p*ro*phecy;
And if þat he be fals, [[1] leaf 19, bk.]
It sal be knawen fulle sone;
His saghes, his takens als
Salle dye and be fordone. 444

(38)

When syngnes ware schewed thurgh [Moyses
Tille Faraon þe kyng*e*,
Twa witches, Ia*m*nes and Mambres,
Did hym ful grett*e* hethyng*e*; 448
Syngnes þat he schewed þai mad*e* þam [les
With þaire enchauntisyng,
Als goddes þam helde alle haythenes;
Bot lithe þe laste endyng; 452

ADDITIONAL.

(36)

And he þat calles hym gods son,
hym falles to be stoned to dede;
He says hys fadr*e* made sone & mone,
Bot we knawe wele all his kynrede;
He says þat he sall sitt in trone, 425
And for thi holy gif we þis rede:
þat he sall on a crosse be done
Or þat he passe out of þis stede; 428
ffor if he regne þus sikirly,
All sall leue vpon his lare;
And bet*er* is þat on man dye
þen alle folke sulde þus mysfare."

(37)

In come sir*e* nichodem*us* þan,
þat was p*r*ince of all Iuwery
And sayde: "I rede ȝowe do þis man
No more harme ne vilany; 436
ffor siche tokenes als he do kan
And shewes till vs here opynly
Was neu*er* sithen þis worlde began
ffonden here be p*ro*phecye; 440
If he be fals or faynte, [leaf 122]
It sall be knawen full sone;
His sawes, his tokenes quaynt
Sall dye & be fordone. 444

(38)

When tokenes were shewed thurgh [moyses
Vnto pharaho þe kynge,
Two wycches, Iames & Membres,
Did to moyses gret lettynge; [leese
Disprufed his signes & made þai*m*e
All thurgh þair*e* fals enchauntynge,
Als gods þai*m*e helde all hethenes;
Bot harkenes nowe þe last endynge;

435. *yo* marked for erasure before *rede*.
438. *swe* marked for erasure after *has*.

426. *holy*: *y* above line. *rede*: *jugemēt* has been erased before *rede*.
450. *fals*: *s* above line.

GALBA.

for his dedes war suthfast
  and þaires bot sorcery;
his dedes sall euermore last,
  and þaires bud nedely dy.

(39)

[1] And *par*chance þis man may be sent
  a prophet vs forto lere; [[1] leaf 60]
i n[e] wat by wham þat moises ment
  þat telles on þis manere:
'a prophet till oure lawes bese lent
  and born omanges vs here;'
he said þai sall be schamely schent
  þat him þis will noght here."
þe iews bifor pilate
  sayd vnto nichodeme:
"his lare be þine algate,
  and his pese might þe ȝeme."

(40)

Nichodeme answerd and said "a-[men,"
  and held up bath his hend,
"vnto his lare I tak me þen,
  his pese in me might lend."
into þe hall þan come þare ten
  þat for lazars war kend,
þai said: "we war vnclene, ȝe ken,
  hale thurgh his word we wend."
in come anoþer and said:
  "sir, blind born was I,
handes on mine eghen he layd,
  þus sagh I sekerly."

(41)

Anoþer said: "sirs, seke I lay
  fourty ȝere al bot twa,

HARLEY.

ffor his dedes war sothfast
  And þaires bot sorcery;
His dedes sall euermore last,
  And þaires bot nedely dy.

(39)

And *par*chaunce þis man may be sent
  A *pro*phet vs forto lere;
I ne wate by whame *þat* moyses ment
  þat telles on þis manere:
'A *pro*phet tyll our lawes bese lent
  And borne omanges vs here;'
He said þai sall be schamely schent
  þ*at* him þis will noght here."
þe Iewes byfor Pilate
  Said vnto Nichodeme:
"His lare be þine allgate,
  And his pese myght þe yheme."

(40)

Nichodeme answerd & said "amen,"
  And held vp both his hend,
"vntyll his lare I tak me þen,
  His pese in me myght lend."
Into þe hall þan come þare ten
  þat for Lazars war kend,
þai said: "we war vnclene, yhe ken,
  Hale thurgh his word we wend."
In come aneother & sayd:
  "Sir, blynd borne was I,
[1] Handes on myne eghen he layd,
  þus saw I sykerly." [[1] leaf 208, bk.]

(41)

Aneother said: "syrs, seke I lay
  ffourty yhere all bot twa,

459. MS. *in what* for *i ne wat.*

SION.

ffor his dedes ware suthefaste
And þairs ware sorcery;
his dedes sall euermare last,
And þairs byhoued nedelyngs dye.

(39)

And p*er*chaunce he may be sent
A p*ro*phete vs to lere;
I ne wate by wham þat moyses ment,
He telles on þis manere:
'A p*ro*phete till yhoure laghe be sent
þat bes born omang yow here;'
He says alle þase bes schamely schent
Of hym þat wille noght lere."
þire Iewes byfore Pilate
Sayde vntille Nichodeme:
"his strenghe be þin allegate,
And his pees mote þe yheme."

(40)

And Nichodeme aswered "amen,"
And helde vppe bathe his hende,
"Vnto his strenghe I me byken,
his pees mote on me lende."
Byfor Pilate þan come þar ten
þat ware for lazars kende:
"We ware lazars," þai sayde, "we ken,
[1] Hale thurgh his word we wende."
In come anothir and sayde: [[1] leaf 20]
"loured, blynde born was I,
Handes on myn eghen he layde,
and sone saghe I þus sykerly."

(41)

Ane sayde: "Pilate, bedred I lay
ffourty yhere alle bot twa;

453. *Sorcery* marked for erasure after *ware*.
461. *be*: Horst. *be(s)*; *s* in *sent* corrected from *l*; Horst. *lent*. 464. Horst. *here*.
469. Horst. *a(n)swerd*.

ADDITIONAL.

ffor moyses dedes were sothfast
And þaire bot sorcery;
Moyses signes gan last,
And þaires gan falle & dye.

(39)

And so may be þis man is sent
Als p*ro*phete trewe vs alle to lere;
I not be wham þat moyses ment,
Bot moyses sayde on þis manere:
'A p*ro*phete sall be to ȝowe sent
þat sall be borne amonge ȝowe here;'
And sayd þat alle þos sall be shent
þat will noȝt of his techynge lere.
þe Iuwes befor pilat
Sayde vnto Nychodeme:
"His trone be þin allgate,
And his pece mot þe ȝheme."

(40)

And Nichodem*us* sayde "Ame*n*,"
And þ*er*ewit*h* helde vp both his hende,
"Vnto his trone I me bekenne,
I p*ra*y his pece myght wit*h* me lende."
Before pilat þ*er*e come forth tene
þat su*m*tyme were for lazares kende:
[1] "We were Lazares, als ȝhe wele kenne,
And þus has ihe*s*u vs amende."
In come anothire & sayde: [[1] lf. 122, bk.]
"Lorde, blynde borne was I,
His handes on me he layde,
And I sawe sikirly."

(41)

Anothire saide: "bedrede I lay
ffourty ȝhere fully sawe two;

454. *sorcery*: *r* is blotted.

478. MS. *bore blynde born*. Horst. *blynde-bore*.

GALBA.

I asked mercy, and he gan say:
'tyte tak þi bed and ga!'
sone was I helid and went my way."
þus come ay ma and ma,
þai said: "sirs, no man nowmber may
how many he has helid swa."
all haly say þai þus:
"a grete prophet es he,
oure sauiore dere Ihesus,
blisced ay mot he be."

(42)

"ʒowre prestes, ʒowre bisschoppes," [q*ua*d pilate,
"þusgat why hele noght þai?"
and þai answerd and said: "we ne [wate,
bot þus wirkes he alway;
ane lazar þat was ded now late
and in his graue lang lay,
he lifes ogain in ful gude state,
þis es suth þat we say."
hereof had pilat drede
and said: "whi will ʒe spill
þe man þat helpis in nede
all þat will call him till?"

(43)

He cald nichodeme and þat quest
þat he fand trew algate
and said: "lordinges, how hald ʒe best?
þir folk falles in debate."
and þai said: "sir, als haue we reste,
what es to do we ne wate;
þam forto pay er we noght p*r*est,
forto les his astate;
we pray god þat he send
right dome þam omang,
on þam self moght it lend
wha dose right and who wrang."

HARLEY.

I asked m*er*cy, & he gan say:
'Tyte tak þi bed and ga!'
Sone was I heled & went my way."
þus come ay ma and ma,
þai said: "syrs, no man nowmbre may
How many he has heled swa."
All halely say þai þus:
"A gret p*ro*phet es he,
Our sauyo*ur* dere Ih*esu*s,
Blyssed ay myght he be."

(42)

"Yho*ur* p*r*estes, yho*ur* bysschopes," [q*ua*d Pilate,
"þusgate whi hele noght þai?"
And þai answerd & said: "we ne wate,
Bot þus wirkes he allway;
Ane Lazar þ*at* was ded now late
And in his graue lang lay,
He lyfes ogayne in full gud state,
þis es soth þat we say."
Hereof had Pilate dred
And said: "whi will yhe spyll
þe man þ*at* helpes in nede
All þ*at* will call him tyll?"

(43)

He called Nichodeme & þ*at* quest
þ*at* he fand trew allgate
And said: "lordynges, how hald yhe best?
þir folk falles in debate."
And þai said: "syr, als haue we rest,
what es to do we ne wate;
þam forto pay er we noght p*r*est,
fforto less his astate;
we pray god þat he send
Ryght dome þam omang,
On þam self mot it lend
wha dose ryght & wha wrang."

SION.

I asked mercy, and he gun say :
'Tite ta þi beddo and ga !'
þare was I heled and went my way."
þus come ay ma and ma,
þai sayde : "it ware ful mekel at say
How many he had heled swa."
Alle halely sayde þai þus :
"A greete prophete es he,
Our saueor Ihesus,
Euer blissed mot he be."

(42)

"yhour prestes, yhoure bisschope,
þusgate why heele þai noght?"
And aswerd : "sire, we wate,
Bot þis werk Ihesu wroght;
Ane lazare þat was deede nowe late
And tille his berying broght,
He leues ogayne in ful gude state,
Hereof wonder vs thoght."
Hereof had pilate drede
And sayde : "whi wille þai spille
þe man þat helpes in nede
Alle þat calle to hym wille?"

(43)

He called Nichodeme and þe quest
þat he fand trewe algate,
He sayd : "lordyng, qwhat hald ye best?
þise folk falles in debate."
And þai of answere ware ful prest
And sayd : "syre, we ne wate ;
[1]Tille þaire counsayle, als haue we rest,
We wille assent nanega ; [1 leaf 20, bk.]
We pray god þat he sende
Ryghtwis dome þaime omange,
On þaire saules mot it lende
Whethir þai do right or wrange."

495. Horst. *þai a(n)swerd* ; *we* (*ne*).
507. Horst. *qwat*. 512. Horst. *ga*(*te*).

ADDITIONAL.

I asked mercy, & he gan say :
'Anon take vp þi bedde & go !'
þus was I helde & went my way."
And on þis wyse come mo & mo,
þai saide : "it were to mych at say
Howe mony þat ihesu helid so."
All holy sayde þai þus :
"A gret prophet is he,
Oure sauyoure ihesus,
Euere blessed mot he be."

(42)

"To ȝoure prestes," quod pilate,
"þes wordes whi shewe ȝhe noȝt?"
And þai answerde : "sir, we ne wate,
Bot all thus ihesu has wroght ;
A lazare þat was ded nowe late
And forth vnto his beryinge broght,
He liffes agayne in full gud state,
And þereof gret wondre vs thoght."
Pilat hereof hade drede
And saide : "whi will ȝhe spille
þat man þat helpes at nede
Alle þat calles hym vntille?"

(43)

He called Nychodeme & þe quest
þat he before fonde trewe allgate
And saide ; "lordynges, what hald ȝhe best?
Alle þes folke are in gret bate."
And þai of answere were full preste
And sayde ilk one ; "sire, we ne wate ;
To þaire consayle, so haue we rest,
[1]We will noȝt sent for drede ne hate ;
We pray god þat he sende [1 leaf 123]
Rightwis dome þaime amange,
On þaire sawes mot it lende
Whethire þai do ryght or wrange."

GALBA.

(44)

At pasch of Iews þe custom was
ane of preson to slake,
withowten dome to lat him pas
for þat high fest sake.
a prison þai had hight barabas
þat many murthers gan make;
wheþer him or ihesu, pilat ass,
þai will fro presoun take,
þai cried fast: "baraban!"
and pilat askes þam all:
"what sall Ihesus do þan?"
þai say: "cros him þou sall;

(45)

Bot þou do so, it es wele sene
þou es noght Cesares frende;
who makes þam kyng, withowten [wene
ogains cesar þai wende."
and pilat said þan in a tene:
"ȝe folk ful of þe fende,
till ȝowre belders ay haue ȝe bene
schrewes and ill at þe ende."
for wroth þai wex nere wode
and said: "why says þou so?
who did vs euer ȝit gude,
[þ]at we ne did þam slike two?"

(46)

"Fro egipt," said he, "war ȝe led
with moyses þe trew p*ro*phete,
fro pharao thurgh þe se ȝe fled
and filed noght ȝowre fete;
in wildernes, when god ȝow fed
with angell mete ful swete,
owles to ȝowre fode þ*at* neu*er* war bred
and rayn fro heuyn he lete;

HARLEY.

(44)

At Pasch of Iewes þe custom was
Ane of p*re*son to slake,
wit*h*outen dome to latt him pas
ffor þ*at* hegh fest sake.
A pryson þai had hight Barabas
þat murthers gan make;
Whether him or Ih*es*u, pilate ass,
þai will fro presone take,
þai cryed fast: "Baraban!"
And Pilate askes þam all:
"What sall Ih*esus* do þan?"
þai say: "cross him þou sall;

(45)

Bot þou do so, it es wele sene
þou ert noght Cesares frende;
who makes þam kyng, wit*h*outen wene
Ogayns Cesare þai wende."
And Pilate said þan in a tene:
"yhe folk full of þe fende,
Tyll yhou*r* belders ay haue yhe bene
Schrewes & ill ay at þe ende."
ffor wroth þai wex nere wode
And said: "whi says þou so?
who did vs eu*er* yhit gud,
þ*at* we ne dyd þam slyke two?"

(46)

"ffro Egypp," said he, "yhe war led
wit*h* moyses þe trew p*ro*phete,
ffro Pharao thurgh þe cee yhe fled
And fyled noght yhou*r* fette;
In wildernes, when god yhow fed
Wit*h* aungell mete full swete,
ffowles to yhou*r* fode þ*at* neu*er* war bred
And rayne fro heuen he lete;

520. *hegh*: *gh* inserted above line.

SION.

(44)

þire Iewes at Paches euer wont was
Anne oute of prisoun take [pas
And withouten dome quyte late hym
ffor þaire grette feste sake. 520
Ane was prisound hight Barabas
ffor murthers þat he gun make;
Whethir hym or Ihesu, Pilate asked
þai sall of prisoun take, [has,
And þai sayd all: "Baraban!" 525
And Pilate asked þayme alle:
"Of Ihesu what sal be þan?"
þai sayde: "croyse hym þou salle;

(45)

And botte þou do, it es wele sene
þou ert noght Cesar frende;
ffor whaso makes þayme kynge, we
Ogayne Cesar þai wende." [wene,
And Pilate saide right in a tene: 533
"Yhe folke fulle of þe fende,
Tille yhoure ay haue ye bene [ende."
Grotchant and ay schrewes at þe
ffore wrethe þai wex nere wode 537
And sayde: "why say þou swa?
Wha dide vs euer any gode, 539
Botte we did þaime swilke twa?"

(46)

He sayde: "fra egipte when ware
Thurgh Moyses þe prophete, [ledde
Euen thurgh þe se euen yhe fledde
And wette noghte anes youre fette;
[1] In þe wildernes god yhow fedde 545
With aungel meete fulle swete,
ffogheles til yhoure fode þat neuer
was bredde, [1 leaf 21]
Rayne fra þe heuen he lete; 548

ADDITIONAL.

(44)

þe Iuwes were wont euere at þe pace
A man out of þaire prisone take,
Withoutyn dome to lat hym passe
And gif hym lyfe for þat fest sake.
On was in prison hight Barabas 521
ffor manslaghter þat he did make;
Pilat þe Iuwes asked in þat place
whethire ihesu or hym þai wolde lat
And þai saide: "Baraban!" [skape,
And pilat asked þaime alle:
"What sall ihesu do þan?"
þai saide: "on crosse he salle; 528

(45)

And bot he be þat it be sene,
We say þou art noȝt Cesare frende;
ffor whoso makis hym kynge, I wene,
Agaynes Cesare lordschippe þai
wende." 532
And pilat saide right þan for tene:
"ȝhe fals felons full of þe fende,
To ȝoure helpers euere haue ȝhe bene
Grucchande & shrewes at ilk ane
þe Iuwes þen wex alle woude [ende."
And saide: "whi says þou so?
who did vs euere ȝhit gude,
Bot we did hym siche two?" 540

(46)

"When þat god ȝowe fro egipte ledde
Thurgh moyses þat was his prophete,
ffro pharaho thurgh þe see ȝhe fledde
þat on of ȝowe wett noȝt ȝowre fete;
In þe wildrenes he ȝowe fedde 545
with angeles foude gostly & swete,
ffloure to ȝoure foude þat neuer was
bredde [lete;
And rayne fro heuene þat lorde ȝowe

541. Horst. *when* (*ye*).

543. *ȝe* erased after *ȝhe*.

GALBA.

out of þe stane he sent
  fress water weterly;
ȝe brac his cumandment
  and lifed on maumetry; 552

(47)

[1] Bot þat moyses gan for ȝow pray,
  god had fordone ȝow þare; [[1] lf. 60, bk.]
and here þis man þat ilka day
  heles ȝow seke and sare, 556
for I deme noght vnto ȝowre pay
  bot wald þe giltles spare;
I am noght Cesars frende, ȝe say,
  þis es vnrightwis fare." 560
þai sai: "we haue no king
  bot þe Emp*er*oure of rome;
to trow on þis tratilling
  þat war no rightwis dome. 564

(48)

We find how thre kinges her biforn
  fro perse to bedlem soght,
þai asked whare þe king of iews was born
  and till him ofrandes broght; 568
bot when herod wist on þe morn
  on what wise þai had wroght,
þat he and þai both suld be lorn,
  þis was in herodes thoght; 572
for he knew noght him þis,
  al childer bad he sla
þat of twa ȝere oght mys,
  and ȝit he scapid him fra." 576

(49)

Pilat hereof had grete pete
  and bad all men be still:
"withowten caus þa kinges thre
  soght noght so fer him till." 580

HARLEY.

Out of þe stane he sent
  ffressch wat*er* wyterly;
yhe brak his comament
  & lyfed on mawmetry; 552

(47)

Bot þ*at* Moyses gan for yhow p*ra*y,
  God had fordone yhow þare;
And here þis man þ*at* ilka day
  heles yhow seke and sare, 556
ffor I deme noght vnto yho*ur* pay
  Bot wald þe gyltles spare;
I am noght Cesars frend, yhe say,
  þis es vnryghtwyse fare." 560
þai say: "we haue no kyng
  Bot þe Emp*er*oure of Rome;
To trow on þis tratylling
  þ*at* war no ryghtwys dome. 564

(48)

We fynd how thre kynges here biforne
  ffro Perse to bethleem soght,
þai asked whare þe kyng of Iewes was borne
  And tyll him offrandes broght; 568
Bot when Herod wist on þe morne
  On what wise þai had wroght,
þ*at* he & þai both suld be lorne,
  þis was in herodes thoght; 572
ffor he knew noght him þis,
  All childer bad he sla
[1] þat of twa yhere oght mys, [leaf 209]
  And yhit he skaped him fra." 576

(49)

Pilate hereof had gret Pete
  And bad all men be styll:
"w*ith*outen cause þa kynges thre
  Soght noght so fer him tyll." 580

[1] þ very large and ornamental.

SION.

Oute of þe stane he sent
yhow water witerly;
And yhe brak hys comandement
And lyfed on mawmettry;

(47)

Bot moyses gun for yhow pray,
he had elles fordone yhow þare;
And here es a man þat ilk day
heles yhoure seke and yhoure sare,
ffor I deme hym noght tille yhoure paye
Bot wald þe giltles spare;
I am noght cesar frend, yhe say,
þis es vnryghtwise fare."
Þai sayd: "we haf na kyng
Bot e*mpero*ure of rome;
To hald hym for hys Iangelyng
ware na ryghtwyse dome.

(48)

Bot for thre kynges of peers byforn
ffra peers tille bethelem soght,
Sayde: 'kynge of Iewes whare es he born?'
And til hym offrandes broght;
When herod wiste sone on þe morn
What wyrschipe þai hym wroght,
Omang othyr he suld haf bene lorn,
þis was in herodes thoght;
ffor he neuer rome suld welde,
Betheelem barnes gert he slaa,
Alle withein twa yhere elde,
Bot he eschapyd hym fra."

(49)

when pilate hard, he had pite
And gert alle men be stille, [1 lf. 21, bk.]
[1] He sayde: "whethir þis þat Ihe*s*u be
Þat Horode pursued with ille?"

555. Horst. *ilk(a)*. 558. þe: *e* above.
568. Horst. *till*. 570. Horst. *wyrshipe*.

ADDITIONAL.

Oute of þe stone he sent [leaf 123, bk.]
ȝhowe watre wondrely;
Ȝhe brake his comaundeme*n*t
And leuyd in maumetry;

(47)

Bot at moyses gan for ȝowe pray,
God had dredles fordone ȝowe þare;
And nowe þis man þ*at* ilka day
Helis ȝowe alle bothe seke & sare,
ffor I hym deme noȝt to ȝowre pay
Bot wolde hym þat is gilteles spare;
I am noȝt Cesar frende, ȝhe say,
And þis me thynke a wondre fare."
Þai saide: "We haue no kynge
Bot þe Emp*erour* of Rome;
Holde hym for his saynge
Kynge RightWise in dome.

(48)

Bot thre kynges here beforne
ffro colayne vnto bethelem soght
And sayde þe kynge of Iuwes was borne
And gret offrynge to hym þai broght;
When herode wist sone on þe morne
what wyrschip þat þe kynges hym wroght,
Amonges outhire he sulde be lorne,
And þus cast herode in his thoght;
ffor ihe*s*u sulde noȝt Bethelem welde,
Alle childre gart he sloo
Wi*th*in two ȝhere of Elde,
And ȝit he skappid þai*m*e fro."

(49)

When pilat herde, he hade pyte
And bad ilke man he sulde be stille,
and askid gif þis ihe*s*u be
þ*at* herode hade so soght wi*th* ille.

553. MS. *at* for *þat*.

GALBA.

water wighty askes he
  and wesse his hend by skill:
"I am giltles, als ȝe sall se,
  þis rightwis blode to spill."
þan cried þe Iews all:
  "þareof haue þou no dout,
his blode on vs might fall,
  put vs in and þe out."

(50)

þan gert pilat vnto bar bring
  knightes ful grete plente,
he sais: "his folk vnproues him king,
  and kingdom claymes he;
þarfore with scowrges ȝe sall him ding,
  þus byd I þat it be,
seþen on a cros ȝe sall him hing
  high þat þe men may se;
a thef on aiþer syde
  ȝo do at my biding,
als king of mekill pride
  in middes ȝe sall him hing."

(51)

þase knightes kene laid hand him on
  and led whare he suld dy,
his clathes of him þai don,
  a white towayle in hy,
a purpure mantell þareopon
  and hid his eghen hastily;
þare þai defouled him als a fon
  and king of iews gan cry;

HARLEY.

water wightly askes he
  And wessch his hend by skyll:
"I am gyltles, als yhe sall se,
  þis ryghtwys blode to spyll."
þan cryed þe Iewes all:
  "þareof haue þou no dout,
þis blode on vs myght fall,
  Put vs in & þe out."

(50)

þan gert Pilate vnto bar bryng
  Knyghtes full gret plente,
He says: "his folk vnproues him kyng,
  And kyngdom claymes he;
þarfore *with* skourges yhe sall him dyng,
  þus byd I þat it be,
Sythen on a cross yhe sall him hyng
  Hegh *þat* þe men may se;
A thef on ayther syde
  yhe do at my byddyng,
Als kyng of mykell pryde
  In myddes yhe sall him hyng."

(51)

þase knyghtes kene layd hand him on
  And led whare he suld dy,
His clothes þai dof, on him þai don
  A whyte towayle in hy,
A purpure mantyll þareopon
  And hyd his eghen hastily;
þare þai defouled him als a fon
  And kyng of Iewes gan cry;

603. *þai* erased before *of*; *on* erased before *don*.

SION.

þai sayd : " ya." Water þan asked he
And wesshe his hende by þat skille,
He sayd : " I am giltles, ye se,
þis rightwis man to spille."
þan cryed þire Iewes alle :
" þareof haue þou na doute,
þe gilte mote on vs falle,
Putte vs In and þe oute."

(50)

þan gart Pilate til bar brynge
Kynghtes ful grette plente, [kynge,
He says : " his folke vnproues hym
ffor kyngdome claymes he ;
þarefore with scourges yhe him dynge,
þus wille þe laghe it be,
Sithen on croys yhe sal hym hynge
Heghe þat alle men may see ;
A thefe on ayther syde
yhe hynge hym at my bedynge,
Als kynge of mykel pride
Imyddes heghe sal he hynge."

(51)

þe kynghtes þan his clathes of hente
And band hym tille a piler faste,
And with scharpe scourges aboute hym went [braste ;
And dange hym alto þe hyde
A corked mantil þai hym þan lent
And aboute hym lapped it at þe laste ;
Bott when it cleuede to þai it of rent,
þusgate to pyne hym was þaire caste.

583. Horst. *giltes.*
602. Horst. *bad.*
603. *scharpe :* above.
603. *fast* marked for erasure before *went.*

ADDITIONAL.

þai saide : "ȝhae." þen watre asked he
To wasche his handes by þis skille,
And saide : " giltles I am, ȝhe se,
þis ryghtwise man þus forto spille."
þen saide þes Iuwes alle : [leaf 124.]
" þereof haue þou no dowte,
þe gilte on vs mot falle,
Put vs in & þe oute."

(50)

þen gart pilat to barre brynge
Armed knyghtes gret plente,
And sayde : " þes folke disprufes him kynge,
And ȝit þis kyngedome claymes he ;
With skourges first ȝe sall hym
þus þe lawȝ will þat it be, [swynge,
And þen on crosse ȝe sall hym hynge
So heeȝ þat alle men may hym se ;
A thefe on aythir syde
ȝhe hange at my biddynge,
As kynge of mykill pride
Betwix þaim sall he hynge."

(51)

þes knyghtes on ihesu layde þaire handes [dye ;
And hym þai led whare he sulde
þai bonde hym þare with bittere bandes
And bobbed hym dispitusely ;
A purpull mantill þat þai fonde
Vpon ihesu þai cast in hye ;
Hym to wemme þai walde noȝt wonde,
Bot gaue hym buffetes full felly ;

581. *water :* *was* before *watre* erased.
585. This line written in lower margin of leaf 123, and repeated at top of following page ; but first three words of second line almost faded out.
604. MS. possibly *bebbed.*

GALBA.

a crown of thorn ful sare
to threst þai haue bygun
on his heuid, till þe hare
was all of blude biron;

(52)

On rode þai raised him þan gude spede,
a thef on ayther syde;
aysell and gall raised on a rede
within a spounge þai hide,
vntill his mowth at drink þai bede,
and ihesus sayd þat tyde:
"fader, forgif þir men þaire dede
of þis bale þat I byde."
þe Iews þan þat þare stode
said: "god sun if þou be,
cum doun now fro þat rode,
and we sall trow in þe."

(53)

A blind knight, so thoght þam best,
a spere þai gaf gude spede;
to ihesu side þai gan it threst,
and blude and water out ȝede.
pilat, for folk bi est and west
suld haue mynde of þat dede,
a bill obouen his heuid he fest
þat ilka man myght rede,
latin, Ebrew and gru;
his titill was þusgate:
"þis ilk man es Ihesu,
king of iews," þus he wrate.

(54)

On his left side hanged Iestas
and said to him bi name:
"if þou be god, hethin lat vs pas,
saue þe and vs fro schame!"

HARLEY.

A crowne of thorne full sare
To threst þai haue bygon
On his heued, tyll þe hare
was all of blode byron;

(52)

On rode þai raysed him þan gud spede,
A thefe on ayther syde;
Aysell & gall raysed on a rede
*with*in a spownge þai hyde,
vntyll his mowthe at drynk þai bede,
And Ih*esu*s said þ*at* tyde:
"ffader, forgyf þir men þair dede
Of þis bale þat I byde."
þe Iewes þan þat þare stode
said: "god son if þou be,
Come doune now fro þ*at* rode,
And we sall trow in þe."

(53)

A blynd knyght, so thoght þam best,
A spere þai gaf gud spede;
To Ih*esu* syde þai gan it threst,
And blode and wat*er* out yhede.
Pilate, for folk by est & west
Suld haue mynde of þ*at* dede,
A byll obouen his heued he fest
þ*at* ilka man myht rede,
Latyn, Ebrew and grew;
His tytell was þusgate:
"þis ilk man es Ihesu,
kyng of Iewes," þus he wrate.

(54)

On his left syde hang Iesmas
And said to him bi name:
"If þou be god, hethen lat vs pas,
Saue þe & vs fro schame!"

SION.

Sone ogayne þai hym cledde,
And a croun of thornes thrested on his heuede;
And forthe þan þai hym ledde 611
Whare he sulde be demed to deede;

(52)

To raise hym on rode þai gun þaime [sped
And hyngede a thefe on ayther syde;
[1] Ayssel and galle raysed on a rede
withIn a spounge þai gun hyde
And tille his mouthe þat drynk gun [bede,
And Ihesu sayde þat tyde:
"ffader, forgyf þam þis mysdede
þat I of þam habide." 620
þe Iewes þat þare stode [1 leaf 22.]
Sayde: "goddes sone if þou be,
Come now doun fra þe rode,
And we sall trow on þe." 624

(53)

þai gert longys a spere take,
A blynd knyght of þat route;
And euen tille his hert he strake, 627
And water and blode þan come oute.
Pilate, of dome wittenes to make,
A titel gert write to doute
þat euen obouen his heued stake,
þat alle myght rede aboute, 632
Latyn, Gru and Ebru;
his titel was þusgate:
"he þis, þis ilk es Ihesu,
kyng of Iewes," þus he wrate. 636

(54)

On goddes left hand hynges Iesmas
þat sayd to Ihesu by name:
"If þou be goddes sone, lat vs pas,
saue þe and vs fra schame!" 640

613. MS. *þai hym þai gun*, with *hym* marked for erasure.

ADDITIONAL.

A corone of thorne full sore
þai cast vpon his heued,
þat felle & flesshe and hore
Was all *with* blode beweued; 612

(52)

On rode þai raysed hym, as we rede,
A theue þai honge on aythire side;
Aysell & galle vpon a rede
*With*in a sponge þai gan it hyde,
Put to his mouthe, drynke þai hi*m* bede, 617
And þen sayde ihe*su* þus þat tyde:
"ffadr*e*, forgife þai*m* þis myssedede
þat þai to me do in þair*e* p*ri*de."
þe Iuwes þe*re* þai stode 621
Sayde: "gods son if þou be,
Come done nowe of þis rode,
And we sall trowe on þe." 624

(53)

To longeus on betoke a spere, [lf. 124, bk.]
A blynde knyght was in þat rowte;
To ihe*su* herte he gon it bere, 627
And watr*e* & blode anon went oute
And sprent on longeus eghen þe*re*,
And sone he sawe *with*outen doute.
Pilat a title *with*outen fere 631
Gart write þat men myght aboute,
Latyn, grewe and ebrewe,
Abouen gods hede he wrot:
"Of nazaret þis is ihe*su*
And kynge of Iuwes I wot." 636

(54)

On gods lefte hande honge Iesmas,
To ihe*su* þus he saide be name:
"If þou be gods son, lat vs passe,
And also shilde þiselue fro shame!"

GALBA.

and on his right hand hanged dismas,
his fere fast gan he blame:
"als þou haues serued so þou has,
and I may say þe same; 644
ouer litill god þou dredes,
we haue þis for oure gilt,
and he for his gude dedes
full wrangwisly es spilt." 648

(55)

Vnto Ihesu þan gan he pray: [leaf 61]
"als þow es high Iustise,
when þou cumes in þi regne for ay,
mend me with þi mercyse." 652
and Ihesus sone to him gan say
ane answer on þis wise:
"I hete þe forto be þis day
with me in paradyse." 656
at vnderon was þis done,
omang þam wex it mirk,
þe son wex dim ful sone,
þe vail rafe in þe kirk. 660

(56)

In þis ilk stori als we rede,
who will it vnderstand,
ane angell was sene do þat dede
with a swerd bright brinand, 664
he said: "I cum, whosom tase hede,
als witnes and warand
of Ihesu ded þat ȝe se blede,
nayled thurgh fote and hand." 668
Ihesus said: "in þi hend,
my fader of mightes maste,
my saul now sall I send."
with þis he gaf þe gaste. 672

HARLEY.

And on his ryght hand hynged Dismas,
His fere fast gan he blame:
"Als þou has serued so þou has,
And I may say þe same; 644
Ouer lytell god þou dredes,
we haue þis for our gylt,
And he for his gud dedes
ffful wrangwisly es spylt." 648

(55)

Vnto Ihesu gan he pray:
"Als þou es heghe Iustyse,
when þou comes in þi regne for ay,
Mend me *with* þi mercyse." 652
And Ihe*sus* sone to him gan say
And answer on þis wyse:
"I hete þe forto be þis day
With me in paradyse." 656
At vnderon was þis done,
Omang þam wex it myrk,
þe son wex dyme full sone,
þe vaile rafe in þe kyrk. 660

(56)

In þis ilk story als we rede,
who will it vnderstand,
Ane aungell was sene do þ*at* dede
with a swerd bryght brynand, 664
He said: "I come, whasom takes hede,
Als witnes and warand
Of Ihe*su* dede þ*at* yhe se blede,
Nayled thurgh fote & hand." 668
Ihe*sus* said: "in þi hend,
My fader of myghtes mast,
My saule now sall I send." [leaf 209, bk.]
with þis he gaf þe gaste. 672

653. Last stroke of *h* in *Ihesus* omitted.

SION.

Opon his ryght hand hynges dismas,
þat fast his felagho gun blame:
"Als þou has serued als þou has,
And I may say þe same;
ffulle litel god þou dredes,
We suffir for oure gilte, [leaf 22, bk.]
And he for his gode dedes
fful wrangwisly es spilte."

(55)

And Dismas gun to Ihesu pray:
"Als þou ert heghe Iustys,
In þi regne when þou comes for ay,
Thyngke on me, kynge rightwys."
Ihesu agayne tille hym gun say
And answerde on þis wise:
"Sothefastly þou sal be to-day
With me In Paradise."
At vndren þis was done,
þe son nyght wex myrke,
Quyte insonder alsone
þe vayle raue in þe kirke.

(56)

And in þe stori als we rede,
Wha wille it vndirstande,
Anne aungel was sene done þat dede
With a swerd brynnande,
And sayde þere wordes ar he yhede:
"Here als wittnes I stande
Of Ihesu deede þat I see blede
And nayled thurght fote and hande."
Ihesu sayd: "in þi hende,
ffadir of myght maste,
My saule to þe mote be bygend."
With þat he gaf þe gaste.

666. Horst. *stand.*

ADDITIONAL.

[1]And on his right hande hange Dismas,
And fast his felawȝ gon he blame:
"As þou erte worthy so þou has,
And I also may say þe same;
ffull litill god þou dredes,
ffull falsely was he spilte,
He dyes for his gud dedes,
And we dye for oure gilte."

(55)

Dismas gon to ihesu pray:
"As þou arte kynge & hye iustice,
In þi blisse when þou comest for ay,
On me haue mynde, þou kynge
ryghtwise."
Ihesu agayne to hym gon say
And mekely answerde on þis wise:
"þou sall surely be þis ilke day
In ioyfull place in paradise."
At vndre þis was done,
þe day as nyght wex darke,
Siche erthe-dynne was þere sene,
þat it brake house & kirke.

(56)

And in þis story as we rede,
þere befelle a wondre thynge,
An aungelle come vnto þis dede [lf. 125]
And in his hande a swerde bren-
And ihesu saide in his manhede [ynge;
Vnto his fadre, heuene kynge:
"ffadre þat all wrought in godhede,
Here nowe at þis ilke endynge
Into þi handes I beteche,
þou fadre of myghtes most,
Mi saule." & with þat speche
Anon he ȝelde þe gost.

[1] On the right-hand margin of this page, the words "Francis Gris Francis" are scribbled in a much later hand.

GALBA.

(57

Centurio said, when he suld dy,
vnto þe iews ful right:
"þis ilk was god sun sekerly,
þat þus to ded es dight."
and many oþer þat stode him by
and saw þis selkuth sight
knocked on þaire brestes & cried [mercy
and mendid þam at þaire might.
of þis wonderful dede
when sir pilate herd say,
for dole and als for drede
he ette no mete þat day.

(58)

þan pilat sembled þe Iews all
and said: "what es ȝowre rede?
swilk ferlis wist we neuer bifall
als fell in Ihesu ded."
þai said: "þir clerkes þe clippes it call
þat made þe sun so rede."
he asked: "what made þe stanes so small
þat none might stir of þe stede?
also, what raf þe vayl
þat in ȝowre temple hang?
vs all to wrotherhail
I dout we haue done wrang."

(59)

Centurio come furth by þan
and oþer þan with him ware;
till all þe iews þus þai bigan
to tell þis ferly fare:
"of wreghing of þis rightwisman
ȝe may ȝow drede ful sare;
þe sun at his ded wex all wan
wele thre mile way or mare,

HARLEY.

(57)

Centurio said, when he suld dy,
vnto þe Iewes full ryght:
"þis ilk was god son sykerly,
þat þus to ded es dyght."
And many other þat stode him by
And saw þis selcouth syght
Knocked on þair brestes & cryed mercy
And mended þam at þair myght.
Of þis wonderfull dede
when sir Pilate herd say,
ffor dole and als for dred
He ette no mete þat day.

(58)

þan Pilate sembled þe Iewes all
And said: "what es yhour rede?
Swilk ferlies wist we neuer bifall
Als fell in Ihesu ded."
þai said: "sir, clerkes þe clyppes it [call
þat made þe son so red."
He asked: "what made þe stanes so small
þat none myght styr of þe stede?
Allso, what raue þe vayle
þat in yhour temple hang?
vs all to wrotherhail
I dout we haue done wrang."

(59)

Centurio come forth bi þan
And other þat with him ware;
Till all þe Iewes þus þai bigan
To tell þis ferly fare:
"Of wreghyng of þis ryghtwisman
yhe may yhow dred full sare;
þe sonne at his ded wex all wan
wele thre myle way or mare,

SION.

(57)

Centurio sayde, when he sulde dye
And þe sone wex myrke als nyght:
"He þis was goddes sone sykirly,
þat þus to dede was dyghte." 676
And many other þat stode hym by,
þat sawe þat selly sighte, [mercy
Knockede on þaire brestes and cryede
[1]And amended þaime at þaire myghte.
Of þis wondirfulle deede [[1] leaf 23]
When sir Pilate hard say,
ffor sorowe and for dreede
He eete na mete þat day. 684

ADDITIONAL.

(57)

Centurio saide, whan he sulde dye
And sawe þe son wex darke as nyght:
"þis man was gods son sikirly, 676
þat on þis wise to dede is dight."
And mony outhire þat stude hym bye
Of Iuwes þat sawe þat sely syght
ffell don to grounde & ast mercy
And mened crist all þat þai myght.
Of þis wondrefull dede 681
When pilat herde þus say
ffor sorowe & for grete drede
He ete no mete þat day. 684

SION.

(58)

Pilate yhede til þire Iewes alle
And sayd: "what es yhoure rede?
Swilke selcouthes wist we neuer by- [falle
Als now at Ihesu deede."
þai sayde: "þire clerkes þe clippes calle
þat þe sone made dym and rede."
Quod Pilate: "what brak youre stanes swa smalle
þat nane myght stire of stede? 692
What raue intw yhoure wayle
þat in yhoure temple hange?
Vs alle till illerhayle
I doute we haf done wrange." 696

ADDITIONAL.

(58)

Pilat ȝede to þe Iuwes alle [rede?
And saide: "sires, what is ȝoure
Siche maruayles wiste we neuere falle
As dos nowe here for ihesu dede."
þai saide: "þes clerkes þe clippes it calle 689
þat makes þe son so blody rede."
"Whi cleue þes stones þus of þis walle?
þere may no stone stande in his [stede,
All shakes bothe heeȝ & lowe
þat in þe temple honge;
It is vengaunce I trowe,
I drede I haue done wronge." 696

SION.

(59)

Centurio come forthe by þan
And alle þat with hym ware;
Tille alle þire Iewes þai bygan
To telle of þis wondir fare: 700
"Of coupynge of þis rightwisman
yhe may yhow drede fulle sare;
þe sone at his deede wex dym and wan
Wele thre myle way and mare, 704

693. Horst. *intw(a)*.

ADDITIONAL.

(59)

Centurio þare come forthe þan [were;
And alle þe folke þat with hym
Till alle þe Iuwes þus he byganne
To telle þe sight þat he sawe þere:
"[1] ffor sleynge of þis ryghtwise man
I leue ȝhe shalle forthynke it sore;
þe sonne at his dede wex alle wanne
And lasted a myle way so & more,
[[1] leaf 125, bk.]

GALBA.

þe stanes in sunder brac,
þe erth trembild and quaked,
with noyse als man it spac,
slike mane for him it maked;

(60)

Ded men er risen out of þaire graue
right in oure aller sight;
þarfore we trow and hope we haue
he was god son ful right."
als þai all þus togeder straue,
to pilat come a knyght,
and ihesu cors fast gan he craue
þat þus to ded was dight;
Pilat granted þat bone
till ioseph of aramathy;
and he fra cros ful sone
toke done þat blisced body.

(61)

He wand þat cors with gude entent
in sendell new and clene
and layd it in his monument
whare nane byfore had bene.
þan said þe iews with ane assent:
"als ill we sall him tene."
men forto seke him haue þai sent,
and he dar noght be sene.
þat quest þat gan him deme
trew in sposage born,
and rightwis nichodeme,
to sla all haue þai sworn;

(62)

And forto sla all haue þai thoght
þat helid of ihesu ware;
þai bad sone þat men spare þam noght,
so war þai greued sare.

HARLEY.

þe stanes in sonder brak,
þe erth trembled & quaked,
with noys als man it spak,
Slyke mane for him it maked;

(60)

Ded men er rysen out of þair g*ra*ue
Ryght in our aller syght;
þarfore we trow & hope we haue
He was god son full ryght."
Als þai all þus togyder straue,
To Pilate come a knyght,
And Ihesu cors fast gan he craue
þ*at* þus to ded was dyght;
Pilate gr*a*unted þ*at* bone
Till Ioseph of Aramathi;
And he fra þe cross full sone
Toke doune þ*at* blyssed body.

(61)

He wand þ*at* cors *with* gud entent
In sendell new & clene
And layd it in his monument
whare nane bifore had bene.
þan said þe Iewes *with* ane assent:
"Als ill we sall him tene."
Men forto seke him haue þai sent,
And he dar noght be sene.
þ*at* quest þ*at* gan him deme
Trew in sposage borne,
And ryghtwise Nichodeme,
To sla all haue þai sworne;

(62)

And forto sla all haue þai thoght
þ*at* heled of Ihesu ware;
þai bad sone þ*at* men spare þam noght,
So war þai greued sare.

707. Horst. *uoys.*

SION.

þe stannes in sundir brake,
þe erthe tremelde and qwakede
And made noys als man it spake,
Swilke mane of hym it makede;

(60)

Deede men er rysen oute of graue
Here in oure aller sight;
Wharefore we trowe and hoope we [haue
He was goddes son full righte."
[1]And als þai þus togyder straue,
Tille Pilate come a knyghte,
And Ihesu body gun he craue
þat þus tille deede was dight;
And Pilate graunted þat bone
Tille Ioseph of Aramathi; [[1] lf. 23, bk.]
And he fra croyce alson
Tuke doun þat blyssed body.

(61)

Sythen he wand hym withe gode en- [ten
In sendel newe and clene
And layd hym in his newe moniment
þare nane byfore had bene.
þe Iewes sayde þan withe alle assente:
"Als ille we sall hym tene."
And hym to seke men had þai sent,
Bot he durst noght be sene.
þe quest þat gun hym deme
Trewe in sposage born,
And ryghtwyse Nichodeme,
at slaa alle had þai sworn;

(62)

And slaa alle þas had þai thoght
þat helede thurgh Ihesu ware;
þai hidde þam þat þai fand þam noght,
þareat þaime tened sare.

713. This line is repeated at top of next page (lf. 23 bk.), with *gydir* instead of *gyder*.
714. *kynge* marked for erasure before *knyghte*. 721. Horst. *enten(t)*.

ADDITIONAL.

ȝour walles asondre cleued,
þo erthe trembled & quaked,
Many one salle be greuyd
ffor þis fare þat is maked;

(60)

Ded men are rysen oute of þaire graue
ffull openly here in ȝour sight;
Wharefore we hope & trouthe we haue
Certys þat he was gods son right."
And as þai þus togidre straue,
Vnto pilat þere come a knyght,
And ihesu body gan he craue
þat þus be dome to dethe was dight;
Pilat graunt hym his bone,
Ioseph of aramathy;
And fro crosse did sone
Take of þat blissed body.

(61)

Sithen he hym wonde with gude en- [tent
In clothes þat were fayre & clene
And layde hym in a monument
þere neuere man before hade bene.
þe Iuwes ȝede by one assent
þat in þaire folyes were full kene;
A newe bargayne ȝit haue þai ment
þat sulde turne þaim to trye & tene.
þe quest þat ihesu gan deme
As man in wedloke borne,
And also Nichodeme,
þaire ded þe Iuwes haue sworne;

(62)

And forto sle þaim alle þai thought
þat thurgh ihesu helede wore;
Bot þai were hidde, þai fonde þaim noȝt,
þerefore þe Iuwes forthought full [sore.

733. *þai* above *bydene* which has been erased.

GALBA.

Sone when þai war togeder broght,
þe maysters of þaire lare,
to þe temple nichodem þam soght,
to speke he wald noght spare,
he said: "ȝe wers þan wode,
how dar ȝe negh þis stede
and ȝowre handes ful of blode
of rightwis ihesus ded?"

(63)

[1] þe iews þan answerd al in fere:
"þou outcast of all men, [[1] lf. 61, bk.]
how dar þou negh þis tempill nere,
his frend se we þe ken?
sen þat þou held his dedis so dere,
his pese we þe biken,
and his lare light opon þe here."
he answerd and said: "amen!"
when all þir saws war said,
Ioseph of Aramathy
þat him in graue had laid
come in al opynly;

(64)

He said: "lordinges, als god ȝow saue,
whi er ȝe wrath with me?
for I layd ihesus in his graue
þat ȝe hanged on rode-tre?
with ful grete wrang slane him ȝe haue,
þat sal men here and se;
when ȝe bifor sir pilat straue,
als ȝe said sall it be;
when pilat wesch his hend
him giltles forto make,
ȝe bad on ȝow decend
his blude, vengance and wrake."

HARLEY.

Sone when þai war togyder broght,
þe maist*er*s of þair lare,
To þe temple Nichodeme þam soght,
To speke he wald noght spare,
He said: "yhe wers þan wode,
How dar yhe negh þis stede
And yho*ur* handes full of blode
Of ryghtwys Ih*esu*s dede?"

(63)

þe Iewes þan answerd all in fere:
"þou outcast of all men,
How dar þou negh þis temple nere,
His frend se we þe ken?
Sen þ*at* þou held his dedes so dere,
. His pese we þe byken,
And his lare lyght opon þe here."
He answerd & said: "ameN!"
when all þir sawes war sayd,
Ioseph of Aramathy
þ*at* him in graue had layd
Come in all openly;

(64)

He said: "lordynges, als god yhow [saue,
whi er yhe wrathe wi*th* me?
ffor I layd Ih*esu*s in his graue
þ*at* yhe hanged on rode-tre?
with full gret wrang slane him yhe [haue,
þ*at* sall men here & se;
when yhe bifor sir Pilate straue,
Als yhe said sall it be;
when Pilate wesch his hend
Him gyltles forto make,
Yhe bad on yhow descend [leaf 210]
His blode, vengance & wrake."

749. *dedis*: first *d* like *b*.

751. MS. possibly *apon*.

SION.

And when þai ware togeder broght,
þe maysters of þaire lare,
at þe temple Nichodeme þam soght,
To speke wald noght spare,
He sayde: "yhe wors and wode,
How dare yhe negh þis stede
and yhoure handes fulle of blode
Of rightwise Ihesu deede?" [leaf 24]

(63)

þe Iewes hym answerde alle in fere:
"þa outecaste of alle men,
How dare þa neghe þis temple nere,
His frende sithen we þe ken?
His pees motte light on þe here."
And he answarde: "Amen,"
And sayde "alswa;" and þai gun answer:
"His pees we þe byken."
And when þai had þus sayde,
Ioseph of Armathy
þan hym in graue had layde
Come forthe þan appertly;

(64)

He sayd: "lordynges, als god yhow saue,
Why er yhe wrathe with me?
ffor I layde Ihesu in my graue
þat yhe hyngede on rode-tre?
with fulle grette wrange slayne hym ye haue,
And that hereaftir sal men see;
When yhe for hym with Pilate straue,
Als yhe sayd mot it be;
When Pilate wesshe his hende
Hym giltles forto make,
Yhe sayd on yhow dessende
His blode, vengaunce and wrake."

740. Horst. (*he*) *wald.*
746. Horst. *þou.*

ADDITIONAL.

Ȝit when þai were alle samen brought,
þe gret maistres of þe lore, [[1] leaf 126.]
[1] To þe temple Nychodeme þai sought,
And þus he saide & nolde noȝt spare:
"Ȝhe felons wars þen wode,
Howe dare ȝhe negh þis stede
And ȝour handes full of blode
Of rightwise ihesu dede?"

(63)

þe Iuwes hym answerde alle yfere:
"ffor ihesu þou myssays alle men,
Howe dare þou come vnto vs here?
þou art his man, full wele we ken,
His pees myght light on þe so dere."
And Nichodeme answerde: "Amen."
And þai for skorne sayd alle yfere:
"Till hym platly we þe bekenne."
And whan þai þus hade saide,
Ioseph of Aramathy
þat ihesu in graue hade layde
Come forth apertly;

(64)

He saide: "sires, so god ȝowe saue,
By what skille are ȝe wrothe with me?
ffor I haue laide ihesu in graue
þat ȝe so hanged on a tre?
With gret wronge slayne hym ȝe haue,
And þat hereafter sall men se;
When ȝhe with pilat so gan raue,
Ryght as ȝowe liste right so did ȝe;
Whan pilat wasshe his hende
Hymselue giltles to make,
ȝhe saide on ȝowe descende
His blode, vengaunce & wrake."

747. Horst. *þou* for *þa.*
762. Horst. *after.*

 The Jews caught Joseph of Arimathea and cast him into a prison that had no windows and but one door.

GALBA.

(65)

Omang þam þare was Ioseph tane,
in presoun þai him kast,
had no window and dore bot ane,
and þat þai sperd ful fast; 772
þai said halely he suld be slane
when þaire sabot war past;
on þe dore þai set þaire seles ilk ane
with lokkes þat wele wald last.
" for he gan ih*es*u graue," 777
þai sai, " fer in þe felde
his beriele sall he haue,
wilde bestes his banes to welde."

HARLEY.

(65)

Omang þam þar*e* was Ioseph tane,
In p*re*soune þai him kast,
Had no wyndow and dore bot ane,
And þ*at* þai sperd full fast; 772
þai said halely he suld be slane
when þair sabot war past;
On þe dore þai sett þair seles ilk ane
wi*th* lokkes þ*at* wele wald last.
"ffor he gan Ih*esu* graue," 777
þai say, " fer in þe feld
His beriele sall he haue,
wyld bestes his banes to weld."

GALBA.

(66)

Efter þaire sabot day alssone
of iosep haue þai thoght:
" he sal be ded bi son and mone
for þat werk he has wroght." 784
þai hied þam withowten hone
and wend him furth haue broght,
þai bad þe dore tite be vndone,
bot Iosep fand þai noght. 788
" allas!" þan gan þai say,
" þis es a wonder thing,
how might he win oway
þus in oure awin kepyng?" 792

HARLEY.

(66)

Aft*er* þair sabot day alssone
Of Ioseph haue þai thoght:
" He sall be ded be son & mone
ffor þ*at* werk he has wroght." 784
þai hyed þam wi*th*outen hone
And wend him furth haue broght,
þai bad þe dore tyte be vndone,
Bot Ioseph fand þai noght. 788
" Allas!" þan gan þai say,
" þis es a wonder thyng,
How myght he wyn oway
þus in our awen kepyng?" 792

GALBA.

(67)

þan come a knight of þam þat woke
ihesus in þe monument:
" þat body þat ȝe vs bitoke
es resin and fro vs went; 796
þe erth trembled and al toschoke,
ane angell doun was sent,

HARLEY.

(67)

þan come a knyght of þam þ*at* woke
Ih*esus* in þe monument:
" þat body þ*at* yhe vs bitoke
Es rysen and fro vs went; 796
þe erth trembled & all toschoke,
Ane aungell doune was sent,

SION.

(65)

Omange þire Iewes Ioseph was tane,
In prisoun þai hym kast,
þat wyndowles was and dore bot ane,
And þat þai sperd ful faste;
Hard þai hym thrette he suld be slaane
ffra þaire sabbaut ware past;
þe dor*e* to kepe knyghtes ware gane,
Meeteles þai gert hym fast. [lf. 24, bk.]
"ffor he gun Ih*esu* craue,"
þai sayde alle, "in þe felde
Na beryels sal he haue,
Wilde bestes his banes sald weld."

(66)

When þair sabbaut was comen and gane,
Ioseph foregat þai noght;
Alle þai hym demed forto be slayne
for þat werk þat he wroght.
Vntil þe presoun þai yhed onane
And wende hym forthe haue broght;
þai oppend þe dore, bot þare was nane,
þai fand noght þat þai soght.
Ilk an til other gun say:
"þis es a wondir thyng,
how myght he wynne away
þus in owre awune kepyng?"

(67)

þan sayde a knyght of þam þat woke
Ih*esu* in þe monument:
"þe body to kepe þat yhe vs tuke,
he ras and fra vs went;
þe erthe trembled and al toschoke,
Ane aungel doun was sent,

775. *knyghtes*: *n* above line.
775. *gare* marked for erasure before *gane*.
792. Horst. *awine*.
794. Horst, *moniment*.

ADDITIONAL.

(65)

þo Iuwes to Ioseph ran anon
And in a depe p*ri*son hym cast,
þ*er*e nas wyndowe ne dore bot one,
And þat þai speryd full wondr*e* fast;
ffast þai thrette Ioseph to slon
ffro tyme þat pair*e* sobot were past;
To kepe þe dore þe knyghtes are gon,
Metlos þ*er*e gart þai Ioseph fast.
ffor he ih*esu* gan graue, [leaf 126, bk.]
þai saide þat in þe felde
No beriynge suld he haue,
Bestes his bones sulde welde.

(66)

When pair*e* sabot was comen & gone,
Ioseph to brynge forth þan þai thought;
Deth þai demyd Ioseph apon
ffor þe warke þat he hade wrought.
To þair*e* p*ri*son þai went anon
And wend forthe Ioseph till haue brought;
þai opned þe dore & made gret mone,
þai fonde noȝt Ioseph þat þai sought.
Ilk on till outhir*e* gan say:
"þis is a wondre thynge,
Howe he myght wyn away
þus in our*e* awen kepynge."

(67)

þen come a knyght þat ih*esu* wooke
When he was layde in monume*nt*:
"þe body," he saide, "þat ȝhe vs toke
To kepe is resen & fro vs went;
þe erthe trembled & al toshouke,
An aungell bright doune was þ*er*e sent,

786. *brought* above *tane* which has been erased.

GALBA.

we dared for drede and durst noght [luke,
ne to him tak no tent;
þe mekill stane þat lay
his rising forto let
þat angell put oway
and þareopon him sett. 804

(68)

He bad wemen be noght affraid
þat war of his menȝe:
"for he es resen, þarfore bese payd,
Cumes nere þe suth to se! 808
þis es þe place whare he was laid,
go biddes his appostels be,
he sal be sene als he þam said
þis day in galile." 812
þe iews grete wonder thoght,
"lifes Ihesus?" gan þai say,
"trayturs, we trow ȝow noght,
sertes he es ded for ay." 816

(69)

þe knightes gaf answer ful swith
till all þat cumpany:
"what wonder werkes gan he ȝow kith
here whils he wond ȝow by! 820
he musterd miracles many sith
omang all þis Iewry;
how suld ȝe leue or till vs lyth
þat left him so lightly? 824
when he was laid in graue,
we kepid him, als ȝe wate;
schortly lorn him we haue,
he es resen and gane his gate. 828

(70)

And als wele wate we ȝisterday
how ioseph presond was,

HARLEY.

we dared for dred & durst noght luke,
Ne to him tak no tent; 800
þe mykell stane þ*at* lay
His rysyng forto lett
þat aungell put oway
And þareopon him sett. 804

(68)

He bad wemen be noght affrayd
þat war of his meneyhe:
"ffor he es rysen, þarfor bese payd,
Comes nere þe soth to se! 808
þis es þe place whare he was layd,
Ga byddes his appestels be,
He sall be sene als he þam sayd
þis day in Galile." 812
þe Iewes gret wonder thoght,
"Lyfes Ihe*sus*?" gan þai say,
"Traytou*r*s, we trow yhow noght,
Sertes he es ded for ay." 816

(69)

þe knyghtes gaf answer full swythe
Till all þ*at* company: [kythe
"what wonder werkes gan he yhow
Here whils he wond yhow by!
He must*er*d miracles many sythe 821
Omang all þis Iewry;
How suld yhe leue or tyll vs lythe
þ*at* left him so lyghtly? 824
When he was layd in graue,
we keped him, als yhe wate;
Schortly lorne him we haue,
He es rysen & gane his gate. 828

(70)

And als wele wate we yhisterday
How Ioseph p*re*sond was,

SION.

We durked for drede, durst noght luke,
Ne take tille hym na tent;
þe mekel stane þat lay
his rysyng for to lette
lyghtly he put oway
And þaroppon hym sette.

(68)

[1] Wemen þare was to þaime he sayd*e*
þat ware of his meynyhe, [[1] leaf 25[2]]
He bad þaime be noght for hym afrayde:
"He es rysen, come nere and see!
þis es þe place þare þai hym laud*e*,
Ga byd hys appostels blithe be,
He sal be sene als he þaime sayd*e*
þis day in Galile."
þise Iewes grette wonder thoght*e*,
"Lyues Ih*esu*?" gun þai say,
"Traytours, we trow yhow noght*e*,
He es deed*e* for euer and ay."

(69)

þhire knyghtes gaf answare als swythe
Tille alle þe company:
"what wondir warkes gun he kythe
whils he was here yhow by,
And mustred miracles many sithe
Tille alle þe Iewery;
How suld yhe trowe or tille vs lithe
þat left hym lightly?
Ih*esu* was layd in graue,
we kepyd hym, als yhe wate;
Scortly lost hym we haue,
He es noght þare nanegate.

(70)

And als wele wate we yhistirday
How Ioseph prisound*e* was,

[2] On this page (as in page 1 of the piece) the initial letters of lines are touched with red.
806. *his* above line.

ADDITIONAL.

We dared for drede, we durst noȝt loke,
We wende ilk one till haue bene [shent;
þat ilke gret stone þat lay
His rysynge forto lette
Lyghtly he put away
And þ*er*evpon hym sette.

(68)

þis angell vnto wym*m*e saide
þat þidr*e* were comen of ih*esu* [meyne:
"Loke þat ȝe be noȝt amayde;
Ih*esu* is risen, come narre & see!
þis is þe place þ*er*e þai hym laide,
Goo biddys his postles redy be,
He sall be sene as he þai*m* saide
þis ilke same day in Galile."
þes Iuwes gret wondr*e* thought,
"Lyues ih*esu*?" gon þai say,
"Traytou*r*, we trowe þe noȝt,
ffor he is ded for ay."

(69)

[1]þes knyghtes answerd þen full swythe
And saide vnto þat company: [[1] lf. 127]
"Siche wondr*e* warkes gon he kythe
Whil þat he was ȝow here fast by,
And shiwed myracles mony sithe
Vnto þe peple of Iuwery;
Howe sulde ȝe trowe or till vs lithe
þat mystrowed hym so pure lightly,
Ih*esu* þat was in graue?
Make ȝhe it neu*er*e so hote,
Shortly lost hym we haue,
Wher*e* he is we ne wote.

(70)

Also we wote þat ȝistirday
Howe þat Ioseph here p*r*isoned was,

807. An erasure before *ȝe*.

809. Horst. *layde*.
827. *als* marked for erasure before *we*.

GALBA.

and how ȝe kepid him vnder kay
for þat he suld noght pas;
we wate wele he es went oway,
þarfore þis thing we ass:
bides þam bring Ioseph if þai may
þat him in kepeing has,
and we sall bring ihesus
withowten langer threpe."
þai say: "bring him till vs,
and we sall bring Ioseph."

(71)

[1] þe knightes said: "warand will we
þarfore to lyf and dy [[1] leaf 62]
þat Iosep es in his cete
at hame in aramathi,
and ihesus gase in Galyle
with his appostels him by."
when þe iews herd it þus suld be,
þai drowped and war drery;
omans þam sone þai say:
"bot if þir wordes fall,
oure folk sall leue oure lay
and trow on ihesu all."

(72)

A sowm of tresore haue þai tane
and to þe knightes þai pay,
and charges þam by ane
þat þai sall algate say,
þat when þai war to sleping gane
and in þaire beddes lay,
his appostels put oway þe stane
and stale þe cors oway;
þe mone made þam faine,
þai toke it ilka dele,
and furth þai talde þis traine,
and ilk man trowed þam wele.

HARLEY.

And how yhe keped him vnder kay
ffor þat he suld noght pas;
we wate wele he es went oway,
þarfor þis thing we ass:
Bydes þam bryng Ioseph if þai may
þat him in kepyng has,
And we sall bryng Ihesus
w*ith*outen langer threpe."
þai say: "bryng him tyll vs,
And we sall bryng Iosepe."

(71)

þe knyghtes sayd: "warand will we
þarfor to lyf and dy
þat Ioseph es in his cete
At hame in Aramathy,
And Ih*esus* gase in Galile
w*ith* his appostels him by."
when þe Iewes herd it þ*us* suld be,
þai drowped & war drery;
Omanges þam sone þai say:
"Bot if þir wordes fall,
Our folk sall leue our lay
And trow on Ih*esu* all."

(72)

A sowme of tresore haue þai tane
And to þe knyghtes þai pay,
And charges þam by ane & ane
þ*at* þai sall allgate say,
þ*at* when þai war to slepyng gane
And in þair beddes lay,
His appostels put oway þe stane
And stale þe cors oway;
þe mone made þam fayne,
þai toke it ilka dele,
And furth þai tald þis trayne, [leaf 210, bk.]
And ilk man trowed þam wele.

SION.

And how yhe kepyd hym vndir kay
ffor he ne sulde fra yow þas;
we ne wate how he es wonden oway,
Botte a thynge we yhow as:
Latte þaime brynge Ioseph if þai may,
þat hym in kepynge has,
And we salle brynge Ihesus."
And hereon gun þai threpe:
"And we graunt, brynge hym tille vs,
And we wille brynge Ioseph."

ADDITIONAL.

And howe ȝe kepid hym vndre kay
Because he sulde noȝt fro ȝowe passe;
We wote not whethire he be away,
Bot one thynge aske we in þis case:
Lat brynge forth Ioseph if ȝe may,
He þat of Ioseph kepynge has,
And we sall brynge Iesus."
And þai agayne gan threpe:
"We graunt, brynge hym till vs,
And we sall brynge Ioseph."

(71)

SION.

þise knyghtes sayde: "warand wille [we
Byfore alle þe Iewery, [lf. 25, bk.]
Ioseph es in his Cete
At hame in Aramathy,
And Ihesu es in Galile,
þis wate we witterly."
When þe Iewes herd it þus sulde be,
þai dredde þaime grettly;
Ilk an tille othir gun say:
"Botte if þire wordes falle,
þis folke sal leue oure lay
And trow on Ihesu alle."

ADDITIONAL.

þe knyghtes saide: "þis proue will we
Here byfor all þis Iuwery
þat Ioseph is in his Cyte
At home in pees in Aramathi,
And ihesus is in Galiley,
þis wote we wele alle witirly."
When þe Iuwes wist it sulde so bee,
Sore þai þam dred þai sulde abye;
Ilk on till outhire gan say:
"Lat þes wordes done falle,
þis folke sall lefe oure lay
And leue on ihesu alle."

(72)

SION.

þe Iewes had grette tresoure tane
To þe knyghtes forto pay,
And examynd þe knyghtes ane be ane
And bad þaime algate say
How, when þai ware to slepe gane
And in þaire beddes lay,
His apostels putte oway þe stane
And stale þe body oway;
Of þe mone ware þai fayne
And toke it ilke a dele,
And aquytte þaime be þis trayne,
And alle men trowed þaime wele.

ADDITIONAL.

[1]þe Iuwes toke tresoure full gude wone
Vnto þos knyghtes forto pay,
And gart examyn one by one [1 leaf 127 bk.]
And þus þai bad þaim forto say:
þat when þai were to slepynge gon
And whiles þai in þaire slepynge [lay,
His postles put away þe stone
And stale þe body so away;
Of þe money were þai fayne
And tolde it ilka dele,
And quit þaim by þis trayne,
And alle men trowed þaim wele.

858. *layde* erased before *lay*.

833. *wh* erased after *we*.

GALBA.

(73)

[1]To ierusalem þat riche cete
 thre prestes þaire way has tane,
vnto þe temple þai went al thre
 and cald þe klerkes onane,
þai said: "Iesus, þis warand we,
 þat ȝe with wrang haue slane,
on þe mount of oliuet þis day sat he
 and his appostels ilk ane;
we saw þam in a rowt
 þat he was won to teche,
þai sat all him obout
 and þir wordes gan he p*re*che:

(74)

'Thurgh all werld I will ȝe wend,
 and wisely luke ȝe wake
and baptiss all men with ȝowre hend
 þat trowth trewly will take;
þat trowes and er for cristen kend
 safe I sall þam make;
and all bese dampned withowten end
 þat right trowth will forsake.'
in þat stede þam omang
 he stegh till heuyn vpright,
and we loked efter him lang
 till clowdes reft vs þe sight."

(75)

Hereof þe iews awonderd ere,
 þai sai: "þus sall noght blin,
þis þat ȝe say all sall ȝe swere."
 a boke þai bid bring in,
þai sayd: "þat may do vs no dere,
 gladly we will bigin;
bot we wald þarof witnes bere,
 for soth we suld haue syn."

[1] This letter is ver large and red.

HARLEY.

(73)

[1]TO Ierusalem þ*at* ryche cete
 Thre p*re*stes þair way has tane,
vnto þe temple þai went all thre
 And called þe clerkes onane,
þai said: "Ih*esus*, þis warand we,
 þ*at* yhe w*ith* wrang haue slane,
On þe mount of Oliuete þis day satt [he
 And his appostels ilk ane;
we saw þam in a rowt
 þ*at* he was won to teche,
þai satt all him obout
 And þir wordes gan he p*re*che:

(74)

'Thurgh all þe werld I will yhe [wende,
 And wysely luke yhe wake
And baptyss all men w*ith* yho*ur* hende
 þ*at* trowth trewly will take;
þ*at* trowes & er for c*ri*sten kend
 Safe I sall þam make;
And all bese damped w*ith*outen end
 þ*at* ryght trowth will forsake.'
In þ*at* stede þam omang
 He steghe tyll heuen vpryght,
And we luked aft*er* him lang
 Till clowdes reft vs þe syght."

(75)

Hereof þe Iewes awondred ere,
 þai say: "þus sall noght blyn,
þis þat yhe say all sall yhe swere."
 A boke þai byd bryng in,
þai said: "þ*at* may do vs no dere,
 Gladly we will bigyn;
Bot we wald þareof witnes bere,
 ffor soth we suld haue syn."

[1] This letter made with a great deal of colour and flourish.

SION.

(73)

To Ie*rusa*lem come on a day
Thre prestes of þe Iewery,
Tille þe temple held þai strek*e* þe way
And saluede þe clergy,
þai sayde: "Ihesu, schorly to say,
þat yhe split wragwisly,
On þe mounte Olyuete satte þis day
And his appostels hym by;
we saghe alle in a route
þat he was wonte to teche,
þai satte alle hym aboute
And þere wordes gun þai preche:

(74)

'Alle thurght þis werd so wide yhe
My message forto make [wende
[1]And baptize men with yhour*e* hende
þat trowely trouthe wille take;
whaso trowes and es for cristen kend
saued I sal hym make; [[1] leaf 26]
And alle bes dampned withouten end
þat þe trouthe sal forsake.'
Als he stode þaime omang
He steye til heuen vpryght,
And we loked aftir lang
Tille þe cloudes reft vs þe sight."

(75)

Hereof þe Iewes forwonderd ware,
þai sayde: "þis sall noght blynne,
If it be þus alle sall yhe swere."
þe haly buke broght þai Inne,
And þai sayde: "þat may vs noght
Gladly wille we begynne; [dere,
If we ne wald hereof wittenes bere,
Suthely we had greete synne."

ADDITIONAL.

(73)

To ierusalem come on a day
Two p*re*stes of þat ilke Iury,
To þe temple þai toke þair*e* way
And gedred alle þe folke in hye,
þai saide: "ih*esu*, shortly at say,
þat ȝhe to dede did wrongefully,
On þe monte olyuete he sat þis day
And his apostles ilk on hym by;
We sawe alle in on route
þat he was wont to teche,
þai satt hym alle aboute
And þes wordes gan he p*re*che:

(74)

'Thurgh alle þe worlde I bid ȝowe [wende
Oue*re*all my message forto make
And baptise þat are gude & hende
And truly trouthe of ȝowe will take;
Whoso is trewe of cristen kynde
Saue & sure I sall hym make;
And dampne alle þos w*ith*outen ende
þat no trouthe of ȝowe will take.'
As he stoude þai*m* amange
he steghe to heuene vpright,
And we loked aft*er* lange,
Two cloudes refte vs þe sight."

(75)

[1]þes Iuwes alle forwondred were [[1] leaf 128]
And saide to þai*m*: "ȝhe shall noȝt [blyn,
If it be þus ȝhe sall it swere,
þe halydome be charged in."
þai saide: "it may vs nothynge dere,
Gladly ynowȝ we wille bygynne
To say þe sothe w*ith*outyn were
Of ihe*su* þat dyed for mans syn*ne*."

870. *wragwisly*: Horst. *wra(n)g.*
876. *þai*: Horst. *he.*
877. *thurght*: Horst. *thurgh.*

GALBA.

handes on þat boke þai laid
  and sware all with a voice:
"al es suth þat we sayd
  of him ȝe hanged on croyce."

(76)

þe iews a buke in handes hent
  and gert þam eft on lay:
"þis þat ȝe speke in oure present
  ȝe sall layn forward ay."
sone fro þat cete er þai sent,
  for þai no suth suld say,
and armed men with þam er went
  to wis þam fast oway.
in [dred] þir iews þus dwell
  and sais: "what may þis mene?
in þe land of irraell
  was neuer slike selkuthes sene."

(77)

To þis spak annas and chaiphas:
  "we sall noght trow," þai said,
"þe knightes þat him miskepid has,
  sen he in graue was layd;"
"þat he rase vp," þaire wordes was,
  "and mad þam all affraid;
bot hou sone gan þat speche ouerpas
  fro we þam siluer payd.
his men, ful wele may be,
  come his cors forto stele
and made þe knightes gre,
  als we did, forto hele."

(78)

All þe iews þan þat þar ware
  answerd and said þus: [mare
"wheþer war oure knightes halden
  vntill his men or till vs?"
"sertainly ȝe say wele þare,"
  þus said nichodemus,

HARLEY.

Handes on þ*at* boke þai layd
  And sware all w*ith* a voyce:
"All es soth þ*at* we sayd
  Of him yhe hanged on croyce."

(76)

þe Iewes a boke in handes hent
  And gert þam eft on lay:
"þis þ*at* yhe speke in our p*re*sent
  yhe sall layne forward ay."
Sone fro þ*at* cete er þai sent,
  ffor þai no soth suld say,
And armed men w*ith* þam er went
  To wyss þam fast oway.
In [dred] þir Iewes þus dwell
  And says: "what may þis mene?
In þe land of Israel
  was neue*r* slyke selcowthes sene."

(77)

To þis spak Annas & Cayphas:
  "we sall noght trow," þai sayd,
"þe knyghtes þ*at* him myskeped has,
  Sen he in graue was layd;"
"þ*at* he rase vp," þare wordes was,
  "And made þam all affrayd;
Bot how sone gan þ*at* speche oue*r*pas
  ffro we þam syluer payd.
His men, full wele may be,
  Come his cors forto stele
And made þe knyghtes gre,
  Als we dyd, forto hele."

(78)

All þe Iewes þan þ*at* þare ware
  Answerd & sayd þus: [mare
"whethe*r* war our knyghtes halden
  vntyll his men or tyll vs?"
"Sertainly yhe say wele þare,"
  þus said Nichodemus,

SION.

Handes on þat buke þai layde
And sware alle withe a voyce:
"Alle es sothe þat we saydo
Of Ihe*su* þat dyed on croyce."

(76)

þe Iewes a buke in handes hent
And gert þaime swere eft þat day:
"þat yhe haue sayde in oure present
yhe sal layne euer and ay."
And fra þe cite þai had þam sent,
fFor þai þe suthe suld say,
And other men withe þaime was went
fForto lede þaime oway.
In dred þire Iewes gun duelle
And sayde: "what may þis mene?
In þe land of Israelle
Slyk selcouthe signes er sene."

(77)

þan spak Annas and cayphas:
"we sall noght trow," þai sayde,
"þe knyghtes þat hym keped has
when he in graue was layde; [leaf 26, bk.]
How he vp rase þe worde was,
And made þaime all afrayde;
Bott*e* how sone gunde þat worde ouer-
ffra yhe þaime siluer payde. [pas
His disciples als may be
His body oway gun stele,
And þire knyghtes gree,
Als we did, forto hele."

(78)

þan alle þe Iewes þat þare ware
Answard*e* ogayn þus:
"whethir wille oure knyghtes hald*e*
with his men or with vs?" [mare
þan spak a Iewe, was wise of lare,
þat hight Nicodem*us*:

ADDITIONAL.

Handes on boke þai layde
And sware alle *with* on voyce:
"All is southe þat we sayde
Of hym þat died on crose."

(76)

þe Iuwes a boke in hande þai hent
And þes men gart swere efte þis day:
"þat ȝhe haue saide in our*e* p*re*sent
ȝhe shall it heele & layne for ay."
And fro þe Cyte þai þam sent,
ffor þai in toune suld no thynge say,
And c*er*tayne men *with* þai*m* forthe
To teche þai*m* sikirly þe way. [went
In drede þes Iuwes nowe duelle
And saide: "what may þis mene?
In þe lande of israell
Siche sightes neu*er*e wer*e* sene."

(77)

þen spake Annas and cayphas: [saide,
"We will noȝt trowe for sothe," þai
"þe knyghtes þat hym kepid has,
I trowe þai haue vs alle betrayde;
þai saide howe þat he rysen was,
And þus þai made vs alle affrayde;
Bot howe sone gan þai lat it passe
ffro tyme þat we þai*m* silu*er* payde.
His postles, wele may be,
His body away gan steele
And made þe knyghtes gre
And gaue þai*m* golde to hele."

(78)

Alle þe Iuwes þat þere wore [lf. 128, bk.]
Anon right þai answerd þus:
"Whethir*e* were our*e* knyghtes holden
Till ihe*su* meyne or till vs?" [more
þen spake a Iuwe, was wise of lore,
þat called was Nichodem*us*:

928. *or* erased before *meyne.*

GALBA.

"for his men saw þai neuer are,
ne noght þai lufed ihesus; 932
þir two men þat sware right
how þai saw him lifand
and stegh to heuyn on hight
with wrang er flemid of land. 936

(79)

[1] We rede when þe prophet Elias
up unto heuyn was tane, [1 leaf 62, bk.]
Elisius, his descipell was, 939
men asked wheder he was gane;
he said: 'till heuyn I saw him pas,'
men for him made grete mane.
'sum spirit,' þai said, 'him rauist has
into þe mountes allane.'
þai gert seke north and sowth 945
þe mowntes of israell,
þai fand no man þat kowth
þam tale of hely tell. 948

(80)

ȝe childer of irraell, listens me,
þat has þis sakles slayne,
in case þat crist so rauist be 951
with spirites to sum mowntayne,
sendes furth men bilyue lat se,
to seke with all þaire mayne;
he sall forgif and haue pete,
when he es funden ogayne." 956
for he suld noght be schent,
þir tales he gan þam tell,
and wight men furth er went
to þe mountes of irraell. 960

(81)

In þe land of irraell haue þai soght
þe mowntaynes fer and nere;

HARLEY.

"ffor his men saw þai neuer are,
Ne noght þai lufed Ihesus; 932
þir two men þat sware ryght
How þai saw him lyfand
And stegh to heuen on hyght
with wrang er flemed of land. 936

(79)

We rede when þe prophete helyas
vp vnto heuen was tane,
Elisius, his discipell was, 939
Men asked whyder he was gane;
He sayd: 'tyll heuen I saw him pas,'
Men for him made gret mane.
'Som spirit,' þai said, 'him rauyst has
Into þe mountes allane.' 944
þai gert seke north & sowth
þe mountes of Israel,
þai fand no man þat couth
þam tale of Hely tell. 948

(80)

Yhe childer of Israel, lystens me,
þat has þis sakles slayne,
In case þat crist so rauyst be 951
with spirites to som mountayne,
Sendes furth men bylyue lat se,
To seke with all þair mayne;
He sall forgyf & haue pete,
When he es fonden ogayne." 956
ffor he suld noght be schent,
þir tales he gan þam tell,
And wight men furth er went [lf. 211]
To þe mountes of Israel. 960

(81)

In þe land of Israel haue þai soght
þe mountanes fer & nere;

SION.

"wele sayde þai saghe þaime neuer [are
And þai er funden of vs;
And þa thre men þat sware
þai saghe Ihesu lyfande 934
And steye tille heuen right þare
with wrange er flemed of lande.

(79)

We rede when þe prophete elyas
Vntil heuen vp was tane,
Helysyus þat his disciple was 939
was askede whare he was gane;
He sayde: 'tille heuen I saght hym pas,'
Men for hym made grette mane
And sayd: 'sum spirite hym rauyst [has
Vnto þe mountayns alane.'
þai gertte seke northe and southe 945
þe mountayns of Iraelle,
þai fand na man þat couthe
Na tale of Ely telle. 948

(80)

Now, Iraelle childer, listens me,
þat haues þis saule slane,
In cas þat Ihesu rauest be 951
[1] By spirit tille some mountayne,
Chese we vs men grette plente [1 lf. 27]
And seke with al þaire mayne;
He sal forgif and haue pete,
when he es funden ogayne." 956
þe Iewes with ane assent,
Als Nichodeme gun telle,
At seke men haue þai sent
þe mountes of Israelle. 960

(81)

Thurgh alle Israell haue þai soght
Mountayns bathes farre and nere;

932. This line was omitted by Horstmann.
958. *say* marked for erasure before *telle*.

ADDITIONAL.

"þe apostles sawe oure men neuere ore
And also oure men loued noȝt [ihesus;
And þos two men þat swore
þai sawe ihesu on lyue stande 934
And steghȝ to heuene þore
With wronge are flemed of lande.

(79)

We rede when þe prophet Elyas
Vp onto heuene was tane,
Eliseus þat his dissiple was 939
Men asked whidre he was gane;
He saide: 'to heuene I sawe hym passe,'
And men for hym þai made gret mone
And saide: 'sum spirit ladde hym has
Into þe montaynes, hym allone.'
þai gart seke northe & southe 945
þe montans of Israell,
þai fonde no man þat couthe
No tale of Ely telle. 948

(80)

Nowe, childre of Israell, listenes to me:
Sen ȝhe ihesu sakelesse haue slayne,
It may so happen þat he be, [tane;
His spirit rauysshed to sum mon-
fforþi I rede þat gret plente 953
Of men seke ihesu with þaire mayne;
He will forgyffe & haue pite
Of ȝowe, if ȝhe hym fynde agayne."
þe Iuwes with on assent, 957
As Nychodeme gan telle,
To seke ihesu þai sent
þe montes of Israell. 960

(81)

Thurgh israell haue þai sought
þe montayns both farre & nere;

GALBA.

þai come and said þai saw him noght,
ne noght might of him here;
"Of Iosep bodword haue we broght
þat ȝe presond to ȝere,
in Aramathi his wanes er wroght
als lord of grete powere."
When þai herd sertaynly
þat Iosep was in quert,
þai thankid god forþi
and war ioyful in hert.

(82)

Sone þai made a grete gadering
and kownsailed þam bitwene
how þai might iosep to þam bring,
als he bifore had bene.
a letter did þai to writeing
þat said þus als I wene:
"pes, frendschip and goddes greting
on þe, sir, mot be senene."
þai said: "we knaw and wate
oure trispas and oure gilt
in god onence þi state,
þat we þe wald haue spilt;

(83)

Syr, vowchesaue to cu*m* vs till,
all halely we þe pray,
and largely mak amendes we will,
whatso þiself will say;
ful oft we stody opon þis skill
how þat þou wan oway,
bot god wald þat þou had none ill,
þi dedes war to his pay;
haue pese with wirschiping,
iosep of Aramathy."
þai close it and þai hing
þaire aller seles þarby.

HARLEY.

þai come & said þai saw him noght,
Ne noght myght of him here;
"Of Ioseph bodword haue we broght
þat yhe presond to yhere,
In Aramathy his wanes er wroght
Als lord of gret powere."
When þai herd sertainly
þ*at* Ioseph was in qwert,
þai thanked god forþi
And war ioyfull in hert.

(82)

Sone þai made a gret gaderyng
And counsayled þam bitwene
How þai myght Ioseph to þam bryng,
Als he before had bene.
A letter dyd þai to wrytyng
And said þus als I wene:
"Pese, frendschip & godes gretyng
On þe, sir, mot be sene."
þai said: "we knaw & wate
Our tryspas & our gylt
In god onence þi state,
þ*at* we þe wald haue spylt;

(83)

Sir, vouchesaue to com vs tyll,
All halely we þe pray,
And largely mak amendes we will,
Whatso þiself will say;
ffful oft we stody opon þis skyll
How þ*at* þou wan oway,
Bot god wald þ*at* þou had none ill,
þi dedes war to his pay;
Haue pese w*ith* wirchipyng,
Ioseph of Aramathy."
þai close it & þai hyng
þair aller seles þareby.

993. *with* repeated in MS.

SION.

And come hame and fande hym noght,
Ne noure myght of hym here;
“Of Ioseph bodeworde haue we broght
þat yhe prisonde to yhere,
In Armathy es his wonynge wroght
Als lord of grette powere.”
When alle þe Iewery
wist Ioseph was in qwerte,
þai thanked god forþi
and ware Ioyfull in harte.

(82)

And þan þai made a greete gaderynge
And counsayled þaime bytwene
How þai myght Ioseph to þaime brynge,
Als he byfore had bene.
A letter þai did to writynge
þat sayd þusgate I wene:
“Pees, frendschepe and goddes gretynge
On þe, sire, mot be sene;
Sire, we knawe bathe and wate
Oure trespas and oure gilte
In god onence þi state,
þat we þe wilde haue spilte;

(83)

þarefore wouchesaue come vntille,
Sire Ioseph, we þe pray,
And largely make amendes we wille,
whatso þiself wille say;
[1]Oftsythes we muse alle of þat skylle
how þat þou wan oway, [1 lf. 27, bk.]
Bot god wald þat þou had nane ille,
his dedes ware to þi pay;
Pees haue with worschipynge,
Ioseph of armathy.”
þan þai it closed and gun hynge
þaire aller seles þareby.

966. *yhe*: *h* above line.
981. On margin these words: *littera missa ad Ioseph a iudeis.*

ADDITIONAL.

þai come agayne & fonde hym noȝt
[1]And sayd þai myght noȝt of hym here; [1 leaf 129]
“Bot worde of Ioseph haue we brought
þat here was prisoned are to ȝere,
In aramathy is wonynge is wrought
Ryght as a lorde of gret powere.”
When þai wiste euereilk one
þat Ioseph was in querte,
þai thanked god in trone
And were ioyfull in herte.

(82)

And þen þai made a gret gadrynge
And helde a consayle þaim bytwene
Howe þai myght hym to þaim brynge,
Ryght as he before hade bene.
A lettre þai wrote all of plesynge,
And þusgates was it wryten I wene:
“Pees, frensshippe & gud gretynge,
Sir, on þe it mot be sene;
We wote wele & confesse
Oure trespasse & oure gilte
þat we thurgh wykednesse
Walde fayne haue hade þe spilte;

(83)

Bot nowe, Ioseph, þou comme vs tille,
And ȝe vouchesaue, sir, we ȝowe pray,
And largely make amendys we will,
Whatso ȝoureselue will deme or say;
ffor mykill we maruayle by what skille
And on what wise ȝhe went away,
Bot god wolde þat ȝhe had non ille,
ffor alle ȝour dedis were till his pay;
Pees be to ȝowe with wirsshippynge,
Ioseph of Aramathy.”
þai it enclosed & sithen gart hynge
þaire sealles full fast þereby.

985. Horst. *come* (*vs*).

GALBA.

(84)

Of iosep frendes seþin haue þai sent
 þe message forto make ;
when þai wist what mate*rs* þai ment,
 þai wald it noght forsake ;
till aramathi wightly þai went,
 ful winly gan þai wake ;
þai tald to Iosep þaire entent,
 þe letter to him þai take.
son when he had it red,
 he thankid god of heuyn ;
he kissed þam and seþin led
 vntill his hows ful euyn.

(85)

Sone on þe morn when it was day,
 Iosep was dight ful tyte,
with þe messangers he went his way
 withowten more respite.
of his come when þe iews herd say,
 withowten lenger lite
with all þe wirschip þat þai may
 ogaynes him went þai quit,
þai said : "at þi cu*m*ing,
 Iosep, be pese and grith."
and he sais : "goddes bliscing
 be all his puple with."

(86)

Nichodeme þat I are of spak
 at his hows gert him ly,
and made grete festes for his sake
 to folk of þe iewry ;
and sone a gadering gan þai make
 in þe temple opynly ;
a boke in hand Iosep þai take
 and bad him swere þarby

1017. *said* above line.

HARLEY.

(84)

Of Ioseph frendes sythen haue þai sent
 þe message forto make ;
when þai wist what mate*rs* þai ment,
 þai wald it noght forsake ;
Till Aramathy wightly þai went,
 ffful wynly gan þai wake ;
þai tald to Ioseph þair entent,
 þe letter to him þai take.
Sone when he had it red,
 He thanked god of heuen ;
He kyssed þam & sythen led
 vntyll his hows full euen.

(85)

Sone on þe morn when it was day,
 Ioseph was dyght full tyte,
w*ith* þe messange*rs* he went his way
 w*ith*outen more respyte.
Of his come when þe Iewes herd say,
 w*ith*outen lenger lyte
w*ith* all þe wirschip þat þai may
 Ogayns him went þai tyte,
þai said : "at þi comyng,
 Ioseph, be pese and gryth."
And he sais : "godes blyssyng
 Be all his pople with."

(86)

Nichodeme þ*at* I are of spake
 At his hows gert him ly,
And made gret festes for his sake
 To folk of þe Iewry ;
And sone a gaderyng gan þai make
 In þe temple openly ;
A boke in hand Ioseph þai take
 And bad him swere þareby

SION.

(84)

Of Ioseph frendes seuen had þai tane
  þe message forto make;
ffurth on þe message ware þai gane,
  þai wald it noght forsake;
Tille armathy þai come onane,
  Ioyfulle for Ioseph sake;
Mekely þai halyst hym onane,
  þe letter þai gun hym take.
When Ioseph had it redde,
  he thanked god of heuen;
he kyssed þam a*n*d sythen þam ledde
  Vntille hys house alle seuen.

(85)

Arely on morne when it was day,
  Ioseph was dyght fulle tite
And with þe messagers went forthe
    hys way,
  Tuke he na langer respite.
Of hys come when þe Iewes hard say,
  Na langer wald þai lette,
with alle worschepe þan wen þai
  Ogayne hys come als tite,
þai sayde at hys comynge:
  "Ioseph, to þe be pees and grethe."
And he sayde: "goddes blyssynge
  Be alle þis pople withe."

(86)

Nichodeme þat we are of spake
  At hys house gart hym ly,
And made greete festynge for hys sake
  Tille alle þe Iewery; [leaf 28]
On þe morne greette gederynge gun
  In þe temple openly; [þai make
A buke Ioseph þai gun take
  In hande, and he swore þareby

999. *fforth*; *th* above line.
1015. Horst. *wen(t)*.

ADDITIONAL.

(84)

Ioseph frendes eu*er*eilk one [make;
  Were ordayned þis message to
fforthe on þaire message are þai gon,
  þai thought noȝt forto lat it slake;
To aramathy þai come anon, [lf. 129, bk.]
  Ioyful ynoghe for Ioseph sake;
Mekely þai haylsed hym eu*er*eilk on
  And sone þis l*ettre* gan hym take.
When Ioseph had it redde,
  He thanked crist of heuene,
And kissed þai*m* & ledde
  Vnto his house full euene.

(85)

Erly at morne when it was day,
  Ioseph to dight hym hade delite,
W*ith* þes men he went his way,
  No lange*re* made he þ*er*e respite.
Of his come when þe Iuwes herde say,
  þai made þai*m* redy more & lasse,
W*ith* all þe wirsshippe þat þai may,
  To welcome hym as worthy wasse;
þai saide at his comynge:
  "Ioseph, haue pees & grithe."
And he saide: "c*r*istes blissynge
  Be all þis peple wythe."

(86)

Nichodeme þat we ere of spake
  At his house gart Ioseph lye,
And made gret festynge for his sake
  To c*er*tayne men of þat Iuwery;
At morne a semble did þai make
  In myddes þaire temple oponly;
A boke in hande Ioseph gan take
  And þ*er*e, I wote, he sware þ*er*eby

1014. *lasse*: effort to correct *a* to *e*.

GALBA.

þat he þe suth sall say ;
  ful depely þai him charge
how þat he wan oway
  fro preson vnto þe large.

(87)

[1]He said : "on gude friday at night
  when I to preson ȝode, [1 leaf 63, bk.]
till þe saterday at midnight right
  in my prayers I stode ;
þe preson in ayre was hinged on hight,
  þat meruaild all my mode ;
I luked and saw byfor my sight
  ihesus þat died on rode ;
till him gude tent I toke,
  his visage schane ful bright,
I might no langer loke,
  for drede I fell doun right.

(88)

He bad me þan rise vp in hy
  and toke me by þe hand,
my mowth he kissed curtaisly,
  ful dredeful gan I stand,
I said to him : 'my lord Ely,
  wher þou be here lifand ?'
and he sayd : 'ȝa, ful faithfully,
  þat sall þou vnderstand ;
of me no drede þou haue,
  Iosep, I am þat ilk
þat þou laid in þi graue
  in sendell and in silk.'

(89)

I answerd þus : 'if þou be he,
  of a thing I þe pray,
þe monument þou lat me se
  whareiu þi body lay.'

HARLEY.

þat he þe soth sall say ;
  ffull depely þai him charge
How that he wan oway
  ffro presoune vnto þe large.

(87)

He said : " on gud fryday at nyght
  when I to presone yhode,
Till þe saterday at mydnyght ryght
  In my prayers I stode ;
þe presone in ayre was hynged on hyght,
  þat meruayld all my mode ;
I luked & saw bifor my syght
  Ihesus þat dyed on rode ;
Till him gud tent I toke,
  His visage schane full bryght,
I myght no langer luke,
  ffor dred I fell doune ryght.

(88)

He bad me þan ryse vp in hy
  And toke me bi þe hand,
Mi mowth he kyssed curtaisly,
  ffull dredfull gan I stand,
I said to him : ' my lord hely,
  wher þou be here lyfand ?'
And he said : 'yha, full faythfully,
  þat sall þou vnderstand ;
Of me no drede þou haue,
  Ioseph, I am þat ilk
þat þou layd in þi graue [leaf 211, bk.]
  In sendell and in sylk.'

(89)

I answerd þus : 'if thou be he,
  Of a thing I þe pray,
þe monument þat lat me se
  wharein þi body lay.'

.SION.

þat he þe suthe sulde say;
  ffulle deply þai gun hym charge
How þat he wan oway
  ffra prisoun tille his large.

(87)

He: "on gude friday at nyght
  when I tille prisoun yhode,
Tille þe settirday obout mydnyght
  In my prayers I stode;
In þe ayer þe prison was hyngede on hight,
  þat merred mykel my mode;
I lukede, þan saghe I by sighte
  Ihesu þat dyed on rode;
Tille hym gude tente I tuke,
  His wisage schane so bright,
I moght no langar luke,
  Bott for drede felle doun right.

(88)

Vp he me raysede smertly
  And toke me be þe hande,
My mouthe he kissede curtoysly,
  And dredefulle gun I stande,
And I sayde: 'my lorde hely,
  whethir þou be here lifande?'
And he sayd: 'nay, but it am I,
  Ihesu, be noght dredande;
Of me na drede þou haue,
  Ioseph, I am þat ilke
þat þou layde in þi graue
  wonden in sendelle and silke.'

(89)

And I sayde: 'sire, if þou be he,
  Of a thynge I þe pray,
þe monument þou lat me see
  þare þi body in lay.' [lf. 28, bk.]

1033. Horst. *He* (*said*).
1050. Horst. *lyfande*.

ADDITIONAL.

þat he þe sothe sulde say;
  Depely þai gon hym charge
Howe þat he wan away
  ffro prisoune to þe large.

(87)

He saide: "at gud fryday at nyght
  When þat I to prisoune ȝode,
To þe satreday aboute mydnyght
  In my prayers euere I stoude;
I lokid vp & sawe a sight,
  Ihesu þat dyed here on þe rode;
[1]þe prisone depe in þe erthe was dight,
  þat made me marred in my mode;
To ihesu gud tent I toke, [[1] leaf 130]
  His visage shone so bright,
I myght no lengere loke,
  ffor dred I fell don right.

(88)

Bot vp he raysed me full smertly
  And streght he toke me by þe hande,
Mi mouthe he kissed curtesly,
  And I sore adred gan stande,
And I saide: 'my lorde haly,
  Whethire þou be noȝt ȝit lyfande?'
And he said: 'nay, bot I am I,
  Ihesu, forþi be noȝt dredand;
Of me no dred þou haue,
  Ioseph, I am þe same
þat þou laide in a graue
  And sithin for me bare blame.'

(89)

And I said: 'if þou be he,
  Of one thynge þen I will þe pray,
þat monyment þou lat me se
  þere þat þi body in with lay.'

GALBA.

out of that preson þan went we,
bot how I can noght say,
his sepulcre sone schewed he me,
þe body was oway ; 1064
þan trowed I stedfastly
when I had sene þat sight,
I asked þat milde mercy 1067
and thanked him at my might.

(90)

In aramathi he set me seine,
and þare I saw him last ;
he bad : 'nonegate luke þou go hein
till fourty dais be past ;' 1072
he said me ȝe suld noght ȝow fein
to pursu cristen fast ;
Sirs, oþerwise went I noght þeine,
right on þis maner wast." 1076
þan said þe ihews halely :
" þis es a ferly fare
to seke all oure iewry,
slike ferlis fell neuer are." 1080

(91)

" Ely þe p*ro*phet in ful gude state,"
þai said, " quik to heuyn ȝede,
and moyses alswa, wele ȝe wate,
of his dede neuer we rede ; 1084
bot Ihesus was done to ded now late
and dampned for his misdede,
he may noght lif ogayne nanegate,
þis es withowten drede." 1088
Iosep sais : " meruail ȝe
þat he es risen to liue ?
to speke of his pouste,
ȝe may meruail slike fiue. 1092

1074. *fast* : *st* almost faded out.
1082. *heuyn* : *e* added above line in different hand.

HARLEY.

Out of þat p*re*sone þan went we,
Bot how I kan noght say,
His sepulcre sone schewed he me,
þe body was oway ; 1064
þan trowed I stedfastly
When I had sene *þat* syght,
I asked þat mylde m*er*cy 1067
And thanked him at my myght.

(90)

In Aramathy he sett me sethen,
And þare I saw him last ;
He bad : 'nogate luke þou go hethen
Till fourty days be past ;' 1072
He said me yhe suld noght yhow [feyne
To pursu cristen fast ;
Syrs, otherwise went I noght þethen,
Ryght on þis maner wast." 1076
þan said þe Iewes halely :
" þis es a ferly fare
To seke all our Iewry,
Slyke ferlyse fell neu*er* are." 1080

(91)

" Ely þe p*ro*phete in full gud state,"
þai said, " whik to heuen yhede,
And moyses allswa, wele yhe wate,
Of his dede neu*er* we rede ; 1084
Bot Ih*esus* was ded now late
And damped for his mysdede,
He may noght lyf ogayne nonegate,
þis es w*ith*outen drede." 1088
Ioseph says : " meruayle yhe
þat he es rysen to lyue ?
To spek of his pouste,
yhe may m*er*uaile slyke fyue. 1092

SION.

Oute of þe prison bathe went we,
  Botte how kan I noght say,
þe sepulcre schewede he me,
  Botte þe body was oway ; 1064
þan trowed I stedfastly
  when I had sene þat sighte,
And cryed hym oft mercy 1067
  And thanked hym at my myght.

(90)

In armathie he sette me sithen,
  And þare sawe I hym laste ;
he bad nagates I suld ga þethen
  Tylle fourty days ware past ; 1072
he sayde þat yhe suld yhow noght
  To pursu þe cristen fast ; [feyne
Othergates was I noght had hethen,
  Suthely ryght þusgates wast."
þire Iewes sayd haly : 1077
  "þis es a wonder fayre,
In alle þe Iewery
  Swylk selcouthe felle neuer are."

(91)

þay sayde : "saynt Hely, wele we [wate,
  Alle qwyk tille heuen yhede,
And enoke yhede þe same gate,
  Of hys deed noure we rede ; 1084
Ihesu was done to deed now late,
  Dampned for hys mysdede,
he may noght leue ogayne nagate,
  And þareof es na drede." 1088
Quod Ioseph þan : "meruayle yhe
  þat he ras fra deed tille lyue ?
Othire ras thurgh hys pouste, 1091
  þis aght yhe meruayle swylk fyue.

ADDITIONAL.

Out of þat p*ri*soune both went we,
  Bot on what wise can I noȝt say,
þe sepulcr*e* þen shewed he me,
  Bot þe body was clene away ; 1064
þen trowed I stedfastly
  When I hade sene þis sight,
And cryed of m*er*cy 1067
  And thanked hym þat I myght.

(90)

In Aramathy he set me þo,
  And þ*er*e for sothe I sawe hym last ;
He bade I suld noȝt þethen go
  Till fourty dayes were come & past ;
He saide no man suld do me wo, [fast ;
  þowȝ þai p*ri*sounde me neu*er*e so
[1]And þus ȝoure p*ri*soune skapped I fro,
  Loke what ȝe her*e*of can cast."
þe Iuwes alle holy [[1] leaf 130, bk.] 1077
  Gretly forwondred were
And saide : "in þis Iury
  Siche thynge fell neu*er*e ere."

(91)

þe Iuwes saide : "holly, wele we wate,
  All quike to heuene for sothe he [ȝede,
And moyses went þe same gate,
  Of his ded can we fully rede ; 1084
Ihe*s*u was don to ded nowe late
  And dampned her*e* for his mysse-
    dede,
He may noȝt lyffe in ryghtfull state,
  Cert*es* þ*er*eof vs thare noȝt drede."
Quod Ioseph : "m*ar*uayle ȝhe, 1089
  He rosse fro ded to lyue ?
He raysed men by pouste,
  Mor wondr*e*ly þen siche fyue. 1092

1061. Second *went* marked for erasure.

GALBA.

(92)

Of saint Simion wele may ȝe mene,
þat kepid ȝowre laws ful right,
and his two suns al haue ȝe sene,
þat Caryn and Lentin hight;
ȝe wate þai war bath ded bidene
and grauen in ȝowre sight;
þaire bodis, I wate withowten wene,
er raysed thurgh Ihesu might;
I warand þat þai both ere
lifand in aramathi,
ay kneleand in praiere
and spekes noght sekerly;

(93)

We will wend to þam, if ȝe rede,
and pray þam, if þai will,
tell vs how þai er raised fro ded
and eft life lent þam till;
parauenture þai sall in þat stede
schew vs sum sertaine skill,
if þai war raised thurgh his godhed,
and what thing to fulfill."
vnto þaire graues went þai,
whare þaire bodis war layd,
and fand þam bath oway,
als Iosep had þam said.

(94)

Iosep, Annas and Caiphas,
and nichodeme alswa,
þaire kownsail halely taken has
till aramathi to ga;
and on þe morn furth gan þai pas,
to þaire iorne þai ta;
fro þeþin sexti mile it was,
and nowþer myn ne ma;

HARLEY.

(92)

Of saint Symon wele may yhe mene,
þ*at* keped yho*ur* lawes full ryght,
And his two sons all haue yhe sene,
þat Caryn & Lentyn hyght;
yhe wate þai war both ded bidene
And grauen in yho*ur* syght;
þair bodyse, I wate *with*outen wene,
Er raysed thurgh Ih*esu* myght;
I warand þat þai both ere
Lyfand in aramathy,
Ay kneland in p*ra*yere
And spekes noght sykerly;

(93)

We will wend to þam, if yhe rede,
And pray þam, if þai will,
Tell vs how þai er raysed fro dede
And eft lyfe lent þam tyll;
P*ar*auenture þai sall in þ*at* stede
Schew vs som sertayne skyll,
If þai war raysed thurgh his godhede,
And what thyng to fullfyll."
vnto þair graues went þai,
whare þare bodyse war layd,
And fand þam both oway,
Als Ioseph had þam sayd.

(94)

Ioseph, Annas and Cayphas,
And Nichodeme allswa,
þair counsayle halely taken has
Till Aramathy tyll ga;
And on þe morn furth gan þai pass,
To þair iorne þai ta;
ffro þethen sexty myle it was,
And nowth*er* myn ne ma;

1120. *tyll*: Horst. *till*.

SION.

(92)

Of saynt symeon alle may yhow mene,
þat kepyd oure lawes fulle ryght;
His twa sones alle haue yhe sene, [lf. 29]
þat Caryn and Lenten hyght; 1096
Alle wate we þare ware deed bydene
And grauen in oure aller syght;
þare bodyse er noght þare I wene,
þai ras thurgh goddes myght;
In my cite þai ere 1101
Lyfand in armathy,
kneland euer in prayer,
þai speke na worde leely; 1104

(93)

Botte wende we to þaime, if yhe rede,
And pray þaime, if þai wille,
Schewe vs how þai ware dreuen fra
And eft putte lyfe vntille; [dede
Perchaunce þai sal schewe yhow in þis
Some resonabel skille, [steede
If þai war raysed thurgh his godehede,
And qwat thynge to fulfille."
Vnto þe graues yhede þai, 1113
þare þe bodys was layde,
And fand þaime bathe oway,
Als Ioseph had þaime sayde. 1116

(94)

Ioseph, Annas and Cayphas,
And Necodeme alsswa,
Halely þaire counsayle taken has
Tille Aramathy to ga, 1120
þat fra þaime sexti myle was,
And nouthir myn na ma;
Sone on þe morne forthe gun þai pas
þaire Iourne forto ta; 1124

1097. *þare*: Horst. *þai*. 1105. Second *wende* marked for erasure before *we*.
1111. MS. *goddehede*, with second *d* marked for erasure.

ADDITIONAL.

(92)

Of saynt symeon ȝhe alle may mene,
þat keppid here ȝ*our* lawes right;
His two son*n*es bothe haue ȝe sene,
þat Caryn & Letyn hyght; 1096
Alle wote ȝe wele þai dyed bedene
And also grauen in ȝ*our* sight;
þaire bodys arne noȝt þare I wene,
Rysyn þai are by gods myght;
þai are bothe holle & fere 1101
Lyfand in Aramathy,
Kneland in þaire prayere,
þai speke noȝt sikerly; 1104

(93)

Go we to þai*m*, if þat ȝhe rede,
And pray þai*m*, if it be þaire wille,
To shewe howe þai are risen fro ded
And eftesones put þe life vntille;
Perchaunse þai sall shewe in þat stede
Sum sikire resonable skille, 1110
If þai were raised thurgh his godhede,
And what thynge þat þai sall full-
[1]Vnto þaire graues ȝhede þai, [fille."
Whare þaire bodys ware layde,
And fonde þai*m* bothe away, [[1] leaf 131]
As Ioseph hade þai*m* sayde. 1116

(94)

Ioseph, Annas and cayphas,
And Nichodem*us* eke also,
Holly þaire consaile taken has
To Aramathy ryght forto go, 1120
þat þethen sexty myle was,
And nouthire myle lesse ne mo;
Sone on þe morne forthe gan þai passe
On þaire iourney wit*h*outen hoo;

1116. Horst. *sayd*.
1118. Second *als* marked for erasure before *swa*.

GALBA.

þir two men in þat toune
 fand þai at þe last
on bare erth kneland doun,
 praiand till god ful fast; 1128

(95)

[1] þai kissed þam als men þat þai kend
 and of þam war ful fayne, [[1] lf. 63, bk.]
to iherusalem þai gert þam wend
 wightly with þam ogayne; 1132
right in þe temple þai gert þame lend
 and þare of þam þai fraine,
þe halidom put þai in þaire hend
 to swere þe suth to sayne: 1136
"by god of israell
 and by god adonay,
þe suth of þis thing vs tell
 þat we ask, if ȝe may; 1140

(96)

Alswa bi grete god we ȝow ath,
 þat till oure faders spak,
if þat war ihesus þat raised ȝow bath,
 sertayne ȝe vs mak; 1144
how ȝe war raised ȝe schew vs rath,
 þat we right trowth may tak."
and for þir wordes þai wex ful wrath,
 both gan þai tremble and quake;
till heuyn vp gan þai stare, 1149
 and þan takin of þe croyce
on þaire mowthes mak þai þare
 and spak with symple voyce: 1152

(97)

"Lordinges," þai said withowten lite,
 "tak vs p*ar*chemyn and pen;

1129. Initial letter flourished in yellow and black representing faces of two cherubs.

HARLEY.

þir two men in þ*at* toune
 ffand þai at þe last
On bare erth kneland doune,
 Prayand tyll god full fast; 1128

(95)

þai kyssed þam als men þ*at* þai kend
 And of þam war full fayne,
To Ier*usal*em þai gert þam wende
 wightly w*ith* þam ogayne; 1132
Ryght in þe temple þai gert þam lend
 And þare of þam þai frayne,
þe halydom putt þai in þair hend
 To swere þe soth to sayne: 1136
"Bi god of Israel
 And bi god Adonay,
þe soth of þis thing vs tell
 þ*at* we ask, if yhe may; 1140

(96)

Allswa bi gret god we yhow athe,
 þat tyll our fade*r*s spak,
If þat war Ih*esus* þ*at* raysed yhow [bathe,
 Sertayne yhe vs make;
How yhe war raysed yhe schew vs [rathe,
 þat we ryght trowthe may take."
And for þir wordes þai wex full wrathe,
 Both gan þai tremble & qwake;
Tyll heuen vp gan þai stare, 1149
 And þan taken of þe croyce
On þair mowthes mak þai þare [lf. 212.]
 And spak w*ith* symple voyce: 1152

(97)

"Lordynges," þai said w*ith*outen lyte,
 "Tak vs p*ar*chemyn & pen;

SION.

When þai come tille þe toun,
 þai fande þaime at þe laste
On þe erthe bathe knelande doun,
 Prayand to godde fulle fast*e*;

(95)

þai kissed*e* þaime als men þat þai kende [[1] leaf 29, bk.]
 [1] And of þaime was fulle fayne,
To Ierusalem þai gert þaime wende
 with þaime smerltly ogayne;
In þe temple domini þai lende,
 At þam þus bygan þai frayne,
And putted þaime a buke In hende
 And swere þe sothe to sayne:
"By god of Irael
 And by god of adonay,
þe suthe þat yhe vs telle
 þat we ask*e*, if yhe may;

(96)

And by grette god we yow athe,
 . . . .
 . . . .
 Certayne ye vs make; [rathe,
How yhe ware raised*e* schewe vs
 þat we þe trouthe may take."
And for þa wordes þai wex alle wrathe,
 Bathe gun tremble and qwake;
Tille heuen vp gun þai stare,
 Sythen þe taken of þe croyce
On þaire tunges made þai þare
 And spak with simple voyce;

(97)

þai saide: "lordyngs, withouten lyte
 Graunte vs parchemen and penne,

1132. Horst. *smertly.*
1135. *hende*: first *e* above and corrected from *a*.

ADDITIONAL.

And when þai come to toune,
 þai fonde þai*m* at þe laste
On þe erthe kneland doune,
 Prayand to god full fast;

(95) [kende

þai kiste þai*m* as men þ*at* þai wele
 And of þair*e* lyues were full fayne,
To Ierusalem þai praide þai*m* wende
 To þair*e* owen contrey agayne;
In templu*m* domini gon þai lende
 And þer*e* þai gan þes two men frayne,
A boke þai put vnto þaire hende
 To swere þe southe & no3t to layne:
"By god of Israelle
 And by god adonay,
þe sothe þat 3he vs telle
 þat we aske, if 3he may;

(96)

By gret god swere sall 3e nowe,
 þat su*m*tyme to 3our*e* fadr*e* spake,
If it were ihesu þat raysed 3owe;
 þer*e*of c*er*tayne 3he sall vs make,
On what wise 3he wer*e* raysed & howe,
 þat 3e þe sadde truthe till vs take."
þes wordes made þai*m* forto bowe
 And bothe for drede tremble &
To heuene vp gan þai stare, [quake;
 And tokenynge of þe crosse
Made on þaire tonges bare [leaf 131, bk.]
 And spake wit*h* symple voysse;

(97)

þai saide: "lordynge*s*, vnto þis plitte
 We p*ra*y 3ow for pa*r*chemyn & penne,

GALBA.

þe preuetese we sall ȝow write
þat we for suthfast ken." 1156
and sone withowten more respite
serely þai sett þam þen,
and þusgat bigan þai to write:
"In þe name of god, amen! 1160
to þe, Ihesu, we pray,
rayser till life fro ded,
lat vs witnes þis day
þe might of þi godhed; 1164

(98)

Sen we er coniord forto tell
þat we saw thurgh þi might,
þe selkuths þat oftsithes byfell
we sall reherce ful right. 1168
al Adams kind we war in hell,
ful many a waful wight,
till on a time it so bifell
of sun we had a sight; 1172
when we in mirknes ware,
a light gan on vs leme,
till vs it semid þare
like a bright suns beme. 1176

(99)

Oure form faders þat was in wa,
Adam and Eue his wife,
and patriarkes and p*ro*phettes ma,
spak all þaire resons rife: 1180
'þis light es cu*m*en oure sorow to sla,
oure dirknes downe to drife,
als oure lord ihesus schewed vs swa
whils we war in life.' 1184
'þis light,' said ysai,
'es sun of þe fader of heuyn,
in my lif so said I
omang mi sawes ful euyn; 1188

HARLEY.

þe p*re*uetese we sall yhow wryte
þat we for sothfast ken." 1156
And sone w*ith*outen more respyte
Serely þai sett þam þen,
And þusgate bygan þai to wryte:
"In þe name of god, amen! 1160
To þe, Ih*e*su, we pray,
Rayser tyll lyfe fro ded,
Lat vs witnes þis day
þe myght of his godhed; 1164

(98)

Sen we er coniornd forto tell
þ*at* we saw thurgh þi myght,
þe selcouthes þat oftsythes bifell
we sall reherce full ryght. 1168
All Adams kynd we war in hell,
ffull many a wafull wight,
Till on a tyme it so bifell
Of sun we had a syght; 1172
when we in myrknes ware,
A lyght gan on vs leme,
Till vs it semed þare
Lyke a bryght sons beme. 1176

(99)

Oure form faders þ*at* was in wa,
Adam and Eue his wife,
And Patryarkes & p*ro*phetes ma,
Spak all þair resons ryfe: 1180
'þis lyght es comen our sorow to sla,
Our dyrknes doune to dryue,
Als our lord Ih*esu*s schewed vs swa
whils we war in lyfe.' 1184
'þis lyght,' said ysai,
'Es son of þe fader of heuen,
In my lyfe so said I
Omang my sawes full euen; 1188

SION.

þat we þire pryuetes may writte
  þat we for suthefast ken."
And þai þaime gaf withouthen respite
  þare omange alle þa men,
And þusgate þai bygan als tite:
  "In þe name of god, amen!
Lorde Ihesu, we þe pray,
  Rayser to lyfe fra deede,
Latte vs writte ryght þis day
  þe myght of þi godhede;

(98)

For we er coniurde forto telle
  Thurgh þi mykel myghte [leaf 30]
þe selcouthes þat of þe byfelle
  Sithen þou tille deede was dighte.
Alle Adams kyn we ware in helle,
  Many a wafulle wighte,
Tille on a tyme þat it byfelle
  Of þe son we had a sighte;
A lightynge schewede þare
  Als it ware a sons beme;
when we in mirknes ware,
  A light gun on vs leme.

(99)

Oure forme fadir þat was In wa,
  Adam and Eue his wife,
Patriarkes and prophetes many ma,
  Spake alle at anes bylyue:
'þis light es comen oure sorow to slaa,
  Oure dirknes doun to dryue,
God hymself schewed to vs swa'
  . . . .
'þis light,' sayde Isay,
  'Es þe son of þe fadir of heue,
lyfande yhow þus sayde I
  In my bokes fulle euen;

1166. *Thong* erased before *Thurgh*.
1186. Horst. *fader . . . . heue(n)*.

ADDITIONAL.

þat we þes priuaytise may write
  þat we trowe & sothefast kenne."
And þai þaim gaue withoute respite
  Openly amonge alle men,
And right þus þai gan endyte:
  "In þe name of god, Amen!
Lorde ihesu, we þe pray,
  Rayser to lyfe fro dede,
So late vs write þis day
  þe myght of þi godhede;

(98)

Gif vs grace nowe forto telle,
  As þou art lorde so mykill of myght,
þe maruayles þat on þe befelle
  Sen þat þe Iuwes to dethe þe dight.
All Adam kyn we were in helle,
  many a drery sorowefull wyght,
Till on a tyme þat it befelle
  þat of þe son we hade a sight;
A lyghtnes shyned þere
  Ryght as a sonnes beme;
When we in merkenes were,
  A light gan on vs leme.

(99)

Oure forme fadre þat was in wo
  And Eue also þat was his wife,
Patriarkes, prophetes many moo,
  Alle at ones þai spake belyue:
'þis son is comen oure sorowe to slo
  And done þis darknes forto dryfe,
Als god hymselue shewed vs vnto
  Whill þat we were alle on lyue.'
'þis lyght,' sayd ysay,
  'Is þe fadre son of heuene,
Lyueand þis tolde I
  In my bokes full euene;

1187. *þus* marked for erasure before *yhow*.

GALBA.	HARLEY.
(100)	(100)
I prechid and said: "allneptalym land	I preched & said: "all Neptalim land
and Zabulon land withall,	And Zabulon land *with*all,
þat es als mekill to vnderstand	þat es als mykell to vnderstand
als fre bicomen es thrall,	Als fre bicomen es thrall,
men in mirknes of ded walkand	Men in myknes of ded walkand
light vnto þam schine sall."	Lyght vnto þam schyne sall."
þus I said whils I was lifand,	þus I said whils I was lyfand,
I se it now bifall;	I se it now bifall;
now all fulfild it es	Now all fullfyld it es
in vs, þat prophecy:	In vs, þ*at* prophecy:
"light schines in oure mirknes	"Lyght schynes in our myrknes
oure thraldom forto by."'	Oure thraldom forto by."'
(101)	(101)
Omang vs mekill mirth made we	Omang vs mykell myrthe made we
and grete ioy for þis thing.	And gret ioy for þis thing.
oure fader Simion þan come he	Our fader Symon þan come he
and tald vs new tything,	And tald vs new tythyng,
he said: 'ȝe mai mak gamyn & gle,	He said: 'yhe may mak gamen & gle,
gude bodword I ȝow bring,	Gud bodword I yhow bryng,
he cumes þat oure bier sall be	He comes þat our bier sall be
oway fro þis woning;	Oway from þis wonyng;
right in þe temple I toke	Ryght in þe temple I toke
þat barn in bath my handes,	þat barn in bath my handes,
myne eghen gan on him loke	Myne eghen gan on him luke
þat sall vs bring of bandes;	þat sall vs bryng of bandes;
(102)	(102)
Thurgh þe haly gaste þus gan I say:	Thurgh þe haly gast þ*us* gan I say:
"lord, leue þi seruand lele	"Lord, leue þi seruand lele
in pese to rest, lord, I þe pray,	In pese to rest, lord, I þe p*r*ay,
for myne eghen saw þi hele	ffor myne eghen saw þi hele
þat þou ordand for euer and ay	þ*at* þou ordand for eue*r* and ay
omang mankinde to dele	Omang mankynd to dele
light to schew folk night and day	Lyght to schew folk nyght & day
and ioy to all irraele."'	And ioy to all israele."'

1193. Horst. *my(r)knes.*

SION.

(100)

I pr*o*phetede : "neptalym lande
And Zabulon withalle,
þat es als mykill at vndirstande
Als fre become thralle, 1192
Men of þaire folk*e* in myrk*e* walkande
Tille þaime light schyne sal."
þat I sayd wils I was lyfand*e*,
I see it now byfalle ; 1196
Right now fulfild*e* it es
In vs, þat pr*o*phecy :
"Lyght*e* schynes In oure myrknes
Oure thraldome forto by." ' [lf. 30, bk.]

ADDITIONAL.

(100)

[1] I pr*o*phecyed by Neptalym lande
And by zabulon alegged w*ith*all ;
And is þus myche to vndrestande,
þat on fre man sall bye alle thralle ;
Vnto folke in m*er*kenes dwellande,
To þai*m* þis lyght shyne ȝit it shalle;
þat I saide whils I was lyfande, 1195
Nowe se I wele þat it sall falle ;
Right nowe fullfilled is [[1] lf. 132, bk.]
In vs þe prophecye :
"Lyght shynes in merkenes
Our*e* thraldome forto bye." ' 1200

SION.

(101)

And we made alle grett*e* myrite
Of þat light schewyng*e*.
Oure fadir Symeon þan come he,
Broght vs in a newe tithyng*e*,
He sayd : 'makes al gamen and gle,
Gude tythandes I yhow bryng*e*,
He es comen þat sal oure byer be
ffra þis laythe wony*nge* ; 1208
In þe temple I hym tuke,
A barne borne in my handes,
My eghen gun on hym luke
þat sal vs bryng*e* of bandes ; 1212

ADDITIONAL.

(101)

And we made gret sole*m*pnyte,
When we sawe þat lyght shynynge.
Our*e* fadr*e* symeon þen come he
And w*ith* hym brought a newe tithynge, 1204
He saide : 'loke ȝe make gam & gle,
ffull gude tithynges nowe I brynge,
He is comen þat sall our*e* byer*e* be
To fetche vs fro þis foule wonynge ;
In þe temple ihe*s*u I toke 1209
And helde hym in my handes,
Myn eyne on hym gan loke
þat salle lawse alle oure bandes ;

SION.

(102)

þus gert þe haly gast*e* me say :
"Leue now þi seruaunt leele
In pees to reste, lord*e*, I þe pray,
ffor myn eghen saghe þi hele 1216
þat þou ordaynd*e* for euer and ay
Omang*e* mankynde to dele
Light*e* to schewyng*e* of folk*e* to-day
and Ioye tille Israell." ' 1220

ADDITIONAL.

(102)

þe holy gost þus gart me say : 1213
"Leue now here þi s*er*uante lealle
In pees & rest, lorde, I þe pray,
ffor myn eyen haue sene þi hele
þat þowe ordand for eu*er*e & ay,
And amonges mankynd gan dele
Lyght to þe shewynge of þi folke, I say,
And ioy to men of yraelle." '

1211. *Men on h* erased at beginning of line.

GALBA.

þe saintes þat ful ill ferd,
  ilk one in þaire degre,
when þai þir tithinges herd,
  made grete solempnite.

(103)

[1] Ane said þan þat semyd bi liknes
  ane hermyt in pouer state,
what he was spird we more and les,
  and he answerd þusgate : [1 leaf 64]
'a voice criand in wildernes,
  and Iohn þe Baptist I hate,
of syns I prechid forgifnes
  thurgh baptyme gifen now late ;
when þat he come me by
  þat vs fro wa sall wyn,
" þis es goddes lamb," said I,
  " þat wastes þe werldes sin."

(104)

I baptist him right with my hend
  in þe water of flom Iordan,
þe haly gaste on him gan lend
  in a dowue liknes þan,
þe voice of þe fader doun was send
  and þus to speke bigan :
" þis es my son withowten end,
  herkins him ilk man,
in whilk sun me likes best."
  þus am I foreriner
to schew ȝow signes of rest,
  bese faine, he es noght ferr.'

(105)

And sone when Adam herd him say
  of þe flum baptissing,
he said : 'my son seth, I þe pray,
  tell vs a litill thing ;

HARLEY.

þe saintes þat full ill ferd,
  Ilk one in þair degre,
when þai þir tythynges herd,
  Made gret sollempnite.

(103)

Ane said þan þat semed by lyknes
  Ane hermyte in pouer state,
What he was spyrd we more & les,
  And he answerd þusgate :
'A voyce cryand in wildernes,
  And Iohan þe baptyst I hate,
Of synnes I preched forgyfnes
  Thurgh baptym gyfen now late ;
when þat he come me by
  þat vs fra wa sall wyn,
" þis es godes lamb," said I,
  " þat wastes þe worldes syn."

(104)

I baptyst him ryght *with* my hend
  In þe water of flom Iordan,
þe haly gast on him gan lend
  In a dowfe lyknes þan,
þe voyce of þe fader doune was send
  And þus to speke bygan :
" þis es my son *with*outen end,
  Herkens him ilk man,
In whilk sun me lykes best."
  þus am I forthermer
To schew yhow signes of rest, [lf.212,bk.]
  Bese fayne, he es noght fer.'

(105)

And sone when Adam herd him say
  Of þe flum baptyssyng,
He said : 'my son Seth, I þe pray,
  Tell vs a lytell thing ;

SION.

þe sayntes þat war in handes
Made greete solempnite
ffor Ioy of þire tithandes,
Ilk ane in hys degree.

(103)

Ane come þare þan þat semede by
Ane heremete pure of state, [liknes
what he was spirede we mare and les,
and he answarde þusgate:
'I voice criande in wildirnes,
And Iohan Baptist I hate,
Of synnes I prechede forgifnes
Thurgh baptyme gyuen now late;
I saghe h . . .[1]
þat vs fr . . .
þis es g . . .
þat dus . . .

(104)

And I hy . . .
In þe . . .
þe haly . . .
In a d . . .
þe fadr . . .
And þar . . .
þis es . . .
Lithes . . .
In wh . . .
þus a . . .
At sch . . .
Bes . . .

(105)

Whe . . .
Of þ . . .
He . . .
T . . . [leaf 32]

ADDITIONAL.

þe sayntes þat were in bandes
Made gret solempnite
ffor solace of þes sondes,
Ilk one in þaire degre

(103)

þen come on forth þat be liknes [lf.132,bk.]
Semed an hermyte of pore estate,
What he was asked more & lesse,
And he agayne answerd þusgate:
'A voysse cryand in wildrenes,
Iohn Baptiste for sothe I hate,
Of synnes I preched forgifnes
Thurgh baptym þat is gyfen late;
I sawe hym come me by
þat vs fro wo sall wynne,
"þis is gods lombe," saide I,
"þat dos away worldes synne;"

(104)

And I, Iohn, baptist hym *with* my
In þe watre of flom iordane, [hende
þe holy gost on hym gan lende
In likenes of a doue anon,
þe fadres voysse done gan descende
And þes wordes sayde he ilk one:
"þis is my dere son *with*outen ende,
ffor whom sall made be mykill
In whome me likes best, [mone,
No thynge is to me darre;
I brynge bode of ȝour rest,
Bes glad, he is noȝt farre."'

(105)

When Adam herde Iohn baptiste say
And speke of þe flom baptisynge,
He sayde: 'son, swithe I þe pray,
Telle vs here a litille thynge;

1229. MS. *ind*, with *d* marked for erasure.

[1] Here a leaf (31) has been torn out from the Sion College MS. containing 69 lines,—a small strip of leaf with the beginning of a few lines remaining.

GALBA.

in erth lifand, seke when I lay,
  I had a grete langing;
till paradis þou toke þe way
  oile of mercy me to bring;
all if þou gat none þare,
  vntill vs ȝit may þou tell
what þou had to answare
  of mighell, goddes angell.'

(106)

þan said seth: 'I stode lang and praid
  at þe ȝates of paradise,
and ane angell þan to me said
  þir wordes on þis wise:
"trauell þe noght on þis manere,
  herof no help may rise,
þe oile of þe tre of mercy here
  gettes þou by nonkins prise;
bot if it be at þe last
  þat þe nowmber may fulfill,
fiue thowsand ȝeres be past
  and fiue hundreth þartill,

(107)

Goddes sun sall þan vntill erth cum
  to mend þi faders mys,
he sall be baptist in þe flom
  and bring ȝowre bale to blis;
of þe oile of mercy þai sall haue sum
  þat he haldes for his,
þai þat with noy er now bynom
  sall win to welth Iwis."'
both patriark and prophete
  all thanked þai god at anes
þat cumes, als he gan hete,
  to win vs fro þir wanes.

HARLEY.

In erth lyfand, seke when I lay,
  I had a gret langyng;
Till Paradyse þou toke þe way
  Oyle of m*er*cy me to bryng;
All if þou gat none þare,
  vntyll vs yhit may þou tell
What þou had to answare
  Of Michael, godes aungell.'

(106)

þan said Seth: 'I stode lang & prayd
  At þe yhates of Paradyse,
And ane aungell þan to me said
  þir wordes on þis wyse:
"Trauell þe noght on þis manere,
  Hereof no help may ryse,
þe oyle of þe tre of m*er*cy here
  Gettes þou by nonkyns pryse;
Bot if it be at þe last
  þat þe nowmbre may fullfyll,
ffyue thowsand yheres be past
  And fyue hundreth þaretyll,

(107)

Godes son sall þan vntyll erth com
  To mend þi faders mys,
He sall be baptist in þe flom
  And bryng yho*ur* bale to blys;
Of þe oyle of m*er*cy þai sall haue som
  þat he haldes for his,
þai þat w*ith* noy er now bynom
  Sall wyn to welth Iwys."'
Both Patryarke and p*ro*phete
  All thanked þai god at anes
þ*at* comes, als he gan hete,
  To wyn vs fro þir wanes.

1271. on margin of MS. in later hand: *ffyve thousand V. honderde.*

SION. | ADDITIONAL.

In erthe lyueand seke I lay,
  To dye I had full gret longynge ;
My son to paradise went his way
  þe ole of mercy forto brynge ;
Come forthe my son so dere,
  Sum dele nowe þou vs telle
Of saynt Michel answere,
  þat þere was gods angelle.'

(106)

[1]Seth sayd : 'longe stoude I in prayere
  At þe ʒates of paradise ;
At þe last an Angell come me nere
  And said : "childe, þou art noʒt wise, [1 leaf 133]
Trauayle þe noʒt in þis manere,
  þare may no helpe þereof arise,
þe oleo of þe tre of mercy here
  þou getis it noʒt in nonkyns wise ;
Bot it sall be at þe last,
  When þis nombre is filled,
ffyue thousand ʒeres sall be past
  And fyue hondret ʒere þeretille,

(107)

þen sall gods son to þe erthe come
  Ryght forto bye þi fadres myssse
And be baptist in þe flome
  To brynge þi fadres bale to blisse
Of þe ole of mercy þou sall haue som
  And alle þat ben holden as his,
Alle þat here are in þis dongoune
  He sall þaim brynge to welthe I-wisse."'
Patriarke and prophete
  Alle thanked god at ones
þat comes, als he gan hete,
  To brynge þaim of þes wones.

1266. *of* above line.

Soon after that Satan, the master in hell, ordered the porter to open the gates and allow Jesus of Israel to come in.

GALBA.

(108)

Sone efter þat spak satanas,
 þat mayster was in hell,
and said till him þat porter was
 whare we presons gan dwell:
'opin ȝowre ȝates, lat him in pas,
 ihesus of irraell!
sen he him god sun maked has,
 in wa here sall he well;
he es made of manhede
 for all his frankis fare,
in my hert haue I drede
 for dedis he has done are;

(109)

[1] He has oft put me fro my pray,
 ful dere now bese it boght,
þam þat I turned vntill oure lay
 has he gert chaunge þaire thoght,
he has me tenid and trauerst ay
 in all þe werkes I haue wroght,
and many sawles gert wend oway
 þat I till vs had broght.'
he asked whethir þis be he
 þat cald lazar vs fra,
þat we had in powste,
 and þai said ilk ane, 'ȝa.'

(110)

'Satan,' þai said, 'we þe forbede
 in all thinges þat we may,
bring him noght hider for no nede,
 bot haue him heþyn oway;
for cum he here, we haue grete drede
 þat alls sall we say;

[1] Large flourish above in yellow and black in form of oak leaf, with comic face at lower end of leaf.

HARLEY.

(108)

Sone eft*er* þat spak Sathanas,
 þat maister was in hell,
And said tyll him þat Port*er* was
 whare we p*re*sons gan dwell:
'Open yho*ur* yhates, lat him in pas,
 Ihesus of Israel!
Sen he him god son maked has,
 In wa here sall he dwell;
He es made of manhede
 ffor all his frankys fare,
In my hert haue I dred
 ffor dedes he has done are;

(109)

He has oft put me fro my pray,
 fful dere now bese it boght,
þam þ*at* I turned vntyll our lay
 Has he gert chaunge þair thoght,
He has me tende and trauerst ay
 In all þe werkes I haue wroght,
And many saules gert wend oway
 þat I tyll vs had broght.'
He asked whether þis be he
 þat called Lazar vs fra,
þ*at* we had in pouste,
 And þai said ilk ane, 'yha.'

(110)

'Sathan,' þai said, 'we þe forbede
 In all thynges þ*at* we may,
Bryng him noght hyder for no nede,
 Bot haue him hethen oway;
ffor come he here, we haue gret drede
 þat all sall we say;

SION.

[1] He has me tenede and trauerste ay
Alle werkes þat I haue wroghte,
Saules fra vs haues he had oway
þat I haue tille vs broghte.'
He asked whethir þat be he [1 leaf 82]
þat calde Lazar vs fra,
þat was in oure pouste,
And satanas sayde hym, 'yha.'

(110)

He sayd : 'satan, I þe forbede
On alle thynghes þat I may,
Brynge hym tille vs for nakyn nede,
Botte haue hym forthe oway;
ffor come he here, I haue greete drede
we sal say waloway!

ADDITIONAL.

(108)

þan anon spak sathanas,
þat was maystre of alle helle,
And saide to hym þat portere was
þere as þe prisons were dressed to dwelle:
'Open þe ȝhates & lat in passe
Ihesu crist of israelle!
He þat gods son hym maked has,
Hidre sall he com full snelle;
He is man in pure manhede
ffor all his frankishe fare;
"Mi saule of þe dethe has drede,"
þus sayde ihesu full ȝhare;

(109)

[1] Ofte has he refte fro me my pray,
And nowe full dere it sall be bought, [1 leaf 133, bk.]
þos þat I turned till oure lay,
Anon he gart þaim turne þaire thought,
He has me tened & trauyst ay
In alle þe workes þat I haue wrought,
Saules fro vs he had away
þat I hade vnto vs brought.'
þat outhire deuyl sayd : 'is þis he
þat called lazare vs fra,
þat was put in oure pouste?'
And sathanas sayde, 'ȝhay.'

(110)

'Lat be, sathan, I þe forbede
In als mykill as I may,
Brynge hym noȝt hidre for no nede,
Bot fast þat he were hethen away;
ffor come he hidre, I haue gret drede
þat we mon synge alle wele away!

1312. MS. *forthe hym*, but the change of order is indicated.

1295. *ha* erased after *saule*.
1304. *bought* erased before *brought*.

GALBA.

all þat him likes heþin will he lede
  and we be pined for ay ;
he es a strenkithi swayn,
  when we all might noght hald
a wofull sawl ogayne,
  when he did noght bot cald.

(111)

[1] Sen he was slike and was bot man,
  to þe, satanas, we say, [1 leaf 64, bk]
wenes þou, wrtht, to maister þan
  both god and man verray ?
trowes þou þat þou close him can
  þat he ne sall win oway,
þat his pouer seruand fro þe wan
  and was dampned for ay ?'
þan answerd satanas :
  'of him haue I no drede,
I knaw wele what he was
  and what life he gan lede ;

(112)

His fourty dayes when he had fast,
  þat tyme him tempid I ;
and to þe iews counsailes I cast
  þat þai suld ger him dy ;
when pilat wald þat he had past,
  I egged him egerly,
till he was hanged at þe last
  with oþer theues him by ;
and þarfore als I ȝow say,
  ordans for him a stede,
he cumes heder þis day,
  by þis I hald hym dede.'

(113)

þus als þai gan togeder chide,
  a voice spak loud and clere :

HARLEY.

All þat him lykes hethen will he lede
  And we be pyned for ay ;
He es a strenkithy swayne,
  when we all myght noght hald
A wafull saule ogayne,
  when he did noght bot cald.

(111)

Sen he was slyke & was bot man,
  To þe, Sathanas, we say,
wenes þou, wreche, to maist*er* þan
  Both god & man v*er*ray ?
Trowes þou þ*at* þou close him kan
  þ*at* he ne sall wyn oway,
þ*at* his pouer seruand fro þe wan
  And was damped for ay ?'
þan answerd Sathanas :
  'Of him haue I no drede,
I knaw wele what he was
  And what lyfe he gan lede ;

(112)

His fourty days when he had fast,
  þat tyme him temped I ;
And to þe Iewes counsayles I kast
  þat þai suld ger him dy ;
when Pilate wald þ*at* he had past,
  I egged him egerly,
Till he was hynged at þe last
  with other theues him by ;
And þarfore als I yhow say,
  Ordayns for him a stede,
He comes hyder þis day, [leaf 213]
  Be þis I hald him dede.'

(113)

þus als þai gan togyder chyde,
  A voyce spak loud & clere :

SION.

Alle þat here er hethen sal he lede
and we be prynede for ay;
He es a myghty swayne,
whe we twa myght noght halde
A caytif saule ogayne,
when he did noght bot calde.

ADDITIONAL.

Alle þes soules will he with hym lede,
And þan sall we be pyned for ay;
He is a myghty swayne,
When we two myght noȝt halde
Lazare saule agayne,
And he did noȝt bot called.

(111)

SION.

Sithen he was swilke þat was bot man,
þou, satanas, I say,
with myghte wenes þou to mayster þan
Bathe god and man verray?
wenes þou þat lorde enclose þou kan
þat he ne sal wyn oway,
Sithen his poure seruaunt he fra þe wan
þat was dampned for ay?'
And þan sayde satanas:
'Of hym haue þou na drede,
I knawe wele what he was
And what lyfe he gun lede;

ADDITIONAL.

Sen he did so þat was bot man,
þou wreched wyght, to þe I say,
Who myght maistre hym nowe þan
þat is bothe man & god veray?
Sen he his seruaunte fro vs wan
þat was dampned hidre for ay,
Wenes þou, wreche, þat þou nowe can
Holde hym he suld noȝt wyn away?'
þen sayde sir sathanas:
'ffelawe, haue þou no drede,
I knowe wele what he was
And what lyue he gan lede;

(112)

SION.

his fourty days whe he gun faste
I tempte him sykerly;
[1] I procurde alle þe Iewes fulle faste
þat þai sulde ger hym dye;
when Pilate walde þat he had paste,
I egede ay egerly, [1 leaf 32, bk.]
Tille he ware hynged at þe laste
On a rode rewefully;
And þarefore I þe say,
Ordayne fore hym a stede,
He comes tille vs þis day,
By þis I halde hym dede.'

ADDITIONAL.

His fourty dayes þat he fast [leaf 134]
I hym temped sikirly;
I procurde alle þe Iuwes full fast
þat þai suld dresse hym forto dye;
When Pilat wolde þat he had past,
I stirde þe Iuwes full egrely,
Till he was hanged at þe last
Vpon þe rode full rufully;
And þerefore I þe say,
Ordayne for hym a stede,
He comes till vs þis day,
Be þis I holde hym dede.'

(113)

SION.

And whils þe fendes straue þusgats,
A voice spake loude and clere:

ADDITIONAL.

And whille þe fendys made all þis dray,
þere spake a voysse bothe loude & clere:

1318. Horst. *whe(n)*.
1333. *he* above line; *whe*: Horst. *whe(n)*.
1345. Horst. *þusgate*.

GALBA.

'ȝe princes, I bid ȝe opin wide
ȝowre endles ȝates here,
þe king of blis now in sall glide.'
and þan spac lucifere:
'satanas, turn him ogayn þis tide,
als þou lufes me dere.'
þan satanas sperd þe ȝates
and his felows he cald:
'haldes him þareout algates,
or we foreuer be thrald.'

(114)

þan said saint dauid þare he lay
vnto þai sayntes all:
'in erth lifand þus gan I say
als I se now byfall;
þat god has made, þis es þe day,
mak ioy þarin we sall;
brasen ȝates he brac for ay
and Iren barres ful small;
fro waies of wilsumnes,
I tald, he has þam taken;
I se now suth it es,
he has vs noght forsaken.'

(115)

[1]þan on þis wise said ysai:
'whils I had life in land,
on þis same maner þan said I,
whoso kowth vnderstand:
"ded men þat in þaire graues ly
sall rise and be lifand,
al sall mak Ioy and melody
þat erth has in his hand."
eftsones I said alwa
to ded: "whare es þi might,
sen he fetches vs þarfra?"
now se I all þis right.'

[1] Large flourish in yellow and black with bearded face of man.

HARLEY.

'yhe p*r*inces, I byd ye open wyde
yho*ur* endeles yhates here,
þe kyng of blys now in sall glyde.'
And þan spak Lucifere:
'Satanas, turn him ogayne þis tyde,
Als þou lufes me dere.'
þan sathanas sperd þe yhates
And his felawes he cald:
'Haldes him þareout allgates,
Or we foreuer be thrald.'

(114)

þan said saint Dauid þare he lay
vnto þa saintes all:
'In erth lyfand þus gan I say
Als I se now bifall;
þat god has made, þis es þe day,
Mak ioy þarein we sall;
Brasen yhates he brak for ay
And Iren barres full small;
ffro wayes of wilsomnes,
I tald, he has þam taken;
I se now soth it es,
He has vs noght forsaken.'

(115)

þan on þis wise said Isay:
'whils I had lyf in land,
On þis same man*er*e þan said I,
whoso couth vnderstand:
"Ded men þat in þair graues ly
Sall ryse & be lyfand,
All sall mak ioy & melody
þat erth has in his hand."
Eftsones I said allswa
To ded: "whare es þi myght,
Sen he fecches vs þarefra?"
Now se I all þis ryght.'

SION.

'I bid yow, prynces, vndo yhoure
Endles yhates remous here, [yhates,
ffor þe kynge of glorio þat al ille abats
Comes ;' and þan spake lucifere :
'Ryse, satan, ger hym gange his gats,
Als þou ert me leeue and dere.'
þire prynces þa yhates sperde at þe laste
And alle his feres he callede :
'ffende þire yhates and bare þam faste,
Or we for euer be thrallede.'

(114)

And þan sayd dauid þare he lay
Vntille þire sayntes alle :
'In erthe lyfande þus gun I say,
I see it now befalle ;
þat god has made, þis es þe day,
Make myrthe and Ioye we salle ;
ffor brasen yhates god brake for ay
And iren barres withalle ;
ffra wayes of wilsomnes,
[1] I sayd, he haues þaime taken ;
I see now sothe it es, [[1] leaf 33]
He haues vs noght forsaken.'

(115)

And þan sayd saynt Isay :
'þus whils I lyfede in lande,
Right on þis wise prophetede I,
whaso cuthe vndirstande :
"Deede men þat in þaire graues ly
Salle ryse vppe and be lifande,
Alle salle make Ioye and melody
þat erthe haues in hys hande."
Eftsones I sayd alsswa
Tille deede : "whare es þi myghte,
Deede sen he fotchede vs fra
Tille life ?" sayde I noght ryghte ?'

1348. *remous*, scribal error for *remouf* (?).
1354. *calde* marked for erasure.
1359. *lyfande* : *f* above line.

ADDITIONAL.

'þou, prince, I bidde withouten nay,
Vndo þes ȝates anon right here,
þe kynge of blisse comes in þis day.'
And þen anon spake lucifere :
'Sathanas, sparre þe ȝates, I þe pray,
Lat hym noȝt in be no manere.'
þe prince of helle þe ȝates he sparde
And his felowes gan calle :
'Bot þes ȝates be wele bared,
fforeuere we mon be thralle.'

(114)

þan said Dauid þere he lay
To þes sayntes gret & smalle :
'In erthe lyueand þen gan I say,
þat I saide þen nowe is befalle,
It is befallen þis day ;
Makys myrthe noȝt one bot alle ;
ffor brasyn ȝhates god brake for ay
And yrenen bandes brast withalle ;
ffro ways of wildrenes
His seruantes has he taken ;
I see nowe sothe it is,
He has vs noȝt forsaken.'

(115)

And after þis sayde ysay : [leaf 134, bk.]
'Whiles I lyueand was in land,
Ryght on þis wyse prophecyde I,
Whaso it kan vndrestand :
"Dede men þat in þaire graues lye
Rise þai sall & be lyueand,
Alle shall make ioy & melody
þat erthe thurgh ded þus has in [hand."
And ȝhitte I sayde also :
"Ded, where is þi myght
Sen þou lyue takes vs fro ?
To lyue þou ledes vs ryght."'

1354. *Alle* erased after *And* ; *gan* above line.

GALBA.

(116)

A voice spak þan ful hidosely,
  als it war thonors blast:
'vndo ȝowre ȝates biliue, bid I,
  þai may no langer last, 1384
þe king of blis cumes in ȝow by.'
  þan hell a voice vpkast:
'what es he þat þai say in hy?
  he sall be set ful fast.' 1388
þan said dauid: 'ȝe ne wate
  how þat I said þus right,
"he es lord of grete state,
  in batayle mekill of might;" 1392

(117)

þe king of blis, trewly I tell,
  right at þi ȝates standes,
he has bihalden fro heuyn to hell
  þe sorow of his seruandes. 1396
þarfore vndo, þou fende so fell,
  þi ȝates right with þi handes,
þe king of blis cu*m*es in ful snell
  to bring vs fro þi bandes 1400
thurgh might of his godhede.'
  þan ihesus strake so fast,
þe ȝates in sunder ȝede
  and Iren bandes al brast. 1404

(118)

He kyd þat he was mekill of might,
  þe fendes pouste he felled,
all lemid þat lathly lake of light
  þat with mirknes was melled. 1408
when all þe saintes saw þat sight
  þat in þat dongon dwellid,
none durst speke a word on hight,
  bot ilk one softly tellid: 1412

HARLEY.

(116)

A voyce spak þan full hydusly,
  Als it war thono*ur*s blast:
'vndo yho*ur* yhates bilyue, byd I,
  þai may no langer last, 1384
þe kyng of blys comes in yhow by.'
  þan hell a voyce vpkast:
'what es he þat þai say in hy?
  He sall be sett full fast.' 1388
þan said Dauid: 'yhe ne wate
  How þ*at* I said þus ryght,
"He es lord of gret state, 1391
  In batayle mykell of myght;"

(117)

þe kyng of blys, trewly I tell,
  Right at þi yhates standes,
He has bihalden fro heuen to hell
  þe sorow of his seruandes. 1396
þarfore vndo, þi fende so fell,
  þi yhates ryght *with* þi handes,
þe kyng of blys comes in full snell
  To bryng vs fro þi bandes 1400
Thurgh myght of his godhede.'
  þan Ih*esu*s strake so fast,
þe yhates in sonder yhede
  And Iren bandes all brast. 1404

(118)

He kyd þ*at* he was mykell of myght,
  þe fendes pouste he felled,
All lemyd þ*at* lathly lake of lyght
  þ*at* *with* myrknes was melled.
When all þe saintes saw þ*at* syght
  þ*at* in þ*at* dongeon dwelled,
None durst speke a word on hyght,
  Bot ilk one softly telled: 1412

1397. þi: Horst. þ*u*.

SION.

(116)

A voice spak þan ful hydusly,
 Als it ware a thunner blaste:
'Vndo yhoure yhates,' it sayd,
 þai may na langer laste, [‘smertly,
Kynge of glori byhoues cum In
 þareby.'
 And helle a voyce þan gan vpcaste:
'what es he, þat kynge of glory?
 He sal be sette fulle faste.' 1388
Dauyde sayde: 'whethir þou ne wate,
 Als I prophetede righte,
"A lorde of ful greete state,
 In batel mykel of fighte;" 1392

(117)

He es kynge of glory, þat I telle,
 þat at þe yhates standes,
And he behelde fra heuen tille helle
 þe sorow of his seruaundes. 1396
Vndo þarefore, þou fende felle,
 þe yhates withe þi handes, [leaf 33, bk.]
for kyng of glory comes fulle snelle
 To bryng vs oute of bandes 1400
Thurgh myght of hys godhede.'
 Ihesu þan strak so fast
þat þe yhates insonder yhede
 And þe Iryn barres al tobrast. 1404

(118)

he mustered he was mekel of myght,
 þe fendes pouste he fellyd,
Alle lemed þat lathely lak of lyght
 þat was with myrknes melled. 1408
When alle þe sayntes saghe þat syght
 þat in þat dongeoun duelled,
Nane durst a worde speke heghe on
 Bot ilk an softly telled: [hight,

1399. Second *fulle* marked for erasure.
1410. Second *þat* above line.

ADDITIONAL.

(116)

þan spake a voysse full hydouscly,
 Ryght as it were a thonor blast:
'Vndo ȝoure ȝates delyuerly, 1383
 ffor certes no langre sall þai last,
þe kynge of blisse here comes in hye.'
 And helle a voysse agayne gan cast,
'What is þat kynge?' alle gan þai crye,
 'Here he sall be sette full fast.'
Dauid sayde withouten were: 1389
 'As I prophecyde ryght,
"A lorde of gret powere,
 In batell mykill of myght;" 1392

(117)

He is þat kynge þat I of telle,
 And at þes ȝhates nowe standes
He behelde fro heuene till helle [here,
 þe sorowe of his seruantes dere.
Vndo þes ȝates, þowe fende so felle,
 Go & vnbarre þe ȝates sere, 1398
þe kynge of blisse comes full snelle
 To lyuere vs thurgh his gret powere,
With þe myght of his godhede.'
 Ihesu þaim helped so fast,
þe ȝates asondre ȝede
 And alle þe barres tobrast. 1404

(118)

[myght,
[1] He showed þat he was mykill of
 þe fendes poustye þere he felled,
All lightened þat before laked light
 þat with merkenesse before had
 melled. [1 leaf 135]
When alle þe sayntes sawe þat sight
 þat in þat depe dongon duelled,
Non durst speke on worde on hyght,
 Bot priuely þus ilk one þai spelled:

GALBA.

'welkum, lord, vntill vs,
  ful lang here has vs thoght;
blisced mot þou be, ihesus,
  ful dere þou has vs boght.'

(119)

He lowsed þan þaire bandes all [lf. 65]
  þat lang had bunden bene,
he made þam fre þat are war thrall,
  of care he clensed þam clene;
þe fendes þat saw slike light bifall
  ware none bifore was sene
said: 'we er clomsed grete and small
  with ȝone caytef so kene.'
ane sais þat mikel him dredes:
  'what ertou schewes slike might
and es so mekill in dedes
  and semes so litell in sight?

(120)

Sen þou was man, on what manere
  was godhede in þe hid? [here?
was þou noght ded? what dose þou
  slike maistris neuer was kyd;
we fendes war all ful fayn in fere
  when þe iews to ded þe did;
how ertou put to slike powere,
  and slike tene vs bytid?
þe sawles þat vs war sent
  has þou won heþin oway,
þou has vs schamly schent
  and priued vs of oure pray.'

(121)

þan ihesus sone toke satanas,
  þat are was lord and sire,
and him in thraldom bunden has
  to brin in endles fire.

HARLEY.

'welcom, lord, vntyll vs,
  ffull lang here has vs thoght;
Blyssed mot þou be, Ihesus,
  ffull dere þou has vs boght.'

(119)

He lowsed þan þare bandell all
  þat lang had bonden bene,
He made þam fre *þat* are war thrall,
  Of care he clensed þam clene;
þe fendes *þat* saw slyke lyght bifall
  whare none before was sene
Said: 'we er clomsed gret & small
  wit*h* yhone kaytyf so kene.'
Ane says þat mykell him dredes:
  'what ertow schewes slyke myght
And es so mykell in dedes
  And semes so lytell in syght?

(120)

Sen þou was man, on what manere
  was godhede in þe hyd? [here?
was þou noght ded? what dose þou
  Slyke maistryse neu*er* was kyd;
we fendes war all full fayne in fere
  when þe Iewes to ded þe dyd;
How ertow put to slyke powere,
  And slyke tene vs bityd?
þe saules *þat* vs war sent
  Has þou won hethen oway,
þou has vs schamely schent [lf. 213, bk.]
  And pryued vs of our pray.'

(121)

þan Ih*esus* sone toke Sathanas,
  þat are was lord & syre,
And him in thraldom bonden has
  To bryn in endeles fyre.

SION.

'Welcom, lorde, vnto vs,
ffful lang þan has vs thoght;
Blyssed be þou, swete Ihesus,
fful dere þou haues vs boght.'

(119)

And he vndyd þaire bandes alle
þat þai with bunden had bene,
And made þaime fre þat are was thralle,
And of care clensed þaime clene;
þe fendes þat sawe swilk light byfalle
þare nan byfor was sene [smalle
Sayde: 'we er ouercomen greete and
with yhon warloghe, we wene.'
Ane spyrres and mekyl he dredes:
'What art þou þat schewes swilk
[1]þat es swa mykel in þi dedes [myght,
And schewes swa littel to sighte?

[1 leaf 34]

(120)

þou þat was man, on what manere
was godhede in þe hidde? [here?
was þou noghte deede? what dus þou
was neuer swylke maystrys kydde;
We fendes alle ware we fayne in fere
when þe Iewes tille deede þe didde;
How ert þou putte to swilk powere,
And slike tene vs betydde?
was neuer na saule vs sente
þat he ne wiste of oure play,
þou haues vs schamely schente
And pryued vs oure pray.'

(121)

þan Ihesu Criste toke Satanas,
þat are was lorde and sire,
And hym in thraldom bunden has
At brynne in endles fire.

ADDITIONAL.

'Lorde, welcome till vs,
ffull lange vs has þe thought;
Blessed be þou, iesus,
ffull dere þowe has vs bought.'

(119)

And he vndide þaire bandes alle
þat þai bonden by hade bene,
He made þaim fre þat ere were thralle,
And of þaire kare þaim clensed clene;
þe fendes þat sawe hes workes alle
þat neuere byfore non siche had
sene
Sayde: 'we are venkesht gret & smalle
With ȝond warlowȝ, as we wene.'
þen sayde þe fende þus nedys:
'What artowe shewes siche myght,
þat is so gret in dedes
And comes so small in sight?

(120)

þowe þat was man, in what manere
Was godhede in þe hydde? [here?
Wastowe noght ded? what dos þou
Neuere here siche maistry was kidde;
We fendes were fayne alle yfere
When þat þe Iuwes to dethe þe did;
Howe artowe put to siche powere,
And siche tene has to vs betidde?
Was neuere saule till vs sent
þat þou ne hast fette away,
þou has vs shamely shent
And priued vs of oure pray;

(121)

[1 lf. 135, bk.]

[1]And taken here sire sathanas,
þat ere þis tyme was lorde & sire,
And in thraldame thrist hym þou has
fforto brenne in endelesse fire.'

1430. MS. *goddhede*, with second *d* marked for erasure.
1440. Second *pray* marked for erasure.

GALBA.

þan said þe fendes þat with him was
  ful of anger and of ire:
'satan, þou has vs lorn, allas,
  þou did noght oure desire;
we bad þe lat him ga
  and noght to cu*m* herein,
oure he feches vs fra,
  oure court waxes ful thin;

(122)

þou duke of ded, leder fro liue,
  hething of goddes angels,
ogains þat strang how durst þou striue
  þat vs þus frekly felles?
þou hight to bind him here biliue,
  it es noght als þo telles;
till endles ded he will þe driue
  and all þat with þe dwelles;
when þou þe iews gan stir
  þat þai suld ger him dy,
þou suld enquere and spir
  first if he war worthi;

(123)

[1]And if þat he had done none ill,
  þou suld haue gert þam blin;
whi suld þou bring a man vs till
  in wham was sene no syn?
all has þou lost now by þis skill
  þe wightes þat war herein,
and þou þaire paines sall ay fulfill
  with wo neuer out to wyn;
þat we wan thurgh þe tre
  when eue þe fruit had etyn,
ilk dele ogayn has he
  now with þe rode-tre getyn.'

HARLEY.

þan said þe fendes þat wi*th* him was
  ffull of angre & of Ire:
'Sathan, þou has vs lorn, allas,
  þou dyd noght oure desyre;
we bad þe latt him ga
  And noght to com herein,
Or he feches vs fra,
  Our court waxes full thyn;

(122)

þou duke of ded, leder fro lyue,
  Hethyng of godes aungels,
Ogayns þ*at* strang how durst þou [stryue
  þat vs þus frekly felles?
þou hyght to bynd him here bilyue,
  It es noght als þou telles;
Till endeles ded he will þe dryue
  And all þ*at* with þe dwelles;
when þou þe Iewes gan styr
  þat þai suld ger him dy,
þou suld enquere & spyr
  ffirst if he war worthy;

(123)

And if þat he had done none ill,
  þou suld haue gert þam blyn;
why suld þou bryng a man vs tyll
  In whame was sene no syn?
All has þou lost now by þis skyll
  þe wightes þ*at* war herein,
And þou þair payns sall all fullfyll
  wi*th* wo neu*er* out to wyn;
þat we wan thurgh þe tre
  when Eue þe fruit had eten,
Ilk dele ogayn has he
  Now wi*th* þe rode-tre geten.'

[1] Large initial, ornamented in yellow and black.

SION.

þan spak*e* þa fendes þat with hym was
 þat ware fulle of angre and Ire:
'Traytoure, what hauos þou done? allas,
 þou dide noght oure desire; 1448
we bad þe latte hym ga,
 Latte hym noght come hereIn;
Alle haues he fochede vs fra,
 Oure court waxes fulle thyn; 1452

(122)

þou duke of deede, leder fra lyue,
 Heghyng*e* of goddes aungels, 1454
Ogayns þat strang*e* how durst þou [stryue
 þat vs þus frekely felles?
þou hyght bryng*e* vs a pray bylyue,
 It es noght*e* als þou telles; [leaf 34, bk.]
ffor euer tille deede he wille þe dryue
 And alle þat with þe duelles; 1460
when þou þe Iewes gun stir
 þat þai suld*e* ger hym dye,
þou suld*e* þan haue done spire
 ffirst if he ware worthy; 1464

(123)

And if in hym ware funden na ille,
 þou suld*e* haue gert*e* þaime blyn;
Traytoure, whi has þou broght vs tille
 In wham es funden na syn? 1468
Alle has þou losed by þis skylle
 þe wightes þat ware he In,
And þou þaire paynes sal fulfille
 In wa neuer oute to wyn; 1472
þat we wan thurgh þe tree
 when Eue þe fruyte had*e* eeten,
Ilk*e* a dele es now, als we see, 1475
 with þe rode-tree fra vs geten.'

1453. *syn* erased before *lyue*.
1454. *aungels*: *e* above line.
1461. Horst. *whan*.

ADDITIONAL.

þan spake fendes þ*at* w*ith* hym was
 ffull of angire & full of ire:
Sathan, whi didest þou þus? allas,
 þou did right noȝt at oure desire;
We bad þe lat hym go 1449
 And noȝt to lat hym in;
Alle has he fette vs fro,
 þis courte waxes full thynne; 1452

(122)

þowe duke of dethe, ledere fro lyue,
 Outcastynge of alle Angelles, [stryfe
Agaynes þat stronge whi woldestowe
 þat w*ith* his myght vs alle þus felles?
þou saide he was þi p*ra*y full ryfe,
 It is no thynge as þou vs telles;
ffor eue*re* to dole he wille vs dryue
 And euereilk one þat w*ith* þe dwelles;
When þou þe Iuwes gan stirre 1461
 þat þai suld gare hym dye,
þou suldest enquire and spirre
 If he had bene worthy; 1464

(123)

And ȝif in hym were fonden non ille,
 þou suldest a gart þai*m* to blynne;
Traytou*r*, whi hastowe brought vs tille
 Hym þ*at* neue*re* was fonden in syn*ne*?
Alle hastowe lost nowe by þis skille
 þe saules þ*at* were su*m*tyme herein,
And nowe sall þou þaire paynes full-fille 1471
 In wo & neue*re* more oute to wynne;
þat we wan thurgh þe tre
 When Eue þe frute had eten,
Eue*re*ilk a dele has he 1475
 Thurgh þe rode-tre fro vs geten.'

1468. *ille* erased before *syn*.
1470. Horst. *he(r) in*.

GALBA.

(124)

[1]Ihesus þan spac with voice ful clere
to þe sayntes þat he has soght:
'cumes vnto me, my childer dere,
þat my liknes war wroght;
ȝe þat for syn war presond here,
to blis ȝe sall be broght.'
þan all þa saintes drogh to him nere
and þanked him in þaire thoght;
on Adam his hand he laid,
and he on knese gan fall,
'pese be to þe,' he sayd,
'and to þi childer all.'

(125)

Adam said þan and for ioy gret:
'lord, I sall wirschip þe,
fro my famen þou has me fett
in blis to bide and be,
in sorows sere whare I was sett
to my sare wald þou se;
me will þou lede withowten let
fro pine thurgh þi pete;
þou fendes vs þat we ne fall
till pine þat es pereles;
makes ioy, ȝe saintes all,
and thankes his grete gudenes.'

(126)

All patriarkes and ilk prophete
and oþer saintes all
fell doun on knese bifor his fete
smertly both grete and small:
'lord, þou es cumen oure bales to bete,
euermore serue þe we sall,
þat þou thurgh p*ro*phecy gan hete
we se it now bifall,

HARLEY.

(124)

Ihesus þan spak w*ith* voyce full clere
To þe sayntes þat he has soght:
'Comes vnto me, my childer dere,
þ*at* my lyknes war wroght;
yhe þat for syn war p*re*sond here,
To blys yhe sall be broght.'
þan all þa saintes drogh to him nere
And thanked him in þair thoght;
On Adam his hand he layd,
And he on knese gan fall,
'Pese be to þe,' he said,
'And to þi childer all.'

(125)

Adam said þan & for ioy gret:
'Lord, I sall wirschip þe,
ffro my famen þou has me fett
In blys to byde and be,
In sorows sere whare I was sett
To my sare wold þou se;
Me will þou lede w*ith*outen lett
ffro pyne thurgh þi pete;
þat fendes vs þ*at* we ne fall
Till pyne þ*at* es pereles;
Makes ioy, yhe saintes all,
And thankes his gret gudenes.'

(126)

All patryarkes and ilk p*ro*phete
And other saintes all
ffell doune on knese bifor his fete
Smertly both gret & small:
'Lord, þou es comen our bales to bete,
Eue*r*more serue þe we will,
þ*at* þou thurgh p*ro*phecy gan hete
we se it now bifall,

[1] Large flourish of leaves in black and yellow, extending to seventh line below.

SION.

(124)

þan spake Ihesu with voice clere
Tille þe payntes mare and les :
'Come to me, my childir dere,
þat er made my lyknes ;
yhe þat for syn er prisounde here,
yhe sal haue forgifnes.'
And alle þa payntes þai droghte hym [nere
And thanked hym of hys godenes;
Hande on adam he layde,
and he on knes gun falle,
'Pees be to þe,' he sayde,
'And to þi childir alle.'

(125)

Adam sayde and for ioy he greete :
'Lorde, I sal worchippe þe,
ffor fra my faas þou haue me fette
þat here war greete plente ; [leaf 35]
I cryed when I sorow was sette,
And þou haues now heled me ;
My saule þou ledde withouten lette
ffra helle thurgh þi pite ;
þou kepes þat we ne falle
Tille þe pitte of myrknes ;
Make Ioye, yhe payntes alles,
And thanke his halynes.'

(126)

þan Patriarks and prophete,
Alle other payntes alle
ffelle doun on knes byfore his fete
Ilk ane, bathe grette and smalle,
And sayde : 'þou erte comen oure bales to bete,
Euermare looue þe we sal,
þat þou in prophecy gun hete
we see it now befalle,

1493. *sorow* : Horst. (*in*) *sorow*.
1497. *kepes* : Horst. *kepes* (*vs*).
1499. *alles* : Horst. *alle*.

ADDITIONAL.

(124)

[1] And þen said ihesu with voysse full [clere
To alle þe payntes more and lesse :
'Comes to me, my children dere,
þat are made to my likenes ;
ȝhe þat for synne are prisoned here,
Alle ȝhe sall haue nowe forgyfnes.'
Alle þe payntes þen drowȝ hym nere
And thanked hym of his gudnes;
On adam handes he layde, [[1] leaf 136]
And he on knees gan falle,
'Pees be to þe,' he sayde,
'And to þin children alle.'

(125)

Adam sayde & for ioy gret :
'Lorde, gif me grace to worsshippe þe,
ffro my foos þou has me fette
þat were aboute me gret plente ;
I cryed when I in payne was sette,
And nowe lorde þou hast herde me ;
My saule þou lede withoutyn lette
ffro þis dongon for þi pite ;
Kepe me þat I ne falle
No more into þis place ;
Makes ioy, ȝhe payntes alle,
And thankes god of his grace.'

(126)

þen many a patriake & prophete
And also outhire payntes alle
ffelle don on knees befor his fete,
Alle þat þere were bothe gret & [smalle :
'And, lorde, oure bales to bete
þou art comen; nowe lyue we shalle,
þat þou in prophecye gan hete,
We thanke þe, lorde, nowe is it falle,

1501. MS. *prophetes*, with *s* marked for erasure.

GALBA.

ded thurgh ded es destroid;
lord, louyng be vnto þe,
all es noght þat vs noyed,
þat war thralles er made fre.'

(127)

[1]By þe right hand gan he adam take
and blisced him right þare,
he led him fro þat lathly lake
and all þat with him ware.
Saint dauid þan ful baldly spake,
als þai fro hell gan fare:
'a new sang till oure lord ȝe make,
als I myself said are;
he þat has bene wirkand
meruailes omang vs here,
he has saue his right hand
to him and his powere;

(128)

Ful mekely has he schewed his might
omang all cristen men,
he has techid ilka werldly wight
his rightwisnes to ken.'
þus all þa sayntes thanked him right
þat slike lane wald þam len:
'blisced be he þat cumes als he hight
in þe name of god, Amen.'
ilk prophet þus gan tell
of þaire awin prophecy
how he suld hery hell,
how he suld for þam dy.

(129)

þus als þai vnto welthis went
þat war won out of wa,

HARLEY.

Ded thurgh ded es destroit;
Lord, loueyng be vnto þe,
All es noght þat vs noyed,
þat war thralles er made fre.'

(127)

By þe ryght hand gan he Adam take
And blyssed him ryght þare,
He led him fro þat lathely lake
And all þat with him ware.
Saint Dauid þan full baldly spake,
Als þai fro hell gan fare:
'A new sang tyll our lord yhe make,
Als I myself said are;
He þat has bene wirkand
Meruayles omang vs here,
He has safe his ryght hand
To him and his powere;

(128)

ffull mekely has he schewed his [myght
Omang all cristen men,
He has teched ilka werldly wight
His ryghtwisnes to ken.'
þus all þa saintes þanked him ryght
þat slyke lane wald þam len:
'Blyssed be he þat comes als he hyght
In þe name of god, Amen.'
Ilk prophete þus gan tell
Of þair awen prophecy
How he suld hery hell, [leaf 214.]
How he suld for þam dy.

(129)

þus als þai vnto welthes went
þat war won out of wa,

[1] leaf 65, back. Flourish of yellow and black with bearded face and foliage where back of head should be.

SION.

Deede thurgh deede es destroed*e*;
Lorde, louynge be to þe,
Nane has nede þat was noyede,
Thraldom es made free.' 1512

(127)

By þe ryght*e* hand*e* he gun adam tak*e*
And blissed hym right*e* þare,
And ledde hym fra þe laythly lake
And alle þat with hym ware. 1516
And dauyd ful baldly spak*e*,
Als þai fra helle gun fare:
'A nowe sang*e* till oure lorde yhe make,
Als I haue p*ro*pheted are; 1520
ffor he haue bene wirkand*e*
Meruayles til vs her*e*,
He has saued*e* his right*e* hand*e* 1523
Tille hym and his powere; [lf. 35, bk.]

(128)

Mekely he haues musterd*e* his myghte
Vntille alle cristen men, 1526
He haues schewed*e* a warldes wyght*e*
His rightwisnes to ken.' [righte
And alle þa sayntes thanked*e* hym
þat swilk*e* grace wald þaime len,
And sayde: 'blyssed be he þ*at* comes als he hight
In þe name of god, Amen.' 1532
Ilk*e* a p*ro*phete þan gun telle
In hys aghen p*ro*phecy
How he suld*e* heright helle, 1535
How he byhoued*e* for þaime dy.

(129)

And als þai ware tille blis wendande,
þere sayntes þat ware in wa,

ADDITIONAL.

Dede *with* ded is distroyed; 1509
Lorde, louynge be to þe,
Alle arne eysed þat were noyed,
Thraldome is maked fre.' 1512

(127)

[1] By þe ryght hand god gan Ad*a*m take
And blissed hym *with*outen more,
He ladde hym fro þat lothely lake
And alle þat eu*er*e þ*er*e *with* hym wore. [1 leaf 136, bk.]
And þan dauyd full baldely spake,
Als he fro hellewarde gan fare: [2]
'A newe songe nowe sall we make
To ihesu, as I p*ro*phecyd are; 1520
ffor he has ben wirkande
Maruayles vnto vs here,
He has saued his right hande
To hym and his powere; 1524

(128)

Mekely has he shewed his myght
Her*e* vnto alle lyueand men,
He has shewed to eu*er*e wyght
þat þai his ryghtwysenes suld ken.'
Alle þe sayntes þanked hym right
þat siche a g*ra*ce walde to pai*m* lene: 1530
'Blissed be he þat comes as he hight
Nowe here in þe name of god, [ame*n*.'
Ilke p*ro*phete þan gon telle
In his awen p*ro*phecye
Howe he suld herye helle
And for mankynde to dye. 1536

(129)

And as þai were to blisse wendand
ffro þe foule fende, þaire faa,

[2] On margin to right in red: Cantate D*omi*no canticu*m* nouu*m* q*uia* mirabilia fecit.

1535. *How* repeated.

1523. *saued: u* corrected from *y*.

GALBA.

a sang þai said with ane assent
  þat was þis, 'Alleluya.'
by þe hand oure lord has Adam hent,
  with michell he bad him ga;
þai toke þe way with gude entent
  vnto paradis ful thra.
Michaell resaiued þam sone
  þat war to him bikend,
in blis he has þam done
  þat lastes withouten end.

(130)

In paradis with ioyes sere
  when all þir saintes war set,
two graihared men with face ful klere
  mildely þare with þam met;
þir saintes asked al what þai were,
  how þai fro hell war fett,
in body and saul: 'how come ȝe here?
  fand ȝe none ȝow to let?'
'oure names er,' þai answerd,
  'Ennoc and als Ely,
we er broght fro midlerd
  to be witnes worthy;

(131)

[1]We died noght ȝit, bot er olyue
  with antcrist forto fight,
in iherusalem þan sall we striue
  and we to ded be dight;
bot right fro ded god sal vs driue
  on þe thrid day thurgh his might,
at þe dome þan sall we rede ful riue
  who dose ill and who right.'
anoþer come þan þare,
  als þai so spac togeder;
þe saintes awonderd ware
  how þat þai so come þeder;

[1] Large flourish in yellow and black representing two bearded faces with backs of heads together.

HARLEY.

A sang þai said w*it*h ane assent
  þat was þis, 'Alleluya.'
By þe hand our lord has Adam hent,
  with Michael he bad him ga;
þai toke þe way w*it*h gud entent
  vntyll Paradyse full thra.
Michael resayued þam sone
  þat war to him bikend,
In blys he has þam done
  þat lastes w*it*houten end.

(130)

In paradyse w*it*h ioyes sere
  When all þir saintes war sett,
Two grayhared men w*it*h face full clere
  Myldely þare with þam mett;
þir saintes asked all what þai were,
  How þai fro hell war fett,
In body & saule: 'how come yhe here?
  ffand yhe none yhow to lett?'
'Our names er,' þai answerd,
  'Ennoc & als Ely,
we er broght fro mydelerd
  To be wytnes worthy;

(131)

We dyed noght yhit, bot er olyue
  w*it*h anticrist forto fyght,
In Ier*usa*lem þan sall we stryue
  And we to ded be dyght;
Bot ryght fro ded god sall vs dryue
  On þe thryd day thurgh his myght,
At þe dome þan sall we rede full ryue
  who dose ill & who ryght.'
Aneother come þan þare,
  Als þai so spak togyder;
þe saintes awondred ware
  How þat þai so come þider;

SION.

A sange of blys þai yhede syngande
þat hat 'Alleluya.'
Ihesu adam be þe hande,
With Michael gert þam ga;
And alle þe payntes yhede folowande
Tille Paradys fulle thra.
Michael receyuede þam sone,
Alle þat ware hym bykende,
In blis he haues þam done
þat lastes withouten ende.

(130)

In endles blys þat haues na pere
when alle þire sayntes ware sette,
Twa grayhared men of faytheful chere
In Paradys þai mette;
And alle þe sayntes asked what þai [ware,
ffra helle how ware þai fette,
Bathe body and saule: 'what do yhe here?
ffande yhe nane wild yhow lette?'
And þai ogayne answerd: [leaf 36]
'we er Ennok and Ely,
We er broght fra myddelerd
Als wittenes witterly;

(131)

We dyed noght yhite, we er left on [lyue
With anticrist forto fight;
In Ierusalem sal we stryue,
Bot we sal tille deede be dight;
Thre days we sal belyue
Ryse vp thurgh goddes myght,
Stande als wittenes when þe dome sal dryue
Wha haues wrang or ryght.'
A pure man come þare,
Als þai stude spekand best;
A cros on hys bak he bare,
A thefe hym semed lykest.

ADDITIONAL.

Alle þe payntes ȝede syngand
A songe þat hyght 'Alleluya.'
Ihesu toke Adam by þe hand [gay;
And *with* saynt Michel gart him
And alle þe sayntes went folowand
To paradise, for sothe to say.
Michell receyued sone
Alle þat were hym bekend,
In blisse he has þai*m* done
þat lastes withouten ende.

(130) [[1] leaf 137]

[1] In endeles blisse þat has no fere
When alle þes sayntes þe*re* sette,
Two grayhored men of face full clere
W*ith*in paradise þai mette;
þes sayntes asked what þai were,
Howe þat þai fro hellè ware fette,
Bothe body and saule: 'what don ȝe here?
ffonde ȝe no thynge þ*at* myght ȝow [lette?'
And þai agayne answerd:
'We are Enoc and Ely,
We come fro mydillerthe
As witnes wytirly;

(131)

Neue*re* dyed we ȝit, we ben alyue,
W*ith* ancrist ȝitt shall we fyght,
In ie*rusa*lem þe*re* mon we stryue,
And þe*re* to ded we sall be dyght;
And thre days afte*r* agayne to lyue
We sall be raysed by gods myght,
And stand as witnes when dome sall dryue
Who þat has don wrange or ryght.'
A pore man þan come þare,
Whiles þai were spekand best;
A crosse on his bake bare,
A theffe he was likest.

GALBA.

(132)

Meruail þai had omang þam all
and said: 'what man es þis?'
he said: 'þe soth say ȝow I sall,
al my life lifed I mys,
on þe cros cristes mercy gan I call,
he sayd þir wordes Iwis:
"þis same day, son, be þou sall
with me in paradis."
his takin he made on me
and þir wordes gan he say:
"when michaell sall þe se,
he sall noght say þe nay."

(133)

Anoþer word of him I had,
he said: "sun, I þe rede,
if þat þe angel be noght glad
þat þou cumes in þat stede,
þou sall say þat Ihesus þe bad,
þat now was done to ded,
þat þou suld in þat stede be stad,
till he come in godhede."
till þe angell sayd I þus,
he opind þe ȝates ful ȝare.'
and all þai thank ihesus
haly both les and mare:

(134)

'God of gudenes, gifer of grace,
blisced be þou euer and ay,
þat gifes lif in so litill space
to cristen sawles;' þai say,
'þai þat will trewly tak þi trace
and mend þam whils þai may,
in lastand liking þou þam laces,
þai wend no wilsom way;

HARLEY.

(132)

Meruail þai had omang þam all
And said: 'what man es þis?'
He said: 'þe soth say yhow I sall,
All my lyfe lyfed I mys,
On þe cross cristes mercy gan I call,
He said þir wordes Iwys:
"þis same day, sun, be þou sall
with me in paradys."
His taken he made on me
And þir wordes gan he say:
"When Michael sall þe se,
He sall noght say þe nay."

(133)

Aneother word of him I had,
He said: "Sun, I þe rede,
If þat þe aungell be noght glad
þat þou comes in þat stede,
þou sall say þat Ihesus þe bad,
þat now was done to ded,
þat þou suld in þat stede be stad,
Till he come in godhede."
Tyll þe aungell said I þus,
He opend þe yhates ful yhare.'
And all þai thank Ihesus
Halely both less & mare:

(134)

'God of gudenes, gyfer of grace,
Blyssed be þou euer & ay,
þat gyfes lyfe in so lytell space
To cristen saules;' þai say,
'þai þat will trewly tak þi trace
And mend þam whils þai may,
In lastand lykyng þou þam lace,
þai wend no wilsom way;

SION.

(132)

‘ leue frende, what ert þou?’ quod þai
‘ A thef semes þou like.’ [alle,
He sayde : ‘ þe suthe say if I salle,
Alle my lyfe was I slyke ;
Bot Ihesu mercy gun I calle,
And he sayde sykerlyke :
“ withe me þis ilk day be þou sall,
with me in heuenryke.”
þis croyce bytuke he me
And sette me in þe way,
He sayde : “ and Michael þe see,
He says noght withe þe nay.”

(133)

Another worde of hym I hadde,
he sayde : “ I þe rede,
If þat þe aungel be noght glade
þou sall come to þat steede,
[1] Say Ihesu criste goddes son bade,
þat now was done to deede, [[1] lf. 36, bk.]
þat þou sulde in þat stede be stade,
Tille he come in godhede.”
Tille þe aungel sayd I þus,
And he opend fulle yhare.’
And alle þai thanke Ihesus
Hereof bathe les and mare ;

(134)

þai sayd : ‘ of gudenes grettes of grace,
Blissed be þou euer and ay,
þat gyues ly in wa littel space
Tille synfulle saules ;’ þai say,
‘ ffolke þat wele folow trewely þi trace
And amend þam whils þai may,
In leele lykynge þou wille þam lace,
witte þai in na wilsom way ;

1587. Second *glade* marked for erasure.
1599. *ly* : Horst. *ly(fe)*. *wa* : Horst. *(s)wa*.

ADDITIONAL.

(132)

‘ Leue frend, what may þou be ?’
With on voysse þai gan say.
And he þaim answerd : ‘ I am he,
A theffe, as ȝe se may ;
I dyed *with* crist vpon a tre,
And þen of helpe I gan hym *pray* ;
He saide sothely þat I suld be
In paradise þis same day ;
þis crosse he gan me bede
And in þis way me sette
And sayd : “ haue þou no dred,
þ*ere* sall no thynge þe lette.”

(133) [[1] leaf 137, bk.]

[1] Anoþ*er* worde of hym I hadde,
He bad me haue no man*ere* drede ;
“ Michel,” he said, “ sall be full glad
þat þou sall come into þat stede,
ffor þou sall say gods son þe badde,
þat ryght nowe was done to dede,
þat þou suld in þat stede be stad,
To tyme hymselue come in god- [hede.
To michel say þou þus,
þat he lette þe in fare.” ’
And þai thanked ihesus
Her*e*of bothe lesse & mare :

(134)

‘ God of godnes, grattest of g*race*,
Blissed be þou eu*er*e and ay,
þat gyffes lyue in so litel a space
To synfull saules nyght and day ;
ffolke þat will filowe þi trace
And will amende þem whill þai [may,
In gud likynge þou will enlace
And lede þai*m* in no wilsome way ;

1599. Two or three letters effaced after *litel*.

GALBA.

þou þat has broght vs all
fro pain in light to lend,
loue þe lely we sall
euer withowten end.' "

(135)

[1] þir childer said : " al þis saw we,
wonand with sayntes in hell, [[1] lf. 66]
it es anly goddes preuete
þat in þis tyme bifell;
and mekill more ȝit gan we se
þat we may no man tell,
we war biden it suld layned be
with michaell, goddes angell;
he bad vs tell no thing
bot þis þat here wretin es;
we rase of his rising
þus forto bere witnes.

(136)

And with vs er resin many ane
þat ded and doluen lay;
þai dwell byȝond þe flum iordane
in prayers nyght and day;
bot vntill þir thre dayes be gane
no langer lif we may,
to blis þan sall we all be tane
and won in welthis ay;
on þis wise er we sent
to schew ȝow in þis stede
þat ȝe may ȝow repent
þat did Ihesus to ded."

(137)

þat Carin wrate he it bytoke
till nichodem and annas,
and Lentyn also gaf his boke
till Iosep and till Cayphas;

HARLEY.

þou þ*a*t has broght vs all
ffro payn in lyght to lend,
Luf þe lely we sall
Euer wit*h*outen end.' "

(135)

þir childer said : " all þis saw we,
wonand wit*h* saintes in hell,
It es anely godes p*re*uete
þat in þis tyme bifell;
And mykell more yhit gan we se
þ*a*t we may no man tell,
we war byden it suld layned be
Wit*h* michael, godes aungell;
He bad vs tell no thing
Bot þis þ*a*t here wryten es;
We rase of his ryseyng
þus forto bere witnes.

(136)

And wit*h* vs er rysen many ane
þ*a*t ded & doluen lay;
þai dwell beyhond þe flum Iordane
In prayers nyght & day;
Bot vntyll þir thre dayes be gane
No langer lyfe we may,
To blys þan sall we all be tane
And won in welthes ay;
On þis wyse er we sent
To schew yhow in þis stede
[1] þat yhe may yhow repent
þat did Ihes*us* to ded." [1] [leaf 214, bk.]

(137)

þat Caryn wrate he it bitoke
Till Nichodeme a*n*d Annas,
And Lentyn allso gaf his boke
Tyll Ioseph and tyll Cayphas;

SION.

þou þat haue broght vs alle
  ffra payne in light to lende,
Euermàre looue þe sal
  In blys withouten ende.'"

(135)

þai sayd: "þis es goddes p*ri*uete
  þat at þis tyme byfelle,
[1]Caryn and lentyn, þis sawe we,
  þat with sayntes in helle;
And mykel mare þan gun we see
  þat we may na man telle,
whe ware beden layned it sulde be
  Of Michel, goddes angel;
He bade vs telle na thynge
  Bote þat here writen es;
we rase of hys risynge
  þus forto bere wittenes.

(136)

And with vs many ane [leaf 37]
  Er rysen þat deede lay;
þai er byyhonde þe flome Iordane
  In paradys nyght and day;
Botte when þire thre days er gane,
  Na lenger lyue we may,
With þaime tille blis we sal be tane
  þat lastes euer and ay;
þus er we tille yhow sente
  At schewe yhow in þis steede
þat ye may yhow repente
  þat haues hym done to deede."

(137)

þat Caryn wrate he it bytuke
  Tille Necodème and Annas,
And lentyn alswa gafe his buke
  Tille Ioseph and Cayphays;

ADDITIONAL.

þowe þat has brought vs alle
  ffro pyne in ioy to lende,
Wirsshippe þe oue*re* we shalle
  In worlde *with*outen ende.'"

(135)

"Caryn & letyn, þis sawe we,
  Whill þat we were *with* syntes in [helle,
And mykill more ȝit gan we se
  þat we darre to no mann tclle;
ffor it is bidden consayle to be
  Of Michel gods dere angelle;
þai saide þis is gods p*ri*uyte
  þat at þis tyme nowe þus befelle;
þe angell bad vs telle no thynge
  Bot þis þat wryten is;
We rose for we of c*ri*stys rysynge
  Sulde þus bere wyttenes.

(136)

And ouþ*er* *with* vs many ane
  Are rysen þat in erthe ded lay,
And are beȝonde þe flom Iordane
  [1] In þaire p*ra*yers nyght and day;
And when þes þre days are gon
  No langere duelle here we ne may,
With hym to blisse we sall ilk one,
  þe*re* whare ioy is lastand ay;
þus are we to ȝowe sent [1 leaf 138]
  To shewe ȝowe in þis stede
þat ȝhe may ȝowe repent
  þat diden ihe*s*u to dede."

(137)

þat Caryn wrot he hit betoke
  To Nychodem*us* and Annas,
And Letyn also gaue his boke
  Vnto Ioseph and Cayphas;

[1] The word Caþin beginning line, erased. The page thus has one line less than usual.
1607. þe: Horst. (*we*) þe.
1611. *sawe*: *a* above line.
1612. MS. *wist* before *with* marked for erasure; Horst. *þat* (*woned*).
1616. Horst. *aungel.*
1636. Horst. *Cayphas.*

1607. ouere: *o* for *e* in MS.

GALBA.

togeder þan þai gan þam luke
  þat serely wretin was,
and þat one wrate noght a letter noke,
  bot euyn als þat oþer has.
when þe iews had of þam tane
  þa rolles þat wreten ware,
þai vanist oway onane,
  of þam þai saw no mare.

HARLEY.

Togyder þan þai gan þam luke
  þat serely wryten was,
A*nd* þat one wrate noght a lett*er* note,
  Bot euen als þat other has.
when þe Iewes had of þam tane
  þa rolles þ*at* wryten ware,
þai vanyst oway onane,
  Of þam þai saw no mare.

GALBA.

(138)

When þai had red þa rolles, alssone
  þe iews haly gan say:
"of grete god þat sites in trone
  es þis werk wroght þis day,
and ilka dele þat here es done
  aledies ogaynes oure lay;
þat þis ilk ihesus was goddes sun
  ful sare drede vs we may."
goddes forbod þan þai fend
  þat euer it suld be swa;
and so þaire waies þai wend,
  ilk one p*ar*tes oþer fra.

HARLEY.

(138)

When þai had red þa rolles, alssone
  þe Iewes halely gan say:
"Of gret god þat syttes in trone
  Es þis werk wroght þis day,
And ilka dele þ*at* here es done
  Aledies ogayn our lay;
þ*at* þis ilk Ih*esus* was godes sone
  ffull sare dred vs we may."
Godes forbod þare þai fend
  þat euer it suld be swa;
A*nd* so þair wayes þai wend,
  Ilk one partes other fra.

GALBA.

(139)

When þis was tald vnto pilate,
  he dred him þan ful sare;
als a dome haly he it wrate
  forto last euermare;
vnto þe temple he toke þe gate
  and gert send efter þare
bisschoppes and all þat he wate
  war best lered on þaire lare.
omang þam sett was he
  and said till all at anes:
"ȝowre bibill lattes me se
  þat es within þir wanes."

HARLEY.

(139)

When þis was tald vnto Pilate,
  He dred him þan full sare;
Als a dome haly he it wrate
  fforto last euermare;
Vntyll þe temple he toke þe gate
  And gert send eft*er* þare
Bysschopes & all þ*at* he wate
  war best lered on þair lare.
Omang þam sett was he
  And said tyll all at anes:
"yho*ur* bybell lattes me se
  þat es wit*h*in þir waues."

1650. *lay*: *law* has been erased in MS.
1655. *wayes*; *s* above line.

SION.

Togydirly þam þai gun luke
  þat sonderly wryten was ;
þe tane wrate noghte a lettre nuke,
  Bot als þe tother has.
When þai þe Iewes had bytane
  þa rolles þat writen ware,
þai wanyst oway onane,
  Of þaime had þai na mare.

(138)

When þai had*e* redde þa rolles, alsone
  þire Iewes haly gun say :
" Of greete god þat syttes in trone
  þis werk*e* es wroght þis day,
Bot ilk*e* a dele þe here es done
  Alleges ogaynne oure lay ;
þa Ihesu crist*e* es goddes sone
  ffful sare drede vs we may."
Goddes forbot þat þai fend*e*
  þat euer it suld be swa ; [leaf 37, bk.]
And þus þaire wayes þai went,
  And ilk ane parted other fra.

(139)

And when þis note was tald pilate,
  he hym dredde full sare ;
als dome halely alle he it wrate
  fforto last euermare ;
Tille þe temple he yhede on a gate
  And gert send aftir þare
Bisshops, prestes and other of greete state
  þat ware oght lere on þaire lare.
þe yhates þan sperd he
  And sayde tille alle at anes :
" yhoure yhe lat me see
  þat es within þire wanes."

1643. *onay* marked for erasure before *oway*.

ADDITIONAL.

þen togedr*e* gan þai loke
  þat sondrely so wryten was ;
þat one wrot no3t a l*e*tre noke
  More sc*ri*pture þen þat outhir*e* has.
Whan þai þe Iuwes had tane in hye
  þe bokes þat wryten ware,
þai vanysshed sodanly,
  Of pai*m* sawe þai ne mare.

(138)

When þai had redde þes rolles, sone
  Holly alle þes Iuwes gan say :
" Of gret god þat sittes in trone
  þis wondr*e* warke is wrought to-day,
Bot eue*re* dele þat here is done
  Expressely is agaynes our*e* lay ;
þat ih*e*su criste is gods son
  ffull sore drede vs nowe we may."
Gods forbode þen þai fende
  þat eue*re* it suld be so ;
And þus þair*e* ways þai wend,
  Ilk one p*ar*ted outhir*e* fro.

(139)

And when all þis was tolde pilat,
  þan he drad hym wondr*e* sore ;
And alle þes wordes þen he wrate
  fforto be witenes eue*re*more ;
To þe temple he toke his gate [lf. 138, bk.]
  And gart anon brynge to hym þore
Bisshoppes and p*re*stes, alle þat he wate
  þat any thynge had witte of lore.
þe 3ates þen sparde he
  And sayd to alle at ones :
" þe bible lat me see
  þat 3he haue in 3our*e* wones."

1651. Horst. þa(*t*).
1667. Horst. *yhoure* (*bible*).

GALBA.

(140)

Foure prestes furth þe bibill broght,
a boke of grete bounte;
Annas and Cayphas sone war soght,
and pilat sais: "lat se, 1672
all þat es written here wate ȝe noght?"
þai say: "sir, ȝis parde."
"a thing," he said, "es in my thoght
þat I will clerid be." 1676
þan by þat boke swere þai,
þai sall leue for no drede,
bot þe suth sal þai say
of þis note als es nede. 1680

(141)

He sais: "by þe faith till god ȝe aw,
of þis þing ȝow avise,
if ȝe find oght wreten in ȝowre law
omang ȝowre prophecise, 1684
or kan ȝe any witnes draw
by kasting of clergise,
if Ihesus war als was his saw,
god sun by any wise; 1688
Also if ȝe oght ken,
hereof tell vs ȝe sall
in whilk ȝeres and when
þat cristes cuming suld fall." 1692

(142)

þus when þat þai charged were,
þai said to sir pilate:
"sir, we will noght þat all men here
of þis thing þat we wate." 1696
he gert haue out þe folk in fere,
and to þam sperd þe ȝate;

HARLEY.

(140)

ffour p*r*estes forth þe bybell broght,
A boke of gret bounte;
Annas & Cayphas sone war soght,
And Pilate says: "lat se, 1672
All þat es wryten here wate yhe noght?"
þai say: "sir, yhis parde."
"A thing," he said, "es in my thoght
þat I will clered be." 1676
þan by þat boke swere þai,
þai sall leue for no dred,
Bot þe soth sall þai say
Of þis note als es nede. 1680

(141)

He sais: "be þe fayth tyll god yhe aw,
Of þis thing yhow avyse,
If yhe fynd oght wryten in yh*our* law
Omang yh*our* p*ro*phecyse, 1684
Or kan yhe any witnes draw
By castyng of clergyse,
If Ih*esus* war als was his saw,
God son be any wyse; 1688
Allso if yhe oght ken,
Hereof tell vs yhe sall
In whilk yheres & when
þ*at* cristes comyng suld fall." 1692

(142)

þus when þ*at* þai charged were,
þai said to sir Pilate:
"Sir, we will noght þ*at* all men here
Of þis thing þat we wate." 1696
He gert haue out þe folk in fere,
And to þam sperd þe yhate;

1673. *noght*: *o* above line.

SION.

(140)

ffoure prestes has forthe þat bible [broght,
A buke of greete bounte;
Annas and Cayphas sone ware soght,
Pilate sayde: "now lat see,
And þat es writen here wate yhe noght?"
þai sayde: "sire yhis p*ar*de!"
Quod Pilat: "a thyng es in my [thoght
þat I wille clered be."
By þat boke bathe swore þai,
þai suld leue for na drede
þat þai ne þe sothe suld say
Ne yhete for luf na mede.

(141)

he sayde: "by þe faythe þat yhe til godde aghe,
hereof yhe yhow auyse;
fynd yhe oure wryten in yhour*e* laghe
Omang yhour prophecyse,
Or may yhe any wittnes draghe [lf. 38]
By castyng*e* of clergy,
þat Ihesu was als was his saghe,
Goddes son on any wise?
Hereof oght*e* if ye ken,
Alswa telle vs yhe sall
In what yheres and when
His comyng*e* suld byfalle."

(142)

when þay ware charged on þis manere,
þai sayd to sire Pilate:
"we wille nanegates þat alle men here
Of þis thyngh þat we wate."
Pilate gert haue oute þat þare were,
And to þaime spered þe yhate;

1697. *were*: *e* above line and corrected from *a*.

ADDITIONAL.

(140)

ffoure p*r*estes forthe þe bible brought,
þat was a boke of gret bonte;
Annas & Cayphas sone þai sought,
And pilat said to þai*m*: "lat se,
All þat is wryten here wote ȝe noȝt?"
And þai answered: "sir, ȝys p*ar*de."
He saide: "a thynge is in my thought
þat I wolde of declared be."
By þat boke þai sware þat day,
þai sulde noȝt layne for no drede
þaten þai þe sothe sulde say
Outhir*e* for loue or mede.

(141)

He saide: "by þe fayth to god ȝe awe,
Hereof ȝhe most ȝowe wele avise;
ffynde ȝhe ought wryten in ȝo*ur* lawe
Anwhere amonge ȝo*ur* p*r*ophecyes,
Or may ȝhe any witnes drawe
By any castynge of clergys,
þat ihesu was as is þe sawe,
Gods son in any wise?
Hereof gif ȝhe ought ken,
Also telle vs ȝe shalle,
And in what ȝeres & when
His comynge shulde befalle."

(142)

When þai were charged on þis man[*ere*,
þan þai saide to sir pilat:
"We will noȝt þat alle men here
Of þis thynge, ne of þe state."
[1] þai gart voide alle þat þe*r*e were,
And when þai had spard fast þe ȝate, [[1] leaf 130]

1669. *Sc.* erased before *prestes*.

GALBA.

þai say: "sir, we war athed ful nere
and we answer þusgate:
we wate withouten wene
þat goddes son was he right;
we wend wichecraft had bene
þat he did thurgh his might;

(143)

Also we wate by sere witnes [lf. 66, bk.]
here of oure awin kinred,
þat he ogayn eft lifand es
sen he was done to dede.
two þat he raysed grete halines
haues schewed vs in þis stede,
whilk we wele wote both more and les
es done thurgh his godhed;
ilk ȝere a tyme we bring
þis haly boke in hand
to luke of his cuming,
and þus þarof we fand:

(144)

In þe first buke of sexty and ten
þat er all contened here,
till Adam son seth, telles it þen,
was spoken on this manere:
'þi fader and all oþer men
sall crist gif grete pouere
efter fiue thousand, we ken,
and als fiue hundreth ȝere.'
þan rekin we þus oureselue:
twa thowsand ȝeres suld be
and twa hundreth and twelue
fro Adam till noe;

HARLEY.

þai say: "sir, we war athed full nere
And we answer þusgate:
we wate w*ith*outen wene
þ*at* godes son was he ryght;
we wend wychecraft had bene
þat he dyd thurgh his myght;

(143)

Allso we wate by sere witnes
Here of our awen kynred,
þat he ogayne eft lyfand es
Sen he was done to ded.
Two þ*at* he raysed gret halynes
Haues schewed vs in þis stede,
whilk we wele wote both more & les
Es done thurgh his godhede;
Ilk yhere a tyme we bryng
þis haly boke in hand
To luke of his comyng,
And þus þareof we fand:

(144)

In þe first boke of sexty and ten
þat er all contened here,
Till Adam son seth, telles it þen,
Was spoken on þis manere:
'þi fader & all other men,
Sall crist gyf gret powere
Eft*er* fyue thowsand, we ken,
And als fyue hundreth yhere.'
þan reken we þus ourselue:
Twa thowsand yheres suld be
And twa hundreth a*nd* twelue
ffro Adam tyll Noe; [leaf 215]

SION.

þai sayd: "we er charged ful nere
And we answere þusgate: 1700
we wate withouton wene
Now goddes son was he right*e*;
we wen wichecrafte had bene
Alle þat he did by myght*e*; 1704

(143)

Sithen haue we witten of sere wittnes
Here of oure aghen kynred*e*,
þat he ogayne eft lyfand*e* es 1707
Sithen he was done tille deede.
Twa þat he raysed thurg*e* halynes
Has tald vs in þis steede
þat we wele wate bathe mare and les,
þat was done thurght*e* goddehede;
Ilk*e* yhere a tyme we bryng*e* 1713
þis haly buke in hadde
At luke of his comyng*e*,
And þis of hym we fande: 1716

(144)

In þe first buke of sexty and ten
þat er contend*e* here,
Tille thridde of adam sons when
was spoken in þis manere: 1720
[1]'Goddes son þi fadir and alle men
Salle putte to þaire power [[1] lf. 38, bk.]
Aftir fyue thousand*e* yheres, we ken,
Alswa fyue hundrethe yhere.' 1724
we reken þus vs oureselfe:
Twa thousand*e* suld*e* be
And twa hundrethe and twelfe 1727
And fourty fra Adam tille Noe;

1703. *wen*: Horst. *wen(d)*.
1714. *hadde*: Horst. *hande*.
1723. Horst. *after*.

ADDITIONAL.

þes foure prestes alle yfere
Sayde to pilat ryght þusgate: 1700
"We wote withouten wene
þat gods son was here dyght;
We wende wychecrafte hade bene
All þat he did be myght; 1704

(143)

Bot nowe we wote by sere witnes
Of men þat come of oure kynrede,
þat he agayne nowe lyueand es
And rysen sen tyme þat he was ded.
Two þat he raysed siche holynes
Of hym haue tolde vs in þis stede,
All þat ihesu did more & lesse 1711
Was don by pure myght of þe godhede;
fforþi shortely to say,
In oure bokes haue we fonde
He was gods son verray
þat we gaffe dedys wounde." 1716

(144)

When pilat herde þe sothe declared,
þat fell of ihesu more & lesse,
ffor gret drede full lowe he dared
þat he put ihesu to siche stres;
And þen no langere he ne spared,
Bot þen his awen errour confesse;
Hym thought his witte was full ille wared, 1723
þerefore he had gret heuynes;
And of his wrongfull dome
Belyue hym gan repent,
And hastily to Rome
His lettres þan he sent; 1728

1726. Two letters erased after *gan*.

GALBA.

(145)

And fro noe flude till Abrah*a*m es
nyen hundreth and twelue ȝere;
fro Abraham þan vntil moyses
foure hundreth and threty were;
fro moyses vntill god dauid chese
king of grete powere,
fiue hundreth and ten withouten lese,
þus telles oure bibill here; 1736
vntill þe t*ra*nsmigracione,
fiue hundreth ȝere fro þeþin,
and till cristes incarnacione 1739
foure hundreth ȝere was seþin.

(146)

þus oure law if we lely luke,
þis proues oure prophecy,
þat Ihesus flessch and blude bath toke
of his moder mary 1744
V thowsand ȝere, als sais þis boke,
and fiue hundreth þarby,
sen þis werld was wroght ilka noke.
and ouer sais ysai: 1748
'of þe rotes of Iesse,'
he sais, 'a wand sall spring
and a flowre faire and fre
þat sall gouern al thing;' 1752

(147)

'And on þat flowre,' he sais, 'sal rest
with al gudenes þe haly gast.'
þan may we se, sir, þusgates est,
he was god sun of mightes maste."
þan said sir pilate: "what es best?
oure werk, I wene, be all in waste."

HARLEY.

(145)

And fro Noe flude tyll Abraham es
Neghen hundreth & twelue yhere;
ffro Abraham þan vntyll Moyses
ffour hundreth & thretty were;
ffro Moyses vntyll god Dauid chese
Kyng of gret powere,
ffyue hundreth & ten *with*outen lese,
þus telles our bybell here; 1736
vntyll þe t*ra*nsmygracione,
ffyue hundreth yhere fro þethen,
And tyll cristes incarnacione 1739
ffour hundreth yhere was sethen.

(146)

þus our law if we lely luke,
þis p*ro*ues our p*ro*phecy,
þat Ihe*su*s flesch & blode both toke
Of his moder Mary 1744
ffyue thowsand yhere, als says þis [boke,
And fyue hundreth þareby,
Sen þis world was wroght ilka noke.
And ouer says ysai: 1748
'Of þe rotes of Iesse,'
He sais, 'a wand sall spryng
And a floure fayre & fre
þ*at* sall gouern all thing;' 1752

(147)

'And on þ*at* flo*ur*,' he sais, 'sall rest
with all gudenes þe haly gast.'
þan may we se, sir, þusgates est,
He was godes son of myghtes mast."
þan said sir Pil[at]e: "what es best?
Our werk, I wene, be all in wast."

1748. Horst. *euer*.

SION.

(145)

ffra Noe flode tille abram es
Neghen hundrethe and (XII) yhere;
ffra Abraham tille Moyses 1731
ffoure hundrethe and thretty were;
ffra Moysen god Dauid chees
Tille kynge of grete powere,
ffyue hundrethe and ten withouten lees,
þus telle oure bible here; 1736
Tille þe transmygracyon,
ffyue hundrethe yhere fra þethen;
Tille þe incarnacion of criste
ffyue hundrethe sithen. 1740

(146)

In oure lawe leely þus if we luke,
we say on þis manere,
þat Ihesu flesshe and blude tuke
Of Mary his modir dere 1744
ffyue thousand yhere aftir buke,
Afftir fyue hundrethe yhere."

1730. *A thousand* written above line and *neghen hundrethe* marked for erasure. Over an erasure VIII is written in later hand.

1732. *thretty*: *yere* erased.

1739. *foure score* after *criste*, possibly in a different hand.

1740. *ffyue* possibly corrected from *ffour; and ten* added at end of line.

ADDITIONAL.

(145)

And in his *lettre* þus he sayde:
"To claudy, was emp*erour* þat tyde,
Nowe late fell vs a wondre brayde;
Amonge vs Iuwes full of pride
[1] Ih*esu* þat borne was of a mayde
Was sent amonges vs forto bide;
A lichire loose on hym we layde,
And all for he wrought wondres wyde; 1736
ffor he went vs amonge [1 leaf 189, bk.]
And helpe bothe blynd & lame,
We Iuwes all *with* wronge
Diden hym dispite & shame; 1740

(146)

ffro ded to lyffe folke raysed he
With gret miracle sothe to say;
And on þe wawes of the see 1743
Drye fote walde he walke & play;
He chased fendes & gart þai*m* fle
ffro diue*rse* bodyes þe*re* þai lay;
Thurgh his witte & his pouste
Siche myracles did he nyght & day,
þe Iuwes sone þai*m* bethought
And plened þai*m* for envye,
And said all þat he wrought
Was done by sorcery; 1752

(147)

And I toke þair*e* tales for gude,
I hade no g*ra*ce ih*esu* to saue,
Bot demed hym to be don on rode,
Iwisse, þis gart I ih*esu* haue; 1756
Sithen when he shad his hert blode,
His body bloudy was layd in g*ra*ue;

1730. *tyme* erased before *tyde*.

GALBA.

þan langer þare wald þai noght rest,
bot ilk one hame sone gan him haste.
þus beres þaire bokes witnes 1761
to þam þe soth will ken.
to won whare welth euer es,
God grant vs grace, amen. 1764
A—M—E—N.

HARLEY.

þan langer þare wald þai noght rest,
Bot ilk one hame sone gan him hast.
þus beres þair bokes witnes 1761
To þam þe soth will ken.
To won whare welth eu*er* es,
God g*ra*unt vs grace, Amen. 1764
A—M—E—N.

SION.

"þan es it he þat we foresuke,"
Quod Pilate tille alle in fere.
þus beres þaire bukes witnes
Of þaime þe suthe wille ken,
And þus oure endyng*e* es,
God Graunte Vs Grace, Amen.

ADDITIONAL.

Knyghtes aboute his tombe þai stode
To kepe his body *with* swerde &
Knyghtes þ*er*e he lay [staue ;
Hym kepid *with* armour bryght,
Bot ȝit on þe thirde day
He rosse vp thurgh his myght ;

(148)

He rose vp þe thirde day
Whill alle þe knyghtes lay & woke,
As mased mysse my men þai lay,
Was non of þai*m* durst speke ne loke ;
Ih*esu* rose and went his way, [leaf 140]
All þis we fynde wele in ou*re* boke.
On my knyghtes felle siche a dray,
As espyn leues þai lay & quoke ;
Bot whan þis was asspied
þat iesu rysen was,
þe Iuwes fast þidr*e* hyed
To wit þis wondr*e* casse ;

(149)

And gaue siluer to ilka knyght
And bad þai*m* say in þis maner*e* :
þat his dissiples come by myght
Mawgr*e* alle þat eu*er* þ*er*e were
And toke his body so by nyght
With armed men of gret powere ;
Mi knyghtes assented anon right
And toke þe money alle yfere ;
Bot noȝt myght it availe,
þaire mede, as I suppose,
þai kept it noȝt consaile,
Bot tolde ryght howe he rose.

(150)

þai hade no myght for all þair*e* mede,
þat nede my knyghtes þe truthe most telle

"I beseech you, Sir Emperor, not to believe the report of the Jews; but believe from this time forth that God's Son suffered on the cross and died and rose again."

ADDITIONAL.

Ryght as it was sothely in dede;
  þai sette on ende & gan to spelle
Howe þ*at* ih*esu* thurgh his godhede
  þe thirde day ros in flesshe & felle,
And howe þai lay in droupand drede
  And non so ȝhepe a worde to ȝelle;
Mi knyghtes myght noȝt layne,
  Bot tolde bothe man & wife
þat c*ri*st wit*h* myght and mayne
  þus rose fro ded to lyue.

(151)

Sir Emp*er*oure to ȝowe þ*er*efore
  þe sothe I sall nowe c*er*tifye,
þat ȝe leue in non Iuwes lore
  þat in þis matere loude will lye;[1]
Bot fro[2] nowe forthe leue eu*er*emore
  And trowe it wele & stedfastly,
þat gods son sufferd full sore
  Vpon þe rode on caluery;
He dyed & rose agayne, [leaf 140, back]
  Of þis bere I witenes;
þus fell it in c*er*tayne
  Of ih*esu* more and lesse."

Explicit Nichodem*us* de passione χri

[1] At bottom of page words *año dñi* 1650 (?), *Elizabeth*, appear in different hand.
[2] *Bot fro:* these two words are almost illegible in MS.

GLOSSARY.

(Only unfamiliar forms are included in this Glossary, and no attempt has been made to give all variants of any particular word. Generally speaking, the unusual and abnormal forms of any one MS. are made clear by familiar forms of another MS.)

A, *adj.* one, G. 431.
A, *v.* have, A. 1466.
ABATS, *pres.* 3 *s.* puts an end to, does away with, S. 1349.
ABOHT, ABOUT, *pp.* paid for, atoned for, L. 57, 59; O. 43.
AGON, *pp.* past, gone, O. 31; L. 47.
AȜEIN (AȜEYN, OGAIN), *adv. prep.* again, against, O. 76; L. 84; E. 88.
AH, *conj.* but, L. 245.
AIWHARE (AYWHARE), *adv.* everywhere, G. 153.
ALEGES (ALLEGES, ALEDIES), *pres.* 3 *s.* alleges, testifies on oath, G. 36, 1650.
ALESED, *pp.* released, redeemed, O. 172.
ALGATE (ALLGATE), *adv.* any how, at any rate, S. 91.
ALONDE, *adv.* in the country, O. 30.
ALS, *conj. adv.* as, also, G. 189, etc.
ALSSONE (ALSONE), *adv.* immediately, G. 1645.
ALWISE, *adv.* in every way, by all means, G. 398.
AMAYDE, *pp.* dismayed, G. 201.
AMBESAAS (AMESAS, AUNBESAS), *s.* both aces, *fig.* misfortune, O. 98; L. 108; E. 114.
APAYDE, *pp.* satisfied, pleased, A. 203.
APERTLY (APPERTLY), *adv.* openly, boldly, A. S. 756.
ARE, *adv.* before, formerly, G. 121.
ARELY, *adv.* early, S. 1009.
AREW, *pret.* 3 *s.* had compassion on, was sorry for, L. 29.
ARNE, *pres. pl.* are, A. 1511.
ARTOW, *pres.* 2 *s.* art thou, E. 220.
ASS, *pres.* 1 *s.* ask, G. 834.
ASSPIED, *pp.* discovered, A. 1773.
ASTATE, *s.* estate, G. 383.
ASTOLDE, *pret.* 2 *s.* established, constituted, O. 231.
ASTOW = as thou, E. 197.
AT, *prep.* of, to, G. 103, etc.
ATH, *pres.* 1 *pl.* charge upon oath, G. 1141; ATHED, *pp.* G. 1699.
AUE = have, O. 109.
AUȜT, *v.* ought, E. 30.
AVED, *v.* had, O. 108.
AW (AGHE), *v.* owe, G. 1681.
AWIN (AGHEN, AUWEN), *adj.* own, G. 76, 1534.
AYSELL, *s.* vinegar, G. 615.

BADE, *pret.* 1 *s.* remained, waited, G. 88.
BALDLY, *adv.* boldly, G. 1517.
BALES, *s. pl.* sorrows, torments, G. 1505.
BANDELL (*corrupt form of* BANDES), *s. pl.* bonds, H. 1417.
BARET, *s.* strife, trouble, G. 152.
BARGAN, *s.* contention, struggle, G. 188.
BARNES, *s. pl.* children, G. 230.
BATE, *s.* debate, strife, A. 508.
BATH, *adj.* both, also, G. 376.
BATHES, *adv.* both, S. 962.
BED, *pret.* 3 *s.* prayed, G. 174.
BEDE, *v.* commend, A. 1581.
BEKENNE, *v.* consecrate, devote, A. 471; BIKEND, *pp.* G. 1546.
BELDERS, *s. pl.* protectors, helpers, G. 535.
BELYUE, *adv.* quickly, A. 213.
BEN (BUEN), *v.* be, O. 51; E. 69; L. 67.
BEREWEþ, *pres.* 3 *s.* repents, commiserates, O. 185.
BES (BESE), *pres. ind. of* BE, G. 319.
BET, *pp.* repented, amended, E. 184.
BETE, *pret.* 3 *pl.* beat, E. 55.
BETE, *v.* remedy, mend, G. 1505.
BETECHE, *v.* commit, entrust, A. 669.
BETEN, *pret.* 3 *pl.* beat, O. 39.
BETOKE, *pret.* 3 *s.* gave, delivered, A. 625.

BEþ, *imperat. pl.* be, O. 3.
BEWEUED, *pp.* stained, covered, A. 612.
BIDE, *v.* beseech, pray, O. 153.
BIDENE, *adv.* at once, the same time, G. 127.
BIER, *s.* rescuer, intercessor, G. 1207.
BIGETEN, *pp.* begotten, O. 190.
BIHETE, *pret.* 2 *s.* promised, O. 177.
BILEUE, *v.* remain, O. 104, 245.
BILEUEN. *See* BILEUE.
BINIM, *v.* deprive, take away, E. 136; BYNOM, *pp.* G. 1279.
BIREUE (BIREUEN), *v.* rob, deprive, O. 112; E. 128.
BIRON, *pp.* surrounded, covered over, G. 612.
BITANE, *pp.* committed, entrusted, G. 333.
BITID, *pret.* 3 *s.* betided, happened, G. 1.
BITWENE, *prep.* þAM BITWENE, among themselves, G. 974.
BIþOUTE, *pret.* 3 *s.* bethought, *refl.* remembered, O. 5.
BLEMIS, *pres.* 3 *s.* defames, discredits, G. 383.
BLIN, *v.* cease, decline, stop, G. 188.
BLOD, *s.* blood, O. 15.
BOBBED, *pret.* 3 *pl.* buffeted, struck, A. 604.
BODE, *s.* message, tidings, A. 1247.
BODWORD, *s.* message, news, G. 965.
BOND, *pret.* 3 *pl.* bound, E. 54.
BONDEN (BUNDEN), *pp.* bound, G. 1418.
BONE, *s.* boon, request, G. 717.
BOREN (IBORE, YBORE), *pp.* born, O. 177, 181; L. 186.
BOHT (BOUȝT), *pp.* bought, E. 59; L. 97.
BOUȝTEST, *pret.* 2 *s.* boughtest.
BOUR, *s.* bour, chamber, L. E. 32.
BOUST, *pp.* bought, O. 100.
BRASTE, *pret.* 3 *s.* burst, S. 604.
BRAYDE, *s.* trick, event, A. 1732.
BREDE, *s.* width, breadth, G. 66, 163.
BRENNE (BRIN), *v.* burn, G. 1444.
BREWE, *sub. pres.* contrive, prepare, A. 207.
BRO, *s.* broth, *fig.* affair, case, G. 415.
BROTHE, *s.* violence, A. 380.
BROUTE = brought, O. 6.
BUD (BOT), *pret*, 3 *s. impers.* it behoved, G. 456.
BUETEN, *pp.* beaten, L. 53.
BUEþ = BEþ, *v.* are, be, L. 82.
BUS, *pres.* 3 *s. impers.* it behoves, G. 309.
BUSKE, *v.* go, haste, prepare, S. 61.
BYGEND, *pp.* entrusted, delivered, S. 671.
BYTUKE, *pret.* 3 *s.* committed to, gave to, S. 1581.

CALDE, *adj.* cold, S. 259.
CARPING, *s.* speech, language, G. 99.
CASTE, *s.* design, purpose, S. 608.
CASTYNG. *s.* arranging, G. 1686.
CERTYS, *adv.* certainly, assuredly, A. 712.
CHARGED, *pp.* bidden, brought, conducted, A. 892.
CHEES, *pret.* 3 *s.* chose, S. 243.
CHELE, *s.* chill, cold, O. 34.
CHERE, *s.* countenance, S. 1551.
CHESED, *v.* chose, G. 243.
CLEDDE, *pret. pl.* clothed, clad, S. 609.
CLEPEDEST, *pret.* 2 *s.* called, O. 176; E. 166, 194.
CLERID, *pp.* made clear; CLERED BE, have explained, G. 1676.
CLOMSED, *pp.* palsied, bereft of sense, S. A. 1423.
COMLYNGS, *s.* strangers, novices, S. 259.
CORKED, *adj.* purple, S. 605.
COUP(E), *v.* accuse, blame, S. 60, 308, 365.
COUPED, *v.* accused, blamed, S. 250.
COUPYNGE, *s.* accusing, S. 701.
COUTH, *v.* could, G. 171; S. 219.
COUTHELY, *adv.* clearly, certainly, S. 228.
CROS, *v.* crucify, G. 528.
CUN, *s.* race, kin, O. 80, etc.
CUNNES, *s. gen.* IN ENI CUNNES WYSE, by any manner of means, O. 85.

DAMPNE, *v.* condemn, A. 883.
DAMPNED, *pp.* *See* DAMPNE, G. 883.
DANGE, *pret. pl.* beat, struck, S. 604.
DARED, *pret. pl.* were dismayed, appalled, G. 799.
DARRE, *adj. comp.* dearer, A. 1246.
DEBATE, *s.* strife, quarrel, G. 508.
DEDE, *s.* death, E. 35, 116.
DEDYS, *s. gen.* of death, A. 1716.
DEFOULED, *pret. pl.* polluted, defiled, G. 607.
DEȜE, *v.* die, L. 54.
DEL, *s.* part, deal, O. 188; E. 200.

DELYUERLY, *adv.* quickly, actively, A. 1383.
DEME, *v.* pass sentence, judge, G. 195.
DEMEDEN (DEMPT), *pret. pl.* *See* DEME, L. 54 ; E. 36.
DEMYD, *pret. pl.* *See* DEME, A. 783.
DEORE (DERE, DUERE), *adj.* dear, L. 59, 174; G. 893.
DERE, *s.* injury, G. 893.
DERYD, *pret. s.* alarmed, disturbed, A. 242.
DIEUX, *Fr. s. pl.* Gods ! S. 72.
DIGHT, *pp.* ordained, appointed, G. 55.
DING, *v.* beat, strike, G. 593.
DISPITUSELY, *adv.* cruelly, insultingly, mercilessly, A. 604.
DOF, *pret. pl.* put off, took off, H. 603.
DOLE, *s.* grief, sorrow, G. 683.
DOMESMAN, *s.* judge, G. 67.
DON (IDON), *pp.* done, O. 17, 20.
DON, *pret. pl.* (?) put on, G. 603.
DOSTOW = dost thou, E. 156.
DOUTE, *s.* doubt, S. 630.
DRAY, *s.* suffering, trouble, G. 60 ; A. 1345.
DRECHID, *pp.* afflicted, troubled, G. 197.
DREDLES, *adv.* without doubt, certainly, A. 554.
DREUEN, *pp.* driven, raised, S. 1107.
DROGH, *pret. pl.* drew, G. 1483.
DROGHTE. *See* DROGH.
DROWȝ. *See* DROGH.
DROWPAND, *pres. part.* drooping, sinking down, S. 176.
DROWPID, *pret. pl.* became dispirited, crouched, cowed, G. 176.
DUDE, *pret. pl.* did, L. 88 ; O. 35, 40.
DURKED, *pret. pl.* trembled, shuddered, S. 799.
DWELLES, *v.* abides, persists, G. 410.
DYN, *s.* noise, G. 225.

EFT, *adv.* again, G. 172.
EFTESONES, *adv.* again, immediately, A. 167.
EGERLY, *adv.* sharply, bitterly, G. 1338.
EGGES, *v.* incites, provokes, G. 30.
EGHEN, *s.* eyes, G. 479.
ENCHAUNTING (ENCHAUNTISYNG), *s.* charm, spell, enchantment, G. 450.
ENCHESON, *s.* cause, reason, motive, G. 84.
ENI, *adj.* any, O. 85.
ENQUEST, *s.* inquiry, A. 257.
ENTENT, *s.* heed, care, A. 78.
ER, *v.* are, E. 137.
ER, *adv.* here, O. 134.
ERE, *v.* are, G. 889.
ERTOU = art thou, G. 1435.
ESPYN, *adj.* aspen, A. 1772.
EST = *es it*, is it, G. 1755.
EUEREILK, *adj.* each, every, A. 969.
EVERUCH, *adj.* every, O. 188 ; L. 194.
EY, *inter.* ah, S. 72.
EYSED, *pp.* eased, A. 1511.

FAA, *s.* foe, A. 1538.
FAILAND, *pres. p.* failing, G. 175.
FALLES, *v.* happens, befalls, pleases ; HYM FALLES, he deserves, G. 269 ; S. 420.
FAMEN, *s.* foemen, G. 1491.
FARE, *pres.* 2 *s.* go, travel, E. 154, 155.
FARE, *s.* procedure, action, G. 441, 700.
FAST, *adv.* strongly, vigorously, G. 525 ; FAST BY, close to, near by, A. 820.
FELD, *pret. pl.* bent, faltered, G. 175.
FELL, *pret. s.* befell, A. 1731.
FELLE, *s.* skin, hide, A. 611.
FELLES, *pres. s.* fells, strikes down, G. 1456.
FELLY, *adv.* cruelly, A. 608.
FENDES, *v.* keepest, defendest, G. 1497.
FER, *adv.* far, G. 102, 778.
FERE, *s.* companion, equal, O. 51; L. 67; G. 642; A. 1549; IN FERE, together, G. 1697.
FERE, *adj.* sound, whole, A. 1100.
FERLIS, *s.* marvels, wonders, G. 687.
FERLY, *adj.* dreadful, wonderful, G. 700.
FEST, *pret.* 3 *s.* fastened, made firm, G. 631.
FETT, *pp.* fetched, G. 1491.
FILED, *pret. pl.* soiled, defiled, G. 544.
FLEMID, *pp.* driven out, put to flight, G. 936.
FLES (FLEYHS), *s.* flesh, O. 15, 190 ; E. 202; L. 196.
FLIM, *s.* stream, river, O. 214.
FON, *s.* fool, G. 607.

FON (FUN), *pp.* found, G. 273.
FOND, *pp.* tried, put to the test, E. 49.
FONDED, *pp.* tried, tempted, O. 61; L. 73.
FONDEN, *pp.* found, A. 1465.
FONDESTOW = foundest thou, E. 77.
FOR, *conj.* in order that, G. 957.
FORBOD(E), *s.* prohibition, command, G. 1653.
FORDONE, *pp.* destroyed, ruined, S. 444.
FORDREDDE, *pp.* dreaded extremely, S. 176.
FORE, *pret. pl.* went, travelled, S. 236.
FORERINER, *s.* forerunner, G. 1246.
FORFARE, *sub. pres.* perish, pass away, G. 432.
FORȜEF, *sub. pres.* 2 *s.* forgive, O. 154.
FORLETEN, *pret. pl.* forsook, abandoned, O. 159.
FORLOREN, *adj.* forlorn, L. 243.
FORLORN, *pp.* lost, G. 232.
FORMAST, *adj.* first, E. 165.
FORME, *adj.* former, earlier, G. 1177.
FORTE, *prep.* for to, L. 5, 67.
FORTHERMER, *s.* forerunner (*corrupt form of* FORERINER ?), H. 1246.
FORTHOUGHT, *pret. pl.* conspired, A. 736.
FORÞI, *adv. conj.* for this reason, therefore, G. 311.
FORWARD, *adv.* afterwards and onwards, G. 904.
FOTT, *imperat.* 2 *s.* fetch, A. 115.
FRA, *adv. prep.* from, G. 195.
FRAINE, *v.* make inquiry about, ask for, G. 1134.
FRAINED, *pp.* questioned, tempted, E. 75.
FRANKIS, *adj.* Frankish, French, G. 1295.
FREKLY, *adv.* eagerly, lustily, G. 1456.
FRO, *adv.* from, from the time that, G. 920.
FRORYNG, *s.* consolation, remission, L. 166.
FUL (FUL), *adj.* full, O. 17; L. 55, etc.
FYNE, *s.* end, confines, L. 11.

GA (GAY), *v.* go, G. 1542.
GACE, *pres. s.* goes, A. 64.
GAMEN, *s.* joy, delight, G. 1205.
GAN, *pret. s.* began, O. 78; S. 1518; A. 1533.
GAN, *pp.* gone, L. 72.
GANGE(N), *v.* go, S. 1351.
GASE. *See* GACE.
GAT (GATE), *s.* way, manner, method, O. 24; G. 69; E. 224.
GATE, *pret. sub.* begot, G. 280.
GATES (GATS). *See* GAT, O. 2, 27; E. 1351, etc.
GER, *v.* make, G. 188.
GERT, *pret. s.* caused, G. 8.
GETEN, *pp.* got, taken, G. 1476.
GLETERAND, *pres. part.* glittering, G. 126.
GOD, *adj.* good, O. 16.
GRAM, *s.* anger, S. 70.
GRAUEN, *pp.* buried, G. 1098.
GRAYTHED, *pp.* furnished, ornamented, G. 126.
GRE, *v.* agree, G. 923.
GREDE, *v.* cry out, L. 80.
GRET (GREETE), *pret. s.* wept, cried out, G. 1489.
GRETTES (GRATTEST), *adj.* greatest, S. 1597.
GRETHE, *s.* power, contrivance, S. 340.
GRILLE, *adj.* fierce, cruel, A. 368.
GRITH, *s.* protection, peace, G. 1018.
GRIÞ (GRYHT). *See* GRITH, O. 116; E. 132.
GROTCHANT (GRUCCHANDE), *pres. part.* grumbling, complaining, S. 536.
GRU (GREWE), *adj.* Greek, G. 633.
GRUNTEN, *v.* wail, murmur, O. 70.
GUL, *adj.* pale, yellow, G. 70.

HABADE = ABADE, abode, S. 88.
HABBE, *v.* have, O. 92.
HABBEÞ, *pres. pl.* have, O. 101.
HAG, *imperat.* cut, chop, G. 164.
HALDE, *s.* support, defence, G. 257.
HALDEN, *pp.* bound, obliged, indebted, G. 927.
HALE, *adj.* whole, hale, G. 43, 476.
HALY, *adv.* wholly, altogether, G. 131.
HALYDOME, *s.* saintly relic, sacrament, A. 892.
HALYNES, *s.* holiness, S. 1500.
HALYST, *pret. pl.* conjured, adjured, besought, S. 1003.
HARDILY, *adv.* boldly, G. 164.
HASTOWE = hast thou, A. 1467.
HATE(N), *v.* call, G. 1230.
HATHENES, *s.* heathen, G. 451.
HAVI (HAVY) = have I, O. 30; L. 46.

HAYLSED. *See* HALYST, A. 1003.
HEELE, *v.* hide, conceal, A. 904.
HEGHE (HEGHT), *adj.* high, G. 173; ON HEGHT, on high.
HEȜE (HEIȜE), *adj.* high, L. E. 31.
HEIN (= HETHEN), *adv.* hence, G. 1071.
HELDE, *v.* bend downwards, lean, G. 131.
HELDES (HELDED). *See* HELDE, G. 163.
HELE, *s.* salvation, G. 1216.
HEM, *pron.* them, L. 6, 29, 30.
HENDE, *adj.* gracious, gentle, A. 879.
HENE (HENNE), *adv.* hence, O. 140.
HENT, *pret. pl.* grasped, seized, G. 901.
HENTE, *pret. pl.* stripped, S. 601.
HEORE, *pron.* their, L. 52.
HERDY, *adj.* bold, audacious, A. 365.
HERIGHT, *v.* rob, despoil, S. 1535.
HEROWEDE. *See* HERWE.
HERTLY, *adv.* sincerely, heartily, G. 234.
HERWE, *v.* harrow, despoil, E. 150.
HERY, *v.* rob, despoil, G. 1535.
HESTE, *s.* injunction, behest, L. 159.
HETE, *pret.* 2. *s.* commanded, bad, O. 230.
HETES, *pres.* 3. *s.* commands, invites, G. 389.
HETHEN, *adv.* hence, H. 1071.
HETHING, *s.* contempt, mockery, G. 134, 448.
HEUEDE, *pret. s.* had, possessed, L. 7, 24.
HEUEDE, *pret. s.* lifted, raised, O. 214.
HEUENRYKE, *s.* the kingdom of heaven, L. 178; S. 1580.
HEUERICHE = HEUENRICHE, HEUENRYKE, O. 250.
HEUIDES, *s.* heads, G. 131.
HI (HEO, HOE, HUE), *pron.* they, O. 37; L. 138, etc.
HIDERTO, *adv.* hitherto, O. 108.
HIHTE, *v,* promised, L. 231.
HINE, *adv.* in, within, O. 74.
HOF = of, O. 165.
HOLLE, *adj.* sound; HOLLE AND FERE, safe and sound, A. 1100.
HOLLY, *adv.* entirely, wholly, A. 1646.
HON = ON, *i.e.* one, O. 28.
HONDEN, *s.* hands, O. 38; E. 54.
HONE, *s.* delay, G. 785.
HOO, *s.* halt, stop, A. 1124.
HORCOP, *s.* bastard, G. 227.
HORE, *s.* hair, A. 163.
HOTE, *adj.* fervent, A. 826.
HOUNBOUNDEN, *pp.* unbound, O. 121.
HOUNDO, *v.* undo, O. 128.
HOUNSTRONGE, *adj.* weak, unstrong, O. 123.
HOURE, *pron.* our, O. 51.
HOUT = out, O. 6.
HUELD = HELD, observed, L. 159.
HYNGMAN, *s.* hangman, A. 164.

IANGELYNG, *s.* wrangling, disputing, S. 563.
ICH (YCH, Y), *pron.* I, O. 47; L. 63.
ICH, *adj.* each, E. 81.
ICHULLE = I will, L. 136.
IDON, *pp.* placed, put, O. 20.
ILK (ILKA), *indef. pron.* each, every, G. 154.
ILLERHAYLE, *s.* misfortune, evil fate, S. 695.
INOGHE (INOWE), *adv.* enough, G. 103.
INUL = I NE WILL, *i.e.* I will not, L. 58.
IREN, *adj.* iron, G. 1364.
IS = his, A. 375, 967.
IWIS, *adv.* surely, certainly, O. 41, etc.

KAY, *s.* key, G. 831.
KEND, *pp.* known, G. 474.
KENE, *adj.* wise, clever, A. 123.
KENEDEN, *v.* confessed, knew, acknowledged, O. 221.
KID, *pp.* well-known, made famous, G. 63.
KIN, *s.* family, race, E. 209.
KITH, *v.* show, make known, G. 819.
KNELEAND, *pres. part.* kneeling, G. 1103.
KYD, *pret. s.* showed, G. 1405.

LACE (LACES), *v.* catch, fasten, seize, G. 1603.
LADDEST = leddest, L. 169.
LAGHE, *s. pl.* laws, S. 461.
LANE, *s.* loan, G. 1530.
LANGARE, *adv.* long ago, long since, G. 289.
LAPPED, *v.* folded, wrapped, S. 606.
LARE, *s.* doctrine, G. 430.
LAT, *v.* let, G. 1449.
LATE, *adv.* lately, G. 497.
LATHLY, *adj.* horrible, loathsome, G. 1515.

LAWED, *adj.* unlearned, untaught, G. 10.
LAWEN, *s.* laws, O. 230.
LAWSE, *v.* loose, break, A. 1212.
LAY, *s.* faith, law, O. 238; G. 1299.
LAYN(E), *v.* conceal, be silent about, G. 233.
LAYTHE, *adj.* unpleasant, loathsome, S. 1208.
LEDES, *s.* people, nation, G. 10.
LEEF, *adj.* dear, beloved, A. 342.
LEEUE (LEOUE, LEUE), *adj.* dear, O. 3.
LEGHES, *s.* lies, falsehoods, S. 98.
LELE, *adj.* loyal, faithful, G. 1214.
LELY, *adv.* loyally, faithfully, G. 354.
LEME, *v.* shine, gleam, G. 1174.
LEMID, *pret.* *See* LEME, G. 1407.
LEN(E), *v.* lend, give, grant possession of, G. 1530.
LEND, *v.* come, light upon, G. 472.
LENGORE. *See* LANGARE, L. 142.
LENT, *v.* bestowed on, put on, S. 605.
LERE, *v.* teach, instruct, learn, G. 458.
LERED, *adj.* learned, G. 10.
LERES. *See* LERE, G. 37.
LERYNGE, *s.* instruction, doctrine, S. 293.
LES(S), *v.* diminish, lessen, G. 512.
LESE (LES, LEESE), *adj.* false, G. 449.
LESE (LEES), *s.* doubt, falsehood, G. 1735.
LESEN, *v.* loose, release, O. 221; L. 215.
LESING, *s.* doubt, denying, E. 92.
LESTEÞ, *imperat. pl.* listen, O. 4.
LETT, *v.* hinder, injure, destroy, G. 192.
LETTYNGE, *s.* hindrance, annoyance, A. 448.
LEUE, *v.* believe, A. 430; G. 1678.
LEUEDEST, *v.* believedst, L. 60.
LIBBE, *v.* live, L. 247.
LICHIRE, *s.* debauché, lewd man, A. 1735.
LIȜTED, *v.* descended, E. 31.
LIKING, *s.* pleasure, enjoyment, G. 1603.
LIS, *s.* prison, dungeon, O. 165.
LITE, *s.* delay, G. 1014.
LITHES, *v.* obey, hearken to, G. 353, 452.
LOKE, *v.* look, examine, A. 1637.
LOKED, *pret.* *See* LOKE.
LOKEN, *v.* keep, take care of, lock, O. 157.
LOME, *adj.* lame, O. 18.
LORDYNGES, *s.* sirs, lords, A. 362, etc.
LORN, *pp.* lost, G. 356.
LOSEN, *v.* loose, release, L. 36.
LOÞE, *adj.* loathsome, O. 150; L. 154.
LOUT, *v.* bow, make obeisance, G. 135.
LOUYNG, *s.* praise, G. 1510.
LOWTYD. *See* LOUT, A. 140.
LURDANS, *s.* vagabonds, rascals, G. 135.
LUTEL, *s.* little, L. 126.
LYHTE, *pret. s.* descended, L. 31.
LYS = lies, S. 353.
LYTH, *v.* hearken, obey, G. 823.
LYUERE, *v.* deliver, A. 1400.

MAISTRIS, *s.* mastery, skill, G. 1432.
MANE, *s.* sorrowing, moaning, G. 708.
MANKIN, *s.* mankind, E. 116.
MANRED (MONRADE), *s.* homage, L. 88.
MASED, *adj.* dazed, confused, A. 1767.
MAUMETRY, *s.* idolatry, heathenism, G. 552.
MAWGRE, *adv. prep.* in spite of, notwithstanding, A. 1780.
MEETELES, *adv.* without food or meat, S. 776.
MELLED, *pp.* mixed, mingled, G. 1408.
MELLES, *v.* meddles, concerns about, maltreats, G. 414.
MELLING, *s.* mingling, meddling, injury, G. 417.
MEND, *v.* remember, be mindful of, G. 652.
MEND, *v.* restore, atone for, G. 1274.
MENE, *v.* remember, have in mind, G. 123, 212, 1093.
MENES, *impers.* US MENES, we are reminded, G. 27.
MENEYHE (MENȜE), *s.* retinue, followers, G. 806.
MENSK, *v.* honour, favour, G. 196.
MENSKES, *s.* honours, dignities, G. 123.
MENT, *pp.* designed, planned, A. 727.
MERRES, *v.* bewilders, troubles, G. 21; S. 295.
MERUAILES, *s.* marvels, G. 217.
MICHEL (MUCHEL, MEKILL), *adj.* much, great, O. 17; G. 242.
MIDLERD, *s.* earth, G. 1559.
MIȜTE, *v.* might, O. 22, 85.
MIN, *pron.* my, G. 38; E. 54.
MIRE, *pron. gen. pl.* my, O. 177.
MIRKNES, *s.* darkness, G. 1173.
MISSE, *v.* miss, fail, O. 194.
MIT, *prep.* with, O. 22.

MODE, *s.* mind, mood, G. 1038.
MON (MUN), *v.* will, G. 200.
MONI, *adj.* many, O. 13, 28.
MOPP, *s.* fool, mop, G. 21.
MORE, *s.* race, stock, O. 177.
MOSTE(N), *v.* must, L. 8, 12.
MOTE, *v.* may, must, L. 151.
MUSTERS, *v.* shows, G. 51.
MYN, *adv.* less, G. 1124.
MYNSTERS, *s.* servants, G. 207.
MYS (MYSSE), *s.* loss, G. 1274.
MYS, *v.* miss, be wanting, G. 575.
MYS, *adv.* wrongly, amiss, G. 1576.
MYSFARE, *v.* go astray, fare ill, A. 432.
MYSSE, *s.* mass, lump, A. 1767.
MYSTROWED, *v.* mistrusted, A. 824.

NAKYN, *adj.* no kind, no sort, S. 1311.
NAM (NOM), *pret. s.* took, E. 39.
NOMEN, *pret. pl.* took, O. 37.
NAN, *adj.* none, E. 77.
NANEGATE (NOGATE), *adv.* by no means, S. 148.
NAS = was not, L. 9.
NEDE (NEODE), *s.* need, necessity, L. 33.
NEDELY, *adv.* necessarily, G. 456.
NEDELYNGES, *adv.* necessarily, S. 77.
NEGH, *v.* approach, draw near, G. 742.
NERE, *adv.* closely, strenuously, G. 1699.
NEUYN, *v.* name, call, G. 24.
NEWEU, *s.* nephew, grandson, O. 10.
NOHT, *s. adv.* nought, not, L. 60.
NOKE (NUKE), *s.* corner, point, stroke, G. 1639, 1747.
NOLDEN, *v.* would not, O. 103.
NON, *s.* noon, O. 19.
NON, *adj.* none, O. 63.
NONKINS, *adj.* no manner of, G. 1268.
NOT, *v.* know not, A. 459.
NOTE, *s.* tenor (*of a letter*), S. 1657.
NOTE, *corrupt form of* NOKE, H. 1639.
NOTES, *s.* business, tricks, G. 77.
NOUȝT, *adv.* not, E. 60; L. 84.
NOURE = nought, S. 964, 1084.
NOUTHIR, *conj.* neither, S. 1122.
NOUÞE, *adv.* now, L. 42.
NOY, *s.* annoyance, hurt, G. 1279.
NOYES, *v.* troubles, annoys, G. 77, 1511.
NULLEÞ = will not, L. 135.

OBLIS, *v.* bind, engage, G. 275.
OBRADE, *adv.* out, abroad, G. 92.
OFRANDES, *s.* offerings, G. 568.
OFTSYTHES, *adv.* oftentimes, S. 989.
OGHE, *v.* be under obligation, ought; VS OGHE, *impers.* it behoves us, A. 37.
OIÞER (OWTHER), *pron. conj.* either, or, G. 329.
ONANE, *adv.* anon, G. 868.
ONENCE, *prep.* anent, in respect to, concerning, G. 983.
OR, *adv.* ere, before, A. 341.
ORDINANCE, *s.* order, contrivance, arrangement, G. 392.
OTHERGATES, *adv.* otherwise, S. 1075.
OU = how, O. 5.
OU = you, L. 2.
OUER, *adv.* further, in addition to, besides, G. 1748.
OUTORYTYE, *s.* authority, A. 330.
OWE, *v.* ought, E. 92.

PARAIS, *s.* paradise, L. 6; O. 157.
PARDE, *inter.* *Fr. par dieu*, G. 239.
PAS, *v.* try, adjudicate, pass upon, G. 243.
PASCH, *s.* Passover, G. 517.
PAY, *v.* pacify, please, G. 511.
PAYDE. *See* APAYDE.
PINE, *s.* pains, torments, O. 45, etc.
PINED, *pp.* tormented, afflicted with pain, G. 1316.
PLATLY, *adv.* plainly, flatly, A. 752.
PLAY, *s.* action, O. 57; E. 71; S. 1438.
PLENED, *pret. pl.* complained, A. 1750.
PLIȝT, *s.* guilt, danger, E. 170.
PLITTE, *s.* plight, purpose, A. 1153.
PORE (POUER), *adj.* poor, L. E. 34.
POUSTE, *s.* power, ability, L. 7; G. 1091.
PRESENT, *s.* presence, G. 370.
PRESENTES, *v.* represents, counterfeits, A. 383.
PREUETESE, *s.* secrets, G. 1155.
PRISOUNS, *s.* prisoners, E. 30.
PRISSE, *s.* esteem, value, A. 257.
PRIUED, *pp.* robbed, deprived, G. 1440.
PRYNEDE, *pp.* tortured, tormented (*corrupt form of* PYNEDE), S. 1316.
PURE, *adj.* very, sheer, S. 387.
PUTTYD, *pp.* raised, brought, A. 54.

QUED, *s.* evil, harm, the devil, L. E. 36.
QUERT, *s.* health, good condition, G. 970.

QUEST, *s.* b.dy of persons appointed to hold an inquiry, jury, G. 243.
QUIT, *adv.* clear, = TYTE, quickly, G. 1016.
QUODE, *v.* said, S. 37.
QUOKE, *v.* trembled, quivered, A. 1772.
QWATE = what, S. 290.

RAFE, *pret. s.* rove, was split, G. 660.
RATH, *adv.* quickly, without delay, G. 1145.
RAUIST, *pp.* carried away, led away, G. 951.
RAW, *s.* row, series; ON RAW, in unison, G. 226.
REALTE, *s.* royalty, G. 2.
RECCHE (REK), *v.* reck, care, O. 110.
RED (REDE), *v.* advise, O. 48; L. 64.
REDES, *s.* counsel, advice, O. 78.
REGNE, *s.* kingdom, dominion, G. 651.
REMAIL, *s.* verse, poetry, G. 12.
REMOUS (*corrupt form of* remouf?), *v.* remove, open, take away, S. 1348.
REN (RENNE), *v.* run, O. 136; L. 144; E. 147.
REUEST, *v.* robbest, deprivest, L. 119.
REW, *v.* rue, grieve, G. 211.
REWEþ, *pres.* 3 *s.* *See* REW, O. 90; L. 100.
REYNE, *pres. pl.* arraign, G. 211.
RIȝT (RYHT), *adj.* right, E. 39; L. 24.
RIGHTWIS, *adj.* righteous, A. 515.
RIȝTWISNESE, *s.* righteousness, O. 185.
RIUE, *adv.* openly, certainly, G. 1567.
RO, *s.* quiet, repose, O. 256.
ROD (RODE), *s.* rood, cross, O. 20, etc.
RYFE, *adv.* openly, certainly, A. 1457.

SAKE, *s.* cause, O. 37; E. 53.
SAKLES, *adv.* without cause, G. 950.
SALUEDE, *v.* greeted, saluted, S. 868.
SAME = shame, O. 35.
SAMEN, *adv.* together, A. 737.
SAUNZ, *Fr. prep.* without, S. 127.
SAWE, *prep.* save, except, A. 482.
SAWES (SAGHES), *s.* saws, sayings, G. 111.
SAYNE, *pres. pl.* say, A. 258.
SCHAFTES, *s.* shafts, G. 125.
SCHALTOW (SHALTOU) = shalt thou, O. 116.
SCHAMLY, *adv.* shamefully, G. 1439.
SCHAPE, *pp.* escaped, S. 240.
SCHAPEN (SHAPED), *pp.* shaped, created, L. 196; E. 202.
SCHENE, *adj.* beautiful, splendid, G. 125.
SCHENT, *pp.* disgraced, reviled, G. 463.
SCHILDE, *v.* shield, protect, G. 114.
SCHO (SHO), *pron.* she, G. 206.
SCHOPE, *pret.* 2 *s.* shaped, created, E. 164.
SCHULD = should, E. 104, etc.
SCHUST = shouldst, E. 195, 219.
SE = SENE (?), *adv.* since, G. 748; (*or it may be for the verb* see.)
SEGE (SUGE, SUGEN), *v.* say, O. 171, 191, 218.
SEID (SEYD) = said, L. 15; E. 97.
SEINE, *adv.* since, G. 1069.
SEKERLY, *adv.* surely, securely, G. 395.
SELCOUTHE, *adj.* strange, wonderful, S. 217.
SELLY, *adj.* strange, marvellous, S. 678.
SEMBLE, *s.* meeting, assembly, A. 1025.
SEN = SETHEN, *conj.* since, A. 53.
SENDELL, *s.* kind of cloth, G. 722.
SENE, *adv. conj.* since, G. 439.
SENT = assent, *v.* A. 512.
SERE, *adj.* several, A. 1398.
SERELY, *adv.* particularly, separately, G. 1638.
SEREWES, *s.* sorrows, O. 28.
SERTES. *See* CERTES, G. 816.
SEþEN (SEþþE, SUþþEN, SYTHEN), *adj. conj.* since, afterwards, L. 10, 48, 49; O. 17, 32, etc.
SHENDE, *v.* confuse, disgrace, O. 22; L. 130.
SHULEN (SULEN), *v.* shall, O. 102; L. 112.
SHUPTEST, *pret.* 2 *s.* shaped, created, L. 158.
SIBNESSE, *s.* peace, kinship, O. 186.
SIKIRE, *adj.* secure, certain, A. 1110.
SITH, *s.* time, occasion, G. 821.
SITTYNGESTEDE, *s.* seat, abode, S. 389.
SKAPE, *v.* escape, depart, G. 380.
SKAPPID, *pret.* 3 *s.* escaped, A. 240.
SKATH, *s.* injury, harm, G. 380.
SKIL(L), *s.* reason, excuse, skill, L. 223; E. 227; G. 308.
SKILFULLY, *adv.* reasonably, right, A. 382.
SLAKE, *v.* loose, release, G. 518.
SLEPAND, *pres. part.* sleeping, G. 210.
SLIKE, *adj.* such, G. 46, etc.
SMERTLY, *adv.* promptly, quickly, A. 74.

SNELLE, *adv*, quickly, A. 1292.
SOBOT = sabbath, A. 774.
SOFFRE (SOFFREN), *v.* suffer, permit, O. 44; L. 58.
SOFFRED, *v.* endured, O. 28; L. 44.
SOME, *s.* shame, O. 17.
SOND(E), *s.* messenger, O. 146; A. 1223.
SONDERLY, *adv.* separately, S. 1638.
SONE, *adv.* immediately, O. 23.
SORWE (SOREWEN), *s.* sorrows, L. 44; E. 84.
SOTELL, *adj.* subtle, G. 437.
SOTHFAST, *adj.* truthful, L. 18.
SOTHFASTNES, *s.* truthfulness, G. 351.
SOÞE, *s.* truth, sooth, E. 40.
SPARRE, *imperat. s.* close, bar, A. 1351.
SPERD, *v.* closed, barred, G. 772.
SPILTE, *pp.* killed, destroyed, A. 646.
SPIR, *v.* search, enquire, investigate, G. 1463.
SPIRD, *pret.* *See* SPIR.
SPOSAGE, *s.* wedlock, G. 730.
SPOWSE, *s.* wedlock, G. 288.
SPRENT, *pret. pl.* sprinkled, wet, A. 629.
SPYRRES. *See* SPIR, S. 1425.
STAD, *pp.* placed, G. 1591.
STEGH (STEYE), *pret. s.* climbed, ascended, G. 886.
STERE, *v.* steer, guide, S. 155.
STEUIN, *s.* agreement, appointment, consent, voice, G. 162.
STIRT, *pret.* started, leapt, G. 253.
STONAYD, *pp.* astonished, G. 360.
STOND (STONDEN), *v.* stand, O. 136; E. 147.
STRAKES, *s.* strokes, G. 419.
STREKE, *adv.* direct, straight, S. 867.
STRENGHE = strength, S. 467.
STRENGHEFULLY, *adv.* strongly, vigorously, S. 155.
STRENKITHI, *adj.* strengthy, powerful, G. 1317.
STRIF, *s.* dispute, debate, L. 2.
STRYFE, *v.* fight, contend, S. 343.
SUETE, *adj.* sweet, O. 189.
SULD = should, G. 55, etc.
SUN (SUNNE, SUNNES), *s.* sins, O. 12; L. 55.
SUTHEFASTE. *See* SOTHFAST.
SWILKE, *adj.* such, S. 79.
SWITH, *adv.* quickly, strongly, G. 817.
SWYNGE, *v.* beat, strike, A. 593.
SYKERLYKE, *adv.* securely, S. 1578.
SYKYR. *See* SIKIRE, S. 154.

TAC, *imperat. s.* take, seize, L. 103.
TAGHT, *pp.* given, entrusted, S. 333.
TAKE, *pret. pl.* gave, delivered, G. 1004.
TAKIN, *s.* token, sign, G. 1150.
TAKYNGS, *s.* takings, seizures. *But here probably a corruption of* TAKENS, S. 437.
TALKINGES, *s. corrupt form of* TAKENS(?) tokens, G. 437.
TANE, *pp.* taken, G. 185.
TE, *prep.* to, L. 8.
TEITEST, *pret.* 2 *s.* showedst, O. 233.
TEMPID, *v.* tempted, G. 1334.
TENE, *s.* vexation, G. 533.
TENE, *v.* irritate, harm, G. 726.
TENED, *pret. of* TENE, S. 736.
TENT, *s.* heed, attention, G. 78.
TENTIFLY, *adv.* securely, attentively, S. 151.
THONORS, *s. gen.* thunder's, G. 1382.
THRA, *adv.* boldly, G. 1544.
THREPE, *s.* contradiction, dispute, G. 838.
THREST, *v.* thrust, cast, G. 610.
THRIST, *pp.* cast, forced, A. 1443.
TOBRAST, *pret. pl.* burst in pieces, burst asunder, S. 1404.
TOKE (TUKE), *pret. pl.* entrusted to, A. 795.
TOSCHOKE, *pret. s.* shook to pieces, G. 797.
TOUN, *s.* town, G. 90.
TOUR, *s.* tower, L. E. 31.
TRACE, *s.* track, course, G. 1601.
TRAINE, *s.* stratagem, snare, G. 185, 863.
TRATILLING, *s.* chattering, gabbling, G. 563.
TRAUERST (TRAUYST), *pp.* crossed, transgressed, G. 1301.
TREULICHE, *adv.* truly, O. 241.
TRONE, *s.* throne, G. 425.
TRYE, *s.* faithfulness, loyalty, A. 728.
TUEN, *v.* go, L. 234.
TWIN, *v.* separate, divide, G. 186.
TYTE, *adv.* quickly, immediately, G. 484.
TYTHING, *s.* tidings, message, G. 1204.

ÞAI, *pron.* they, E. 53.
ÞAIM, *pron.* them, E. 29.

Þan, *conj.* when, E. 37.
Þan (þon), *pron. acc.* this, O. 65; E. 79.
Þare, *adv.* there, E. 65.
Þf, *conj.* when, as, O. 77; L. 41.
Þeine, *adv.* thence, G. 1075.
Þen, *adv.* than, O. 14.
Þen, *pron. acc.* the, L. 10, 39.
Þenne, *adv. conj.* then, when, O. 69, 70.
Þenne, *adv.* thence, L. 5, 13.
Þethen, *adv.* thence, G. 102.
Þilke, *adj.* such, that, L. 135.
Þir, *pron.* these, G. 619.
Þo, *pron.* they, O. 74, 103.
Þo, *adv. conj.* then, when, L. 37, 41.
Þo-þe, *conj.* when, O. 25.
Þoled, *pp.* endured, suffered, O. 33.
Þore, *adv.* there, L. 30, 63.
Þoru (þourh, þurch), *prep.* through, O. 84.
Þouȝ (?), *s.* disgrace, indignity, E. 51.
Þrest, *s.* thirst, E. 50.
Þridde, *adj.* third, L. E. 45.
Þritti, *adj.* thirty, O. 29.
Þuncheþ, *v.* seems, L. 140.
Þusgate, *adv.* thus, in this way, S. 107.

Unbedde, *adj.* unbidden, A. 174.
Underon, *s.* the time from nine to twelve o'clock in the morning, G. 657.
Unhild, *pp.* uncovered, G. 169.
Unrightwis, *adj.* unrighteous, G. 560.
Used, *pp.* was used, was the custom, G. 122.

Vacche, *v.* fetch, L. 5, 30.
Venkesht, *pp.* vanquished, A. 1423.
Veren = weren, were, O. 8.
Visage, *s.* face, countenance, G. 1042.
Voide, *v.* make void, clear out, A. 285, 1697.
Vor = for, L. 15.

Wa, *s.* woe, G. 1538.
Walde, *v.* would, A. 292.
Waloway, *inter.* woe, alas, S. 1314.
Wane, *s.* quantity, number, G. 419.
Wanes, *s.* dwelling, abode, G. 967.
Wankill, *adj.* unstable, A. 340.
War, *v.* were, E. 100.
Warand, *s.* guarantee, safeguard, G. 666.
Ware, *s.* host, inhabitants, O. 217.
Wared, *pp.* defended, spent, A. 1723.
Warloghe (warlowȝ), *s.* wizard, sorcerer, S. 1424.
Wars, *adj.* worse, A. 741.
Wat = what, O. 59; E. 73.
Wath, *s.* hurt, peril, G. 378.
Wed (wedde), *s.* pledge, G. 100.
Wede, *s.* garment, weeds, L. E. 34.
Weder (whyder), *adv.* whither, O. 110; L. 118.
Wedlayk, *s.* wedlock, G. 252.
Weld (wald), *v.* wield, rule, O. 93, 96; L. 106, etc.
Welle, *v.* will, S. 100.
Welth (welthes), *s.* happiness, pleasure, G. 1537, 1763.
Wemme, *s.* crime, stain, A. 607.
Wend (?), *pp. for* wond, woned, lived, dwelt, O. 30.
Wend, *pret. pl.* supposed, G. 1703.
Wend, *v.* go, wend, L. 129; O. 250; G. 476.
Wendest, *pret.* 2 *s.* supposedst, O. 99.
Wene, *s.* doubt, G, 531.
Wenestow = weenest thou.
Wer, *adv.* where, O. 129.
Were, *s.* doubt, A. 1389.
Werldly, *adj.* worldly, G. 1527.
Wes = was, L. 4, 17.
Wex, *v.* wax, G. 70, 537.
Wharethurgh, *adv.* wherethrough, through which, G. 284.
Whatkin, *adv.* what kind of, what manner of, G. 28.
Wher = whether, G. 1050.
Whik = quick, H. 1082.
Whilk, *pron.* which, G. 34.
Whyt, *s.* wight, man, L. 23.
Wiȝt, *s.* whit, E. 169.
Wight, *adj.* brave, valiant, G. 161, 959.
Wightly, *adv.* immediately, quickly, H. 581.
Wike, *s.* dwelling, E. 187; L. 177.
Wild, *v.* would, S. 1556.
Wildrenes, *s.* wilderness, A. 1365.
Willy, *adj.* ready, willing, G. 161.
Willy = will I, O. 75.
Wilsom, *adj.* wilful, obstinate, G. 1604.
Wilsomnes, *s.* wilfulness, obstinacy, G. 1365.
Win, *v.* win, go; win oway, get away, G. 791, 1031, 1472.
Winde, *v.* go, wend, O. 140; E. 152.

WINLY, *adv.* joyously, G. 1002.
WIS (WYSS), *v.* show, guide, G. 908.
WIST (WEST, WYST), *pp.* known, suffered, O. 33; E. L. 49.
WITERLY, *adv.* surely, G. 145.
WITING, *s.* knowing, G. 140.
WITTE, *imperat. s.* guard, keep, S. 1604.
WODE, *adj.* mad, S. 43; G. 537.
WOH, *s.* wickedness, L. 52.
WOKE (WOOKE), *pret. s.* watched, G. 793.
WOLDE (?), *s.* power, dominion, O. 232.
WOLDEST (WOST) = wouldst, O. 122; L. 132; E. 136.
WOLDESTOWE = wouldst thou, A. 1455.
WON, *adj.* accustomed, G. 874.
WONAND, *pres. part.* dwelling, G. 1610.
WONDE, *v.* refrain from, hesitate, A. 607.
WONDEN, *pp.* gone, S. 833.
WOND (WONED), *pp.* dwelt, lived, L. E. 46.
WONE(N), *v.* live, dwell, L. 162, 237.
WONE, *s.* quantity, store, A. 853.
WONYNGE, *s.* dwelling, home, S. 967.
WOR (?) = WORȢ, or WAR (WERE), O. 232.
WORÞ, *adj.* worthy, E. 172.
WOSE = whoso, O. 135.
WOST, *v.* knowest, O. 59; L. 71.
WOUȜ. *See* WOH, E. 52 (?).
WOUNDEN, *s. pl.* wounds, O. 36.
WRAKE, *s.* persecution, injury, G. 768.
WRANGWISLY, *adv.* wrongly, G. 204.
WREGH, *pres. pl.* accuse, G. 204.
WRETH, *s.* wrath (?), G. 80.
WROTHERHAIL, *s.* misfortune, evil fate. G. 695.
WROUȜT, *pp.* worked, committed, E. 167.

ȜA, *adv.* yes, E. 171.
ȜAF (ȜEF), *v.* gave, O. 79; L. 89.
ȜARE (YHARE), *adv.* quickly, G. 1594.
ȜATES, *s.* gates, O. 127.
ȜATEWARD, *s.* gate-warden, porter, O. 129.
ȜE (ȜHE), *pron.* ye, A. 46; E. 142.
ȜEDE, *pret. pl.* went, G. 1403.
ȜELLE, *v.* utter, yell, A. 1796.
ȜEME, *v.* deem, care, regard, L. 24; E. 148, 180; G. 468.
ȜER (ȜERE), *s. pl.* years, O. 29; E. 45; TO ȜERE, this year, long ago, G. 966.
ȜERDE (YHERD), *s.* rod, G. 420.
ȜERNED, *pp.* yearned, desired, L. 164; E. 174.
ȜEUE (ȜOUEN), *pp.* given, E. 189.
ȜHARE, *adv.* readily, clearly, A. 1296.
ȜHEPE, *adj.* bold, A. 1796.
ȜONE (YHONE, ȜOND), *adj.* yon, G. 1424.
ȜONGE (YONGE, GANG), *v.* go, O. 124.
ȜORE, *adv.* long ago, for long, L. 164.
ȜOU = you, E. 141.

YBOHT, *pp.* bought, L. 182.
YCOREN, *pp.* chosen, E. 208.
YFERE, *adv.* together, in unison, A. 361, 751.
YGAN, *pp.* gone, L. 4.
YHEDE, *pret. pl.* went, S. 1113.
YNE, *s.* eyes, A. 210.
YNOH, *adv.* enough, L. 51.
YRENEN, *adj.* iron, A. 1364.
YRON, *pp.* covered, L. 53.
YS = his.

INDEX OF PROPER NAMES.

(All the variant forms of each name are recorded, but no attempt has been made to give all references for each form.)